ATS-119   ADMISSION TEST SERIES

*This is your
PASSBOOK for...*

Liberal Arts & Sciences Test (LAST)

*Test Preparation Study Guide
Questions & Answers*

COPYRIGHT NOTICE

This book is SOLELY intended for, is sold ONLY to, and its use is RESTRICTED to individual, bona fide applicants or candidates who qualify by virtue of having seriously filed applications for appropriate license, certificate, professional and/or promotional advancement, higher school matriculation, scholarship, or other legitimate requirements of education and/or governmental authorities.

This book is NOT intended for use, class instruction, tutoring, training, duplication, copying, reprinting, excerption, or adaptation, etc., by:

1) Other publishers
2) Proprietors and/or Instructors of "Coaching" and/or Preparatory Courses
3) Personnel and/or Training Divisions of commercial, industrial, and governmental organizations
4) Schools, colleges, or universities and/or their departments and staffs, including teachers and other personnel
5) Testing Agencies or Bureaus
6) Study groups which seek by the purchase of a single volume to copy and/or duplicate and/or adapt this material for use by the group as a whole without having purchased individual volumes for each of the members of the group
7) Et al.

Such persons would be in violation of appropriate Federal and State statutes.

PROVISION OF LICENSING AGREEMENTS – Recognized educational, commercial, industrial, and governmental institutions and organizations, and others legitimately engaged in educational pursuits, including training, testing, and measurement activities, may address request for a licensing agreement to the copyright owners, who will determine whether, and under what conditions, including fees and charges, the materials in this book may be used them. In other words, a licensing facility exists for the legitimate use of the material in this book on other than an individual basis. However, it is asseverated and affirmed here that the material in this book CANNOT be used without the receipt of the express permission of such a licensing agreement from the Publishers. Inquiries re licensing should be addressed to the company, attention rights and permissions department.

All rights reserved, including the right of reproduction in whole or in part, in any form or by any means, electronic or mechanical, including photocopying, recording, or by any information storage and retrieval system, without permission in writing from the Publisher.

Copyright © 2025 by
National Learning Corporation

212 Michael Drive, Syosset, NY 11791
(516) 921-8888 • www.passbooks.com
E-mail: info@passbooks.com

PASSBOOK® SERIES

THE *PASSBOOK® SERIES* has been created to prepare applicants and candidates for the ultimate academic battlefield – the examination room.

At some time in our lives, each and every one of us may be required to take an examination – for validation, matriculation, admission, qualification, registration, certification, or licensure.

Based on the assumption that every applicant or candidate has met the basic formal educational standards, has taken the required number of courses, and read the necessary texts, the *PASSBOOK® SERIES* furnishes the one special preparation which may assure passing with confidence, instead of failing with insecurity. Examination questions – together with answers – are furnished as the basic vehicle for study so that the mysteries of the examination and its compounding difficulties may be eliminated or diminished by a sure method.

This book is meant to help you pass your examination provided that you qualify and are serious in your objective.

The entire field is reviewed through the huge store of content information which is succinctly presented through a provocative and challenging approach – the question-and-answer method.

A climate of success is established by furnishing the correct answers at the end of each test.

You soon learn to recognize types of questions, forms of questions, and patterns of questioning. You may even begin to anticipate expected outcomes.

You perceive that many questions are repeated or adapted so that you can gain acute insights, which may enable you to score many sure points.

You learn how to confront new questions, or types of questions, and to attack them confidently and work out the correct answers.

You note objectives and emphases, and recognize pitfalls and dangers, so that you may make positive educational adjustments.

Moreover, you are kept fully informed in relation to new concepts, methods, practices, and directions in the field.

You discover that you are actually taking the examination all the time: you are preparing for the examination by "taking" an examination, not by reading extraneous and/or supererogatory textbooks.

In short, this PASSBOOK®, used directedly, should be an important factor in helping you to pass your test.

The New York State Teacher Certification Examinations

The NYSTCE are criterion-referenced, objective-based tests designed to measure a candidate's knowledge and skills in relation to an established standard rather than in relation to the performance of other candidates. The explicit purpose of these tests is to help identify for certification those candidates who have demonstrated the appropriate level of knowledge and skills that are important for performing the responsibilities of an educator in New York State public schools.

The NYSTCE program includes the following tests that measure a candidate's knowledge and skills in the liberal arts and sciences, in teaching theory and practice, and in the content area of the candidate's field of certification.

Test	Test Description
Liberal Arts and Sciences Test (LAST)	The LAST consists of multiple-choice questions and a written assignment. Examinees are asked to demonstrate conceptual and analytical skills, critical-thinking and communication skills, and multicultural awareness. The test covers scientific, mathematical, and technological processes; historical and social scientific awareness; artistic expression and the humanities; communication and research skills; and written analysis and expression.
Elementary Assessment of Teaching Skills—Written (ATS–W)	The Elementary ATS–W consists of multiple-choice questions and a written assignment. The Elementary ATS–W measures professional and pedagogical knowledge at the Early Childhood (birth–grade 2) and Childhood (grades 1-6) levels.
Secondary Assessment of Teaching Skills—Written (ATS–W)	The Secondary ATS–W consists of multiple-choice questions and a written assignment. The Secondary ATS–W measures professional and pedagogical knowledge at the Middle Childhood (grades 5-9) and Adolescence (grades 7-12) levels.
Content Specialty Tests (CSTs)	The CSTs (except those for languages other than English) consist of multiple-choice questions and a written assignment. The CSTs for languages other than English include recorded listening and/or speaking components and writing components. The American Sign Language CST includes video-recorded signing components. CSTs measure knowledge and skills in the content area of the candidate's field of certification. Refer to "Test Selection" for information about specific CSTs.
Bilingual Education Assessments (BEAs)	The BEAs consist of multiple-choice questions and constructed-response assignments. They include recorded listening and speaking components in English and include listening, speaking, reading, and writing components in the target language. The BEAs are required of candidates seeking a bilingual education extension to a certificate. Refer to "Test Selection" for information about specific BEAs.
Communication and Quantitative Skills Test (CQST)	The CQST consists of multiple-choice questions. The CQST is one of the requirements for a Transitional A certificate and an initial certificate (nondegree route) in career and technical education subjects.

HOW TO TAKE A TEST

I. YOU MUST PASS AN EXAMINATION

A. *WHAT EVERY CANDIDATE SHOULD KNOW*

Examination applicants often ask us for help in preparing for the written test. What can I study in advance? What kinds of questions will be asked? How will the test be given? How will the papers be graded?

As an applicant for a civil service examination, you may be wondering about some of these things. Our purpose here is to suggest effective methods of advance study and to describe civil service examinations.

Your chances for success on this examination can be increased if you know how to prepare. Those "pre-examination jitters" can be reduced if you know what to expect. You can even experience an adventure in good citizenship if you know why civil service exams are given.

B. *WHY ARE CIVIL SERVICE EXAMINATIONS GIVEN?*

Civil service examinations are important to you in two ways. As a citizen, you want public jobs filled by employees who know how to do their work. As a job seeker, you want a fair chance to compete for that job on an equal footing with other candidates. The best-known means of accomplishing this two-fold goal is the competitive examination.

Exams are widely publicized throughout the nation. They may be administered for jobs in federal, state, city, municipal, town or village governments or agencies.

Any citizen may apply, with some limitations, such as the age or residence of applicants. Your experience and education may be reviewed to see whether you meet the requirements for the particular examination. When these requirements exist, they are reasonable and applied consistently to all applicants. Thus, a competitive examination may cause you some uneasiness now, but it is your privilege and safeguard.

C. *HOW ARE CIVIL SERVICE EXAMS DEVELOPED?*

Examinations are carefully written by trained technicians who are specialists in the field known as "psychological measurement," in consultation with recognized authorities in the field of work that the test will cover. These experts recommend the subject matter areas or skills to be tested; only those knowledges or skills important to your success on the job are included. The most reliable books and source materials available are used as references. Together, the experts and technicians judge the difficulty level of the questions.

Test technicians know how to phrase questions so that the problem is clearly stated. Their ethics do not permit "trick" or "catch" questions. Questions may have been tried out on sample groups, or subjected to statistical analysis, to determine their usefulness.

Written tests are often used in combination with performance tests, ratings of training and experience, and oral interviews. All of these measures combine to form the best-known means of finding the right person for the right job.

II. HOW TO PASS THE WRITTEN TEST

A. NATURE OF THE EXAMINATION

To prepare intelligently for civil service examinations, you should know how they differ from school examinations you have taken. In school you were assigned certain definite pages to read or subjects to cover. The examination questions were quite detailed and usually emphasized memory. Civil service exams, on the other hand, try to discover your present ability to perform the duties of a position, plus your potentiality to learn these duties. In other words, a civil service exam attempts to predict how successful you will be. Questions cover such a broad area that they cannot be as minute and detailed as school exam questions.

In the public service similar kinds of work, or positions, are grouped together in one "class." This process is known as *position-classification*. All the positions in a class are paid according to the salary range for that class. One class title covers all of these positions, and they are all tested by the same examination.

B. FOUR BASIC STEPS

1) Study the announcement

How, then, can you know what subjects to study? Our best answer is: "Learn as much as possible about the class of positions for which you've applied." The exam will test the knowledge, skills and abilities needed to do the work.

Your most valuable source of information about the position you want is the official exam announcement. This announcement lists the training and experience qualifications. Check these standards and apply only if you come reasonably close to meeting them.

The brief description of the position in the examination announcement offers some clues to the subjects which will be tested. Think about the job itself. Review the duties in your mind. Can you perform them, or are there some in which you are rusty? Fill in the blank spots in your preparation.

Many jurisdictions preview the written test in the exam announcement by including a section called "Knowledge and Abilities Required," "Scope of the Examination," or some similar heading. Here you will find out specifically what fields will be tested.

2) Review your own background

Once you learn in general what the position is all about, and what you need to know to do the work, ask yourself which subjects you already know fairly well and which need improvement. You may wonder whether to concentrate on improving your strong areas or on building some background in your fields of weakness. When the announcement has specified "some knowledge" or "considerable knowledge," or has used adjectives like "beginning principles of..." or "advanced ... methods," you can get a clue as to the number and difficulty of questions to be asked in any given field. More questions, and hence broader coverage, would be included for those subjects which are more important in the work. Now weigh your strengths and weaknesses against the job requirements and prepare accordingly.

3) Determine the level of the position

Another way to tell how intensively you should prepare is to understand the level of the job for which you are applying. Is it the entering level? In other words, is this the position in which beginners in a field of work are hired? Or is it an intermediate or advanced level? Sometimes this is indicated by such words as "Junior" or "Senior" in the class title. Other jurisdictions use Roman numerals to designate the level – Clerk I, Clerk II, for example. The word "Supervisor" sometimes appears in the title. If the level is not indicated by the title, check the description of duties. Will you be working under very close supervision, or will you have responsibility for independent decisions in this work?

4) Choose appropriate study materials

Now that you know the subjects to be examined and the relative amount of each subject to be covered, you can choose suitable study materials. For beginning level jobs, or even advanced ones, if you have a pronounced weakness in some aspect of your training, read a modern, standard textbook in that field. Be sure it is up to date and has general coverage. Such books are normally available at your library, and the librarian will be glad to help you locate one. For entry-level positions, questions of appropriate difficulty are chosen – neither highly advanced questions, nor those too simple. Such questions require careful thought but not advanced training.

If the position for which you are applying is technical or advanced, you will read more advanced, specialized material. If you are already familiar with the basic principles of your field, elementary textbooks would waste your time. Concentrate on advanced textbooks and technical periodicals. Think through the concepts and review difficult problems in your field.

These are all general sources. You can get more ideas on your own initiative, following these leads. For example, training manuals and publications of the government agency which employs workers in your field can be useful, particularly for technical and professional positions. A letter or visit to the government department involved may result in more specific study suggestions, and certainly will provide you with a more definite idea of the exact nature of the position you are seeking.

III. KINDS OF TESTS

Tests are used for purposes other than measuring knowledge and ability to perform specified duties. For some positions, it is equally important to test ability to make adjustments to new situations or to profit from training. In others, basic mental abilities not dependent on information are essential. Questions which test these things may not appear as pertinent to the duties of the position as those which test for knowledge and information. Yet they are often highly important parts of a fair examination. For very general questions, it is almost impossible to help you direct your study efforts. What we can do is to point out some of the more common of these general abilities needed in public service positions and describe some typical questions.

1) General information

Broad, general information has been found useful for predicting job success in some kinds of work. This is tested in a variety of ways, from vocabulary lists to questions about current events. Basic background in some field of work, such as sociology or economics, may be sampled in a group of questions. Often these are principles which have become familiar to most persons through exposure rather than through formal training. It is difficult to advise you how to study for these questions; being alert to the world around you is our best suggestion.

2) Verbal ability

An example of an ability needed in many positions is verbal or language ability. Verbal ability is, in brief, the ability to use and understand words. Vocabulary and grammar tests are typical measures of this ability. Reading comprehension or paragraph interpretation questions are common in many kinds of civil service tests. You are given a paragraph of written material and asked to find its central meaning.

3) Numerical ability

Number skills can be tested by the familiar arithmetic problem, by checking paired lists of numbers to see which are alike and which are different, or by interpreting charts and graphs. In the latter test, a graph may be printed in the test booklet which you are asked to use as the basis for answering questions.

4) Observation

A popular test for law-enforcement positions is the observation test. A picture is shown to you for several minutes, then taken away. Questions about the picture test your ability to observe both details and larger elements.

5) Following directions

In many positions in the public service, the employee must be able to carry out written instructions dependably and accurately. You may be given a chart with several columns, each column listing a variety of information. The questions require you to carry out directions involving the information given in the chart.

6) Skills and aptitudes

Performance tests effectively measure some manual skills and aptitudes. When the skill is one in which you are trained, such as typing or shorthand, you can practice. These tests are often very much like those given in business school or high school courses. For many of the other skills and aptitudes, however, no short-time preparation can be made. Skills and abilities natural to you or that you have developed throughout your lifetime are being tested.

Many of the general questions just described provide all the data needed to answer the questions and ask you to use your reasoning ability to find the answers. Your best preparation for these tests, as well as for tests of facts and ideas, is to be at your physical and mental best. You, no doubt, have your own methods of getting into an exam-taking mood and keeping "in shape." The next section lists some ideas on this subject.

IV. KINDS OF QUESTIONS

Only rarely is the "essay" question, which you answer in narrative form, used in civil service tests. Civil service tests are usually of the short-answer type. Full instructions for answering these questions will be given to you at the examination. But in case this is your first experience with short-answer questions and separate answer sheets, here is what you need to know:

1) Multiple-choice Questions

Most popular of the short-answer questions is the "multiple choice" or "best answer" question. It can be used, for example, to test for factual knowledge, ability to solve problems or judgment in meeting situations found at work.

A multiple-choice question is normally one of three types—
- It can begin with an incomplete statement followed by several possible endings. You are to find the one ending which *best* completes the statement, although some of the others may not be entirely wrong.
- It can also be a complete statement in the form of a question which is answered by choosing one of the statements listed.

- It can be in the form of a problem – again you select the best answer.

Here is an example of a multiple-choice question with a discussion which should give you some clues as to the method for choosing the right answer:

When an employee has a complaint about his assignment, the action which will *best* help him overcome his difficulty is to
- A. discuss his difficulty with his coworkers
- B. take the problem to the head of the organization
- C. take the problem to the person who gave him the assignment
- D. say nothing to anyone about his complaint

In answering this question, you should study each of the choices to find which is best. Consider choice "A" – Certainly an employee may discuss his complaint with fellow employees, but no change or improvement can result, and the complaint remains unresolved. Choice "B" is a poor choice since the head of the organization probably does not know what assignment you have been given, and taking your problem to him is known as "going over the head" of the supervisor. The supervisor, or person who made the assignment, is the person who can clarify it or correct any injustice. Choice "C" is, therefore, correct. To say nothing, as in choice "D," is unwise. Supervisors have and interest in knowing the problems employees are facing, and the employee is seeking a solution to his problem.

2) True/False Questions

The "true/false" or "right/wrong" form of question is sometimes used. Here a complete statement is given. Your job is to decide whether the statement is right or wrong.

SAMPLE: A roaming cell-phone call to a nearby city costs less than a non-roaming call to a distant city.

This statement is wrong, or false, since roaming calls are more expensive.

This is not a complete list of all possible question forms, although most of the others are variations of these common types. You will always get complete directions for answering questions. Be sure you understand *how* to mark your answers – ask questions until you do.

V. RECORDING YOUR ANSWERS

Computer terminals are used more and more today for many different kinds of exams.
For an examination with very few applicants, you may be told to record your answers in the test booklet itself. Separate answer sheets are much more common. If this separate answer sheet is to be scored by machine – and this is often the case – it is highly important that you mark your answers correctly in order to get credit.
An electronic scoring machine is often used in civil service offices because of the speed with which papers can be scored. Machine-scored answer sheets must be marked with a pencil, which will be given to you. This pencil has a high graphite content which responds to the electronic scoring machine. As a matter of fact, stray dots may register as answers, so do not let your pencil rest on the answer sheet while you are pondering the correct answer. Also, if your pencil lead breaks or is otherwise defective, ask for another.

Since the answer sheet will be dropped in a slot in the scoring machine, be careful not to bend the corners or get the paper crumpled.

The answer sheet normally has five vertical columns of numbers, with 30 numbers to a column. These numbers correspond to the question numbers in your test booklet. After each number, going across the page are four or five pairs of dotted lines. These short dotted lines have small letters or numbers above them. The first two pairs may also have a "T" or "F" above the letters. This indicates that the first two pairs only are to be used if the questions are of the true-false type. If the questions are multiple choice, disregard the "T" and "F" and pay attention only to the small letters or numbers.

Answer your questions in the manner of the sample that follows:

32. The largest city in the United States is
    A. Washington, D.C.
    B. New York City
    C. Chicago
    D. Detroit
    E. San Francisco

1) Choose the answer you think is best. (New York City is the largest, so "B" is correct.)
2) Find the row of dotted lines numbered the same as the question you are answering. (Find row number 32)
3) Find the pair of dotted lines corresponding to the answer. (Find the pair of lines under the mark "B.")
4) Make a solid black mark between the dotted lines.

VI. BEFORE THE TEST

Common sense will help you find procedures to follow to get ready for an examination. Too many of us, however, overlook these sensible measures. Indeed, nervousness and fatigue have been found to be the most serious reasons why applicants fail to do their best on civil service tests. Here is a list of reminders:

- Begin your preparation early – Don't wait until the last minute to go scurrying around for books and materials or to find out what the position is all about.
- Prepare continuously – An hour a night for a week is better than an all-night cram session. This has been definitely established. What is more, a night a week for a month will return better dividends than crowding your study into a shorter period of time.
- Locate the place of the exam – You have been sent a notice telling you when and where to report for the examination. If the location is in a different town or otherwise unfamiliar to you, it would be well to inquire the best route and learn something about the building.
- Relax the night before the test – Allow your mind to rest. Do not study at all that night. Plan some mild recreation or diversion; then go to bed early and get a good night's sleep.
- Get up early enough to make a leisurely trip to the place for the test – This way unforeseen events, traffic snarls, unfamiliar buildings, etc. will not upset you.
- Dress comfortably – A written test is not a fashion show. You will be known by number and not by name, so wear something comfortable.

- Leave excess paraphernalia at home – Shopping bags and odd bundles will get in your way. You need bring only the items mentioned in the official notice you received; usually everything you need is provided. Do not bring reference books to the exam. They will only confuse those last minutes and be taken away from you when in the test room.
- Arrive somewhat ahead of time – If because of transportation schedules you must get there very early, bring a newspaper or magazine to take your mind off yourself while waiting.
- Locate the examination room – When you have found the proper room, you will be directed to the seat or part of the room where you will sit. Sometimes you are given a sheet of instructions to read while you are waiting. Do not fill out any forms until you are told to do so; just read them and be prepared.
- Relax and prepare to listen to the instructions
- If you have any physical problem that may keep you from doing your best, be sure to tell the test administrator. If you are sick or in poor health, you really cannot do your best on the exam. You can come back and take the test some other time.

VII. AT THE TEST

The day of the test is here and you have the test booklet in your hand. The temptation to get going is very strong. Caution! There is more to success than knowing the right answers. You must know how to identify your papers and understand variations in the type of short-answer question used in this particular examination. Follow these suggestions for maximum results from your efforts:

1) Cooperate with the monitor

The test administrator has a duty to create a situation in which you can be as much at ease as possible. He will give instructions, tell you when to begin, check to see that you are marking your answer sheet correctly, and so on. He is not there to guard you, although he will see that your competitors do not take unfair advantage. He wants to help you do your best.

2) Listen to all instructions

Don't jump the gun! Wait until you understand all directions. In most civil service tests you get more time than you need to answer the questions. So don't be in a hurry. Read each word of instructions until you clearly understand the meaning. Study the examples, listen to all announcements and follow directions. Ask questions if you do not understand what to do.

3) Identify your papers

Civil service exams are usually identified by number only. You will be assigned a number; you must not put your name on your test papers. Be sure to copy your number correctly. Since more than one exam may be given, copy your exact examination title.

4) Plan your time

Unless you are told that a test is a "speed" or "rate of work" test, speed itself is usually not important. Time enough to answer all the questions will be provided, but this does not mean that you have all day. An overall time limit has been set. Divide the total time (in minutes) by the number of questions to determine the approximate time you have for each question.

5) Do not linger over difficult questions

If you come across a difficult question, mark it with a paper clip (useful to have along) and come back to it when you have been through the booklet. One caution if you do this – be sure to skip a number on your answer sheet as well. Check often to be sure that you have not lost your place and that you are marking in the row numbered the same as the question you are answering.

6) Read the questions

Be sure you know what the question asks! Many capable people are unsuccessful because they failed to *read* the questions correctly.

7) Answer all questions

Unless you have been instructed that a penalty will be deducted for incorrect answers, it is better to guess than to omit a question.

8) Speed tests

It is often better NOT to guess on speed tests. It has been found that on timed tests people are tempted to spend the last few seconds before time is called in marking answers at random – without even reading them – in the hope of picking up a few extra points. To discourage this practice, the instructions may warn you that your score will be "corrected" for guessing. That is, a penalty will be applied. The incorrect answers will be deducted from the correct ones, or some other penalty formula will be used.

9) Review your answers

If you finish before time is called, go back to the questions you guessed or omitted to give them further thought. Review other answers if you have time.

10) Return your test materials

If you are ready to leave before others have finished or time is called, take ALL your materials to the monitor and leave quietly. Never take any test material with you. The monitor can discover whose papers are not complete, and taking a test booklet may be grounds for disqualification.

VIII. EXAMINATION TECHNIQUES

1) Read the general instructions carefully. These are usually printed on the first page of the exam booklet. As a rule, these instructions refer to the timing of the examination; the fact that you should not start work until the signal and must stop work at a signal, etc. If there are any *special* instructions, such as a choice of questions to be answered, make sure that you note this instruction carefully.

2) When you are ready to start work on the examination, that is as soon as the signal has been given, read the instructions to each question booklet, underline any key words or phrases, such as *least, best, outline, describe* and the like. In this way you will tend to answer as requested rather than discover on reviewing your paper that you *listed without describing*, that you selected the *worst* choice rather than the *best* choice, etc.

3) If the examination is of the objective or multiple-choice type – that is, each question will also give a series of possible answers: A, B, C or D, and you are called upon to select the best answer and write the letter next to that answer on your answer paper – it is advisable to start answering each question in turn. There may be anywhere from 50 to 100 such questions in the three or four hours allotted and you can see how much time would be taken if you read through all the questions before beginning to answer any. Furthermore, if you come across a question or group of questions which you know would be difficult to answer, it would undoubtedly affect your handling of all the other questions.

4) If the examination is of the essay type and contains but a few questions, it is a moot point as to whether you should read all the questions before starting to answer any one. Of course, if you are given a choice – say five out of seven and the like – then it is essential to read all the questions so you can eliminate the two that are most difficult. If, however, you are asked to answer all the questions, there may be danger in trying to answer the easiest one first because you may find that you will spend too much time on it. The best technique is to answer the first question, then proceed to the second, etc.

5) Time your answers. Before the exam begins, write down the time it started, then add the time allowed for the examination and write down the time it must be completed, then divide the time available somewhat as follows:
    - If 3-1/2 hours are allowed, that would be 210 minutes. If you have 80 objective-type questions, that would be an average of 2-1/2 minutes per question. Allow yourself no more than 2 minutes per question, or a total of 160 minutes, which will permit about 50 minutes to review.
    - If for the time allotment of 210 minutes there are 7 essay questions to answer, that would average about 30 minutes a question. Give yourself only 25 minutes per question so that you have about 35 minutes to review.

6) The most important instruction is to *read each question* and make sure you know what is wanted. The second most important instruction is to *time yourself properly* so that you answer every question. The third most important instruction is to *answer every question*. Guess if you have to but include something for each question. Remember that you will receive no credit for a blank and will probably receive some credit if you write something in answer to an essay question. If you guess a letter – say "B" for a multiple-choice question – you may have guessed right. If you leave a blank as an answer to a multiple-choice question, the examiners may respect your feelings but it will not add a point to your score. Some exams may penalize you for wrong answers, so in such cases *only*, you may not want to guess unless you have some basis for your answer.

7) Suggestions
    a. Objective-type questions
        1. Examine the question booklet for proper sequence of pages and questions
        2. Read all instructions carefully
        3. Skip any question which seems too difficult; return to it after all other questions have been answered
        4. Apportion your time properly; do not spend too much time on any single question or group of questions

5. Note and underline key words – *all, most, fewest, least, best, worst, same, opposite,* etc.
6. Pay particular attention to negatives
7. Note unusual option, e.g., unduly long, short, complex, different or similar in content to the body of the question
8. Observe the use of "hedging" words – *probably, may, most likely,* etc.
9. Make sure that your answer is put next to the same number as the question
10. Do not second-guess unless you have good reason to believe the second answer is definitely more correct
11. Cross out original answer if you decide another answer is more accurate; do not erase until you are ready to hand your paper in
12. Answer all questions; guess unless instructed otherwise
13. Leave time for review

b. Essay questions
1. Read each question carefully
2. Determine exactly what is wanted. Underline key words or phrases.
3. Decide on outline or paragraph answer
4. Include many different points and elements unless asked to develop any one or two points or elements
5. Show impartiality by giving pros and cons unless directed to select one side only
6. Make and write down any assumptions you find necessary to answer the questions
7. Watch your English, grammar, punctuation and choice of words
8. Time your answers; don't crowd material

8) Answering the essay question

Most essay questions can be answered by framing the specific response around several key words or ideas. Here are a few such key words or ideas:

M's: manpower, materials, methods, money, management
P's: purpose, program, policy, plan, procedure, practice, problems, pitfalls, personnel, public relations

a. Six basic steps in handling problems:
1. Preliminary plan and background development
2. Collect information, data and facts
3. Analyze and interpret information, data and facts
4. Analyze and develop solutions as well as make recommendations
5. Prepare report and sell recommendations
6. Install recommendations and follow up effectiveness

b. Pitfalls to avoid
1. *Taking things for granted* – A statement of the situation does not necessarily imply that each of the elements is necessarily true; for example, a complaint may be invalid and biased so that all that can be taken for granted is that a complaint has been registered

2. *Considering only one side of a situation* – Wherever possible, indicate several alternatives and then point out the reasons you selected the best one
3. *Failing to indicate follow up* – Whenever your answer indicates action on your part, make certain that you will take proper follow-up action to see how successful your recommendations, procedures or actions turn out to be
4. *Taking too long in answering any single question* – Remember to time your answers properly

IX. AFTER THE TEST

Scoring procedures differ in detail among civil service jurisdictions although the general principles are the same. Whether the papers are hand-scored or graded by machine we have described, they are nearly always graded by number. That is, the person who marks the paper knows only the number – never the name – of the applicant. Not until all the papers have been graded will they be matched with names. If other tests, such as training and experience or oral interview ratings have been given, scores will be combined. Different parts of the examination usually have different weights. For example, the written test might count 60 percent of the final grade, and a rating of training and experience 40 percent. In many jurisdictions, veterans will have a certain number of points added to their grades.

After the final grade has been determined, the names are placed in grade order and an eligible list is established. There are various methods for resolving ties between those who get the same final grade – probably the most common is to place first the name of the person whose application was received first. Job offers are made from the eligible list in the order the names appear on it. You will be notified of your grade and your rank as soon as all these computations have been made. This will be done as rapidly as possible.

People who are found to meet the requirements in the announcement are called "eligibles." Their names are put on a list of eligible candidates. An eligible's chances of getting a job depend on how high he stands on this list and how fast agencies are filling jobs from the list.

When a job is to be filled from a list of eligibles, the agency asks for the names of people on the list of eligibles for that job. When the civil service commission receives this request, it sends to the agency the names of the three people highest on this list. Or, if the job to be filled has specialized requirements, the office sends the agency the names of the top three persons who meet these requirements from the general list.

The appointing officer makes a choice from among the three people whose names were sent to him. If the selected person accepts the appointment, the names of the others are put back on the list to be considered for future openings.

That is the rule in hiring from all kinds of eligible lists, whether they are for typist, carpenter, chemist, or something else. For every vacancy, the appointing officer has his choice of any one of the top three eligibles on the list. This explains why the person whose name is on top of the list sometimes does not get an appointment when some of the persons lower on the list do. If the appointing officer chooses the second or third eligible, the No. 1 eligible does not get a job at once, but stays on the list until he is appointed or the list is terminated.

X. HOW TO PASS THE INTERVIEW TEST

The examination for which you applied requires an oral interview test. You have already taken the written test and you are now being called for the interview test – the final part of the formal examination.

You may think that it is not possible to prepare for an interview test and that there are no procedures to follow during an interview. Our purpose is to point out some things you can do in advance that will help you and some good rules to follow and pitfalls to avoid while you are being interviewed.

What is an interview supposed to test?

The written examination is designed to test the technical knowledge and competence of the candidate; the oral is designed to evaluate intangible qualities, not readily measured otherwise, and to establish a list showing the relative fitness of each candidate – as measured against his competitors – for the position sought. Scoring is not on the basis of "right" and "wrong," but on a sliding scale of values ranging from "not passable" to "outstanding." As a matter of fact, it is possible to achieve a relatively low score without a single "incorrect" answer because of evident weakness in the qualities being measured.

Occasionally, an examination may consist entirely of an oral test – either an individual or a group oral. In such cases, information is sought concerning the technical knowledges and abilities of the candidate, since there has been no written examination for this purpose. More commonly, however, an oral test is used to supplement a written examination.

Who conducts interviews?

The composition of oral boards varies among different jurisdictions. In nearly all, a representative of the personnel department serves as chairman. One of the members of the board may be a representative of the department in which the candidate would work. In some cases, "outside experts" are used, and, frequently, a businessman or some other representative of the general public is asked to serve. Labor and management or other special groups may be represented. The aim is to secure the services of experts in the appropriate field.

However the board is composed, it is a good idea (and not at all improper or unethical) to ascertain in advance of the interview who the members are and what groups they represent. When you are introduced to them, you will have some idea of their backgrounds and interests, and at least you will not stutter and stammer over their names.

What should be done before the interview?

While knowledge about the board members is useful and takes some of the surprise element out of the interview, there is other preparation which is more substantive. It *is* possible to prepare for an oral interview – in several ways:

1) Keep a copy of your application and review it carefully before the interview

This may be the only document before the oral board, and the starting point of the interview. Know what education and experience you have listed there, and the sequence and dates of all of it. Sometimes the board will ask you to review the highlights of your experience for them; you should not have to hem and haw doing it.

2) Study the class specification and the examination announcement

Usually, the oral board has one or both of these to guide them. The qualities, characteristics or knowledges required by the position sought are stated in these documents. They offer valuable clues as to the nature of the oral interview. For example, if the job involves supervisory responsibilities, the announcement will usually indicate that knowledge of modern supervisory methods and the qualifications of the candidate as a supervisor will be tested. If so, you can expect such questions, frequently in the form of a hypothetical situation which you are expected to solve. NEVER go into an oral without knowledge of the duties and responsibilities of the job you seek.

3) Think through each qualification required

Try to visualize the kind of questions you would ask if you were a board member. How well could you answer them? Try especially to appraise your own knowledge and background in each area, *measured against the job sought*, and identify any areas in which you are weak. Be critical and realistic – do not flatter yourself.

4) Do some general reading in areas in which you feel you may be weak

For example, if the job involves supervision and your past experience has NOT, some general reading in supervisory methods and practices, particularly in the field of human relations, might be useful. Do NOT study agency procedures or detailed manuals. The oral board will be testing your understanding and capacity, not your memory.

5) Get a good night's sleep and watch your general health and mental attitude

You will want a clear head at the interview. Take care of a cold or any other minor ailment, and of course, no hangovers.

What should be done on the day of the interview?

Now comes the day of the interview itself. Give yourself plenty of time to get there. Plan to arrive somewhat ahead of the scheduled time, particularly if your appointment is in the fore part of the day. If a previous candidate fails to appear, the board might be ready for you a bit early. By early afternoon an oral board is almost invariably behind schedule if there are many candidates, and you may have to wait. Take along a book or magazine to read, or your application to review, but leave any extraneous material in the waiting room when you go in for your interview. In any event, relax and compose yourself.

The matter of dress is important. The board is forming impressions about you – from your experience, your manners, your attitude, and your appearance. Give your personal appearance careful attention. Dress your best, but not your flashiest. Choose conservative, appropriate clothing, and be sure it is immaculate. This is a business interview, and your appearance should indicate that you regard it as such. Besides, being well groomed and properly dressed will help boost your confidence.

Sooner or later, someone will call your name and escort you into the interview room. *This is it.* From here on you are on your own. It is too late for any more preparation. But remember, you asked for this opportunity to prove your fitness, and you are here because your request was granted.

What happens when you go in?

The usual sequence of events will be as follows: The clerk (who is often the board stenographer) will introduce you to the chairman of the oral board, who will introduce you to the other members of the board. Acknowledge the introductions before you sit down. Do not be surprised if you find a microphone facing you or a stenotypist sitting by. Oral interviews are usually recorded in the event of an appeal or other review.

Usually the chairman of the board will open the interview by reviewing the highlights of your education and work experience from your application – primarily for the benefit of the other members of the board, as well as to get the material into the record. Do not interrupt or comment unless there is an error or significant misinterpretation; if that is the case, do not hesitate. But do not quibble about insignificant matters. Also, he will usually ask you some question about your education, experience or your present job – partly to get you to start talking and to establish the interviewing "rapport." He may start the actual questioning, or turn it over to one of the other members. Frequently, each member undertakes the questioning on a particular area, one in which he is perhaps most competent, so you can expect each member to participate in the examination. Because time is limited, you may also expect some rather abrupt switches in the direction the questioning takes, so do not be upset by it. Normally, a board member will not pursue a single line of questioning unless he discovers a particular strength or weakness.

After each member has participated, the chairman will usually ask whether any member has any further questions, then will ask you if you have anything you wish to add. Unless you are expecting this question, it may floor you. Worse, it may start you off on an extended, extemporaneous speech. The board is not usually seeking more information. The question is principally to offer you a last opportunity to present further qualifications or to indicate that you have nothing to add. So, if you feel that a significant qualification or characteristic has been overlooked, it is proper to point it out in a sentence or so. Do not compliment the board on the thoroughness of their examination – they have been sketchy, and you know it. If you wish, merely say, "No thank you, I have nothing further to add." This is a point where you can "talk yourself out" of a good impression or fail to present an important bit of information. Remember, *you close the interview yourself*.

The chairman will then say, "That is all, Mr. _____, thank you." Do not be startled; the interview is over, and quicker than you think. Thank him, gather your belongings and take your leave. Save your sigh of relief for the other side of the door.

How to put your best foot forward

Throughout this entire process, you may feel that the board individually and collectively is trying to pierce your defenses, seek out your hidden weaknesses and embarrass and confuse you. Actually, this is not true. They are obliged to make an appraisal of your qualifications for the job you are seeking, and they want to see you in your best light. Remember, they must interview all candidates and a non-cooperative candidate may become a failure in spite of their best efforts to bring out his qualifications. Here are 15 suggestions that will help you:

1) Be natural – Keep your attitude confident, not cocky

If you are not confident that you can do the job, do not expect the board to be. Do not apologize for your weaknesses, try to bring out your strong points. The board is interested in a positive, not negative, presentation. Cockiness will antagonize any board member and make him wonder if you are covering up a weakness by a false show of strength.

2) Get comfortable, but don't lounge or sprawl

Sit erectly but not stiffly. A careless posture may lead the board to conclude that you are careless in other things, or at least that you are not impressed by the importance of the occasion. Either conclusion is natural, even if incorrect. Do not fuss with your clothing, a pencil or an ashtray. Your hands may occasionally be useful to emphasize a point; do not let them become a point of distraction.

3) Do not wisecrack or make small talk

This is a serious situation, and your attitude should show that you consider it as such. Further, the time of the board is limited – they do not want to waste it, and neither should you.

4) Do not exaggerate your experience or abilities

In the first place, from information in the application or other interviews and sources, the board may know more about you than you think. Secondly, you probably will not get away with it. An experienced board is rather adept at spotting such a situation, so do not take the chance.

5) If you know a board member, do not make a point of it, yet do not hide it

Certainly you are not fooling him, and probably not the other members of the board. Do not try to take advantage of your acquaintanceship – it will probably do you little good.

6) Do not dominate the interview

Let the board do that. They will give you the clues – do not assume that you have to do all the talking. Realize that the board has a number of questions to ask you, and do not try to take up all the interview time by showing off your extensive knowledge of the answer to the first one.

7) Be attentive

You only have 20 minutes or so, and you should keep your attention at its sharpest throughout. When a member is addressing a problem or question to you, give him your undivided attention. Address your reply principally to him, but do not exclude the other board members.

8) Do not interrupt

A board member may be stating a problem for you to analyze. He will ask you a question when the time comes. Let him state the problem, and wait for the question.

9) Make sure you understand the question

Do not try to answer until you are sure what the question is. If it is not clear, restate it in your own words or ask the board member to clarify it for you. However, do not haggle about minor elements.

10) Reply promptly but not hastily

A common entry on oral board rating sheets is "candidate responded readily," or "candidate hesitated in replies." Respond as promptly and quickly as you can, but do not jump to a hasty, ill-considered answer.

11) Do not be peremptory in your answers

A brief answer is proper – but do not fire your answer back. That is a losing game from your point of view. The board member can probably ask questions much faster than you can answer them.

12) Do not try to create the answer you think the board member wants

He is interested in what kind of mind you have and how it works – not in playing games. Furthermore, he can usually spot this practice and will actually grade you down on it.

13) Do not switch sides in your reply merely to agree with a board member

Frequently, a member will take a contrary position merely to draw you out and to see if you are willing and able to defend your point of view. Do not start a debate, yet do not surrender a good position. If a position is worth taking, it is worth defending.

14) Do not be afraid to admit an error in judgment if you are shown to be wrong

The board knows that you are forced to reply without any opportunity for careful consideration. Your answer may be demonstrably wrong. If so, admit it and get on with the interview.

15) Do not dwell at length on your present job

The opening question may relate to your present assignment. Answer the question but do not go into an extended discussion. You are being examined for a *new* job, not your present one. As a matter of fact, try to phrase ALL your answers in terms of the job for which you are being examined.

Basis of Rating

Probably you will forget most of these "do's" and "don'ts" when you walk into the oral interview room. Even remembering them all will not ensure you a passing grade. Perhaps you did not have the qualifications in the first place. But remembering them will help you to put your best foot forward, without treading on the toes of the board members.

Rumor and popular opinion to the contrary notwithstanding, an oral board wants you to make the best appearance possible. They know you are under pressure – but they also want to see how you respond to it as a guide to what your reaction would be under the pressures of the job you seek. They will be influenced by the degree of poise you display, the personal traits you show and the manner in which you respond.

ABOUT THIS BOOK

This book contains tests divided into Examination Sections. Go through each test, answering every question in the margin. We have also attached a sample answer sheet at the back of the book that can be removed and used. At the end of each test look at the answer key and check your answers. On the ones you got wrong, look at the right answer choice and learn. Do not fill in the answers first. Do not memorize the questions and answers, but understand the answer and principles involved. On your test, the questions will likely be different from the samples. Questions are changed and new ones added. If you understand these past questions you should have success with any changes that arise. Tests may consist of several types of questions. We have additional books on each subject should more study be advisable or necessary for you. Finally, the more you study, the better prepared you will be. This book is intended to be the last thing you study before you walk into the examination room. Prior study of relevant texts is also recommended. NLC publishes some of these in our Fundamental Series. Knowledge and good sense are important factors in passing your exam. Good luck also helps. So now study this Passbook, absorb the material contained within and take that knowledge into the examination. Then do your best to pass that exam.

EXAMINATION SECTION

READING COMPREHENSION
UNDERSTANDING AND INTERPRETING WRITTEN MATERIAL
EXAMINATION SECTION
TEST 1

DIRECTIONS: Each question or incomplete statement is followed by several suggested answers or completions. Select the one that BEST answers the question or completes the statement. PRINT THE LETTER OF THE CORRECT ANSWER IN THE SPACE AT THE RIGHT.

PASSAGE

It is a common belief that a thing is desirable because it is scarce and thereby has ostentation value. The notion that such a standard of value is an inescapable condition of settled social existence rests on one of two implicit assumptions. The first is that the attempt to educate the human race so that the desire to display one's possessions is not a significant feature of man's social behavior, is an infringement against personal freedom. The greatest obstacle to lucid discourse in these matters is the psychological anti-vaccinationist who uses the word freedom to signify the natural right of men and women to be unhappy and unhealthy through scientific ignorance instead of being healthy and happy through the knowledge which science confers. Haunted by a perpetual fear of the dark, the last lesson which man learns in the difficult process of growing up is "ye shall know the truth, and the truth shall make you free." The professional economist who is too sophisticated to retreat Into the obscurities of this curious conception of liberty may prefer to adopt the second assumption, that the truth does not and cannot make us free because the need for ostentation is a universal species characteristic, and all attempts to eradicate the unconscionable nuisance and discord which arise from overdeveloped craving for personal distinction artificially fostered by advertisement propaganda and so-called good breeding are therefore destined to failure. It may be earnestly, hoped that those who entertain this view have divine guidance. No rational basis for it will be found in textbooks of economics. Whatever can be said with any plausibility in the existing state of knowledge rests on the laboratory materials supplied by anthropology and social history.

1. According to the writer, the second assumption

    A. Is fostered by propaganda and so-called good breeding
    B. is basically opposite to the view of the psychological anti-vaccinationist
    C. is not so curious a conception of liberty as Is the first assumption
    D. is unsubstantiated
    E. is a religious explanation of an economic phenomenon

1.____

2. The author's purpose in writing this paragraph is MOST probably to

    A. denounce the psychological anti-vaccinationists
    B. demonstrate that the question under discussion is an economic rather than a psychological problem
    C. prove the maxim "ye shall know the truth, and the truth shall make you free"
    D. prove that ostentation is not an inescapable pheonomenon of settled social existence
    E. prove the inability of economics to account for ostentation

2.____

3. The writer implies that

   A. neither the psychological anti-vaccinationist nor the professional economist recognizes the undesirability of ostentation
   B. our cultural standards are at fault in enhancing ostentation value
   C. scarcity as a criterion of value Is an inexplicable concept
   D. his main objection Is to the inescapable standard of values
   E. the results of studies of ostentation in anthropology and social history are Irrational

4. The writer believes that both assumptions

   A. are invalid because they ignore the lesson "ye shall know the truth, and the truth shall make you free"
   B. are fallacious because they agree that a thing is desirable because it is scarce
   C. arise from overdeveloped craving for personal distinction
   D. are implicit in the conception of ostentation value
   E. dispute the efficacy of education in eliminating ostentation

5. In his reference to divine guidance, the writer is

   A. being ironic
   B. implying that only divine guidance can solve the problem
   C. showing how the professional economist is opposing divine laws
   D. referring to opposition which exists between religion and science
   E. indicating that the problem is not a matter for divine guidance

6. The writer believes that personal freedom is

   A. less important than is scientific knowledge
   B. a requisite for the attainment of truth
   C. attained by eradicating false beliefs
   D. no concern of the professional economist
   E. an unsophisticated concept

7. We may infer that this writer does NOT believe that

   A. education can solve the problem
   B. people have any "natural rights"
   C. science can solve the problem
   D. the psychological anti-vaccinationist is more than a lipservant of the cause of freedom
   E. people can be happy under the present value system

8. The writer would consider as MOST comparable to the effect of a vaccination on the body, the effect of

   A. fear upon personality
   B. science upon the supposed need for ostentation
   C. truth upon the mind
   D. knowledge upon ignorance
   E. knowledge upon happiness

KEY (CORRECT ANSWERS)

1. D
2. D
3. B
4. D
5. A
6. C
7. E
8. C

TEST 2

DIRECTIONS: Each question or incomplete statement is followed by several suggested answers or completions. Select the one that *BEST* answers the question or completes the statement. *PRINT THE LETTER OF THE CORRECT ANSWER IN THE SPACE AT THE RIGHT.*

PASSAGE

In any country the wages commanded by laborers who have comparable skills but who work in various industries are determined by the productivity of the least productive unit of labor, i.e., that unit of labor which works in the industry which has the greatest economic disadvantage. We will represent the various opportunities of employment in a country like the United States by symbols: A, standing for a group of industries in which we have exceptional economic advantages over foreign countries; B, for a group in which our advantages are less; C, one in which they are still less; D, the group of industries in which they are least of all.

When our population is so small that all our labor can be engaged in the group represented by A, productivity of labor (and therefore wages) will be at their maximum. When our population increases so that some of the labor will have to be set to work in group B, the wages of all labor must decline to the level of the productivity in that group. But no employer, without government aid, will yet be able to afford to hire labor to exploit the opportunities represented by C and D, unless there is a further increase in population.

But suppose that the political party in power holds the belief that we should produce everything that we consume, that the opportunities represented by C and D should be exploited. The commodities that the industries composing C and D will produce have been hitherto obtained from abroad in exchange for commodities produced by A and B. The government now renders this difficult by placing high duties upon the former class of commodities. This means that workers in A and B must pay higher prices for what they buy, but do not receive higher prices for what they sell.

After the duty has gone into effect and the prices of commodities that can be produced by C and D have risen sufficiently, enterprisers will be able to hire labor at the wages prevailing in A and B, and establish industries in C and D. So far as the remaining laborers in A and B buy the products of C and D, the difference between the price which they pay for those products and the price that they would pay if they were permitted to import those products duty-free is a tax paid not to the government, but to the producers in C and D, to enable the latter to remain in business. It is an uncompensated deduction from the natural earnings of the laborers in A and B. Nor are the workers in C and D paid as much, estimated in purchasing power, as they would have received if they had been allowed to remain in A and B under the earlier conditions.

1. When C and D are established, workers in these industries   1.___
   A. receive higher wages than do the workers in A and B
   B. receive lower wages than do the workers in A and B
   C. must be paid by government funds collected from the duties on imports
   D. are not affected so adversely by the levying of duties as are workers in A and B
   E. receive wages equal to those workers in A and B

2. We cannot exploit C and D unless

   A. the productivity of labor in all industries is increased
   B. the prices of commodities produced by A and B are raised
   C. we export large quantities of commodities produced by A and B
   D. the producers in C and D are compensated for the disadvantages under which they operate
   E. we allow duties to be paid to the producers in C and D rather than to the government

3. "No employer; without government aid, will yet be able to afford to hire labor to exploit the opportunities represented by C and D" because

   A. productivity of labor is not at the maximum
   B. we cannot produce everything we consume
   C. the population has increased
   D. enterprisers would have to pay wages equivalent to those obtained by workers in A and B, while producing under greater economic disadvantages
   E. productivity would drop correspondingly with the wages of labor

4. The government, when it places high duties on imported commodities of classes C and D,

   A. raises the price of commodities produced by A and B
   B. is, in effect, taxing the workers in A and B
   C. raises the wages of workers in C and D at the expense of the workers in A and B
   D. does not affect the productivity of the workers in A and B, although the wages of these workers are reduced
   E. is adopting a policy made necessary by the stability of the population

5. The author's MAIN point is that

   A. it is impossible to attain national self-sufficiency
   B. the varying productivity of the various industries leads to the inequalities in wages of workers in these industries
   C. a policy that draws labor from the fields of greater natural productiveness to fields of lower natural productiveness tends to reduce purchasing power
   D. wages ought to be independent of international trade
   E. the government ought to subsidize C and D.

6. The author's arguments in this passage could BEST be used to

   A. refute the belief that it is theoretically possible for us to produce everything that we consume
   B. disprove the theory that national self-sufficiency can be obtained by means of protective tariffs
   C. advocate the levying of duties on imported goods
   D. advocate equal wages for workers who have comparable skills but who work in various industries
   E. advocate free trade

7. When could C and D, as here defined, be exploited without the assistance of an artificially boosted price and without resultant lowering of wage levels?

    A. When a duty is placed on competing products from other countries
    B. When the products of C and D are exchanged in trade for other commodities
    C. When the country becomes economically self-sufficient
    D. When there is a favorable balance of trade
    E. At no time

8. In the last sentence in the selection, the statement is made: "Nor are the workers in C and D paid as much, estimated in purchasing power, as they would have received if they had been allowed to remain in A and B under the earlier conditions." This is because

    A. they must pay higher prices for commodities produced by C and D
    B. C and D cannot pay so high wages as can A and B
    C. products of C and D do not command sufficiently high prices
    D. there has not been an increase in population
    E. wages in all groups have declined

KEY (CORRECT ANSWERS)

1. E
2. D
3. D
4. B
5. C
6. E
7. B
8. E

TEST 3

DIRECTIONS: Each question or incomplete statement is followed by several suggested answers or completions. Select the one that BEST answers the question or completes the statement. PRINT THE LETTER OF THE CORRECT ANSWER IN THE SPACE AT THE RIGHT.

PASSAGE

In the Federal Convention of 1787, the members were fairly well agreed as to the desirability of some check on state laws; but there was sharp difference of opinion whether this check should be political in character as in the form of a congressional veto, or whether the principle of judicial review should be adopted.

Madison was one of the most persistent advocates of the congressional veto and in his discussion of the subject he referred several times to the former imperial prerogative of disallowing provincial statutes. In March, 1787, he wrote to Jefferson, urging the necessity of a federal negative upon state laws. He referred to previous colonial experience in the suggestion that there should be "some emanation" of the federal prerogative "within the several states, so far as to enable them to give a temporary sanction to laws of immediate necessity." This had been provided for in the imperial system through the action of the royal governor in giving immediate effect to statutes, which nevertheless remained subject to royal disallowance. In a letter to Randolph a few weeks later, Madison referred more explicitly to the British practice, urging that the national government be given "a negative, in all cases whatsoever, on the Legislative acts of the States, as the King of Great Britain heretofore had." Jefferson did not agree with Madison; on practical grounds rather than as a matter of principle, he expressed his preference for some form of judicial control.

On July 17, Madison came forward with a speech in support of the congressional veto, again supporting his contention by reference to the royal disallowance of colonial laws: "Its utility is sufficiently displayed in the British System. Nothing could maintain the harmony and subordination of the various parts of the empire, but the prerogative by which the Crown stifles in the birth every Act of every part tending to discord or encroachment. It is true the prerogative is sometimes misapplied thro' ignorance or a partiality to one particular part of the empire: but we have not the same reason to fear such misapplications in our System." This is almost precisely Jefferson's theory of the legitimate function of an imperial veto.

This whole issue shows that the leaders who wrestled with confederation problems during and after the war understood, in some measure at least, the attitude of British administrators when confronted with the stubborn localism of a provincial assembly.

1. Madison was advocating

   A. royal disallowance of state legislation
   B. a political check on state laws
   C. the supremacy of the states over the federal government
   D. the maintenance of a royal governor to give immediate effect to statutes
   E. discord and encroachment among the states

1._____

2. From this passage there is no indication

   A. of what the British System entailed
   B. of Jefferson's stand on the question of a check on state laws
   C. that the royal negative had been misapplied in the past
   D. that Jefferson understood the attitude of British administrators
   E. of what judicial review would entail

3. According to this passage, Madison believed that the federal government

   A. ought to legislate for the states
   B. should recognize the sovereignty of the several states
   C. ought to exercise judicial control over state legislation
   D. should assume the king's veto power
   E. was equivalent to a provincial assembly

4. Madison's conception of a congressional veto

   A. was opposed to Jefferson's conception of a congressional veto
   B. developed from fear that the imperial negative might be misused
   C. was that the federal prerogative should be exercised in disallowing state laws
   D. was that its primary function was to give temporary sanction to laws of immediate necessity
   E. was that its primary function was to prevent such injustices as "taxation without representation"

5. Madison believed that

   A. the congressional veto would not be abused
   B. the royal prerogative ought to have some form of check to correct misapplications
   C. the review of state legislation by the federal government ought to remain subject to a higher veto
   D. the imperial veto had not been misused
   E. utility rather than freedom is the criterion for governmental institutions

6. Jefferson believed that

   A. the congressional veto would interfere with states' rights
   B. Madison's proposal smacked of imperialism
   C. the veto of state legislation was outside the limits of the federal prerogative
   D. the British System would be harmful if applied in the United States
   E. an imperial veto should include the disallowance of all legislation leading to discord

7. Madison's MAIN principle was that

   A. the national interest is more important than the interests of any one state
   B. the national government should have compulsive power over the states
   C. the king can do no wrong
   D. the United States should follow the English pattern of government
   E. the veto power of the royal governor should be included in the federal prerogative

8. Madison thought of the states as

    A. emanations of the federal government
    B. comparable to provinces of a colonial empire
    C. incapable of creating sound legislation
    D. having no rights specifically delegated to them
    E. incapable of applying judicial review of their legislation

9. Which of the following is the BEST argument which could be made against Madison's proposition?

    A. The United States has no king.
    B. The federal government is an entity outside the jurisdiction of the states.
    C. Each state has local problems concerning which representatives from other states are not equipped to pass judgment.
    D. The federal prerogative had been misused in the past.
    E. It provides no means of dealing with stubborn localism.

KEY (CORRECT ANSWERS)

1. B   5. A
2. E   6. D
3. D   7. B
4. C   8. B
         9. C

TEST 4

DIRECTIONS: Each question or incomplete statement is followed by several suggested answers or completions. Select the one that BEST answers the question or completes the statement. PRINT THE LETTER OF THE CORRECT ANSWER IN THE SPACE AT THE RIGHT.

PASSAGE

The nucleus of its population is the local businessmen, whose interests constitute the municipal policy and control its municipal administration. These local businessmen are such as the local bankers, merchants of many kinds and degrees, real estate promoters, local lawyers, local clergymen...The businessmen, who take up the local traffic in merchandising, litigation, church enterprise and the like, commonly begin with some share in the real estate speculation. This affords a common bond and a common ground of pecuniary interest, which commonly masquerades under the name of local patriotism, public spirit, civic pride, and the like. This pretense of public spirit is so consistently maintained that most of these men come presently to believe in their own professions on that head. Pecuniary interest in local land values involves an interest in the continued growth of the town. Hence any creditable misrepresentation of the town's volume of business traffic, population, tributary farming community, or natural resources, is rated as serviceable to the common good. And any member of this business-like community will be rated as a meritorious citizen in proportion as he is serviceable to this joint pecuniary interest of these "influential citizens."

1. The tone of the paragraph is

   A. bitter
   B. didactic
   C. complaining
   D. satirical
   E. informative

2. The foundation for the "influential citizens" interest in their community is

   A. their control of the municipal administration
   B. their interests in trade and merchandising
   C. their natural feeling of civic pride
   D. a pretense of public spirit
   E. ownership of land for speculation

3. The "influential citizens" type of civic pride may be compared with the patriotism of believers in

   A. a balance of power in international diplomacy
   B. racial superiority
   C. laissez faire
   D. a high tariff
   E. dollar diplomacy

4. The IMPORTANT men in the town

   A. are consciously insincere in their local patriotism
   B. are drawn together for political reasons
   C. do not scruple to give their community a false boost
   D. regard strict economy as a necessary virtue
   E. are extremely jealous of their prestige

5. The writer considers that the influential men of the town　　　　5._____

   A. are entirely hypocritical in their conception of their motives
   B. are blinded to facts by their patriotic spirit
   C. have deceived themselves into thinking they are altruistic
   D. look upon the welfare of their community as of paramount importance
   E. form a closed corporation devoted to the interests of the town

6. PROBABLY the author's own view of patriotism is that it　　　　6._____

   A. should be a disinterested passion untinged by commercial motives
   B. is found only among the poorer classes
   C. is usually found in urban society
   D. grows out of a combination of the motives of selfinterest and altruism
   E. consists in the main of a feeling of local pride

KEY (CORRECT ANSWERS)

1.	B	4.	C
2.	E	5.	C
3.	E	6.	A

TEST 5

DIRECTIONS: Each question or incomplete statement is followed by several suggested answers or completions. Select the one that *BEST* answers the question or completes the statement. *PRINT THE LETTER OF THE CORRECT ANSWER IN THE SPACE AT THE RIGHT.*

PASSAGE

Negative thinking and lack of confidence in oneself or in the pupils are probably the greatest hindrances to inspirational teaching. Confronted with a new idea, one teacher will exclaim: "Oh, my children couldn't do that! They're too young." Another will mutter, "If I tried that stunt, the whole class would be in an uproar." Such are the self-justifications for mediocrity.

Here and there it is good to see a teacher take a bold step away from the humdrum approach. For example, Natalie Robinson Cole was given a class of fourth-year pupils who could hardly speak English. Yet in her book, THE ARTS IN THE CLASSROOM, she describes how she tried clay work, creative writing, interpretive dancing and many other exciting activities with them. Did her control of the class suffer? Were the results poor? Was morale adversely affected? The answer is *NO* on all three counts.

But someone may point out that what Mrs. Cole could do on the fourth-grade could not be done in the primary grades. Wrong again! The young child is more malleable than his older brother. Furthermore, his radiant heritage of originality has not been enveloped in clouds of self-consciousness. Given the proper encouragement, he will paint an interesting design on the easel, contribute a sparkling expression to the "class poem" as it takes shape on the blackboard, make a puppet speak his innermost thoughts, and react with sensitivity in scores of other ways.

All teachers on all grade levels need to think positively and act confidently. Of course, any departure from the commonplace must be buttressed by careful preparation, firm handling of the situation, and consistent attention to routines. Since these assets are within the reach of all teachers there should be no excuse for not putting some imagination into their work.

1. The central idea of the above passage is BEST conveyed by the

    A. first sentence in the first paragraph
    B. last sentence in the first paragraph
    C. first sentence in the second paragraph
    D. last sentence in the passage
    E. third sentence in the third paragraph

2. If the concepts of this passage were to be expanded into a book, the one of the following titles which would be MOST suitable is

    A. THE ARTS IN THE CLASSROOM
    B. THE POWER OF POSITIVE THINKING
    C. THE HIDDEN PERSUADERS
    D. KIDS SAY THE DARNDEST THINGS
    E. ARMS AND THE MAN

3. Of the following reasons for uninspired teaching, the one which is *NOT* given explicitly in the passage is   3.____

   A. negative thinking
   B. teachers' underestimation of pupils' ability or stability
   C. teachers' failure to broaden themselves culturally
   D. teachers' lack of self-assurance
   E. teachers' rationalizations

4. From reading the passage one can gather that Natalie R. Cole   4.____

   A. teaches in New York City
   B. has been married
   C. is an expert in art
   D. teaches in the primary grades
   E. is a specialist in child psychology

5. An activity for children in the primary grades which is NOT mentioned in the passage is   5.____

   A. creative expression
   B. art work
   C. puppetry
   D. constructing with blocks
   E. work on the blackboard

6. A basic asset of the inspirational teacher NOT mentioned in the passage is   6.____

   A. a pleasant, outgoing personality
   B. a firm hand
   C. a thorough, careful plan
   D. consistent attention to routines
   E. acting confidently

KEY (CORRECT ANSWERS)

1. A   4. B
2. B   5. D
3. C   6. A

TEST 6

DIRECTIONS: Each question or incomplete statement is followed by several suggested answers or completions. Select the one that *BEST* answers the question or completes the statement. *PRINT THE LETTER OF THE CORRECT ANSWER IN THE SPACE AT THE RIGHT.*

PASSAGE

Of all the areas of learning the most important is the development of attitudes. Emotional reactions as well as logical thought processes affect the behavior of most people. "The burnt child fears the fire" is one instance; another is the rise of despots like Hitler. Both these examples also point up the fact that attitudes stem from experience. In the one case the experience was direct and impressive; in the other it was indirect and cumulative. The Nazis were indoctrinated largely by the speeches they heard and the books they read.

The classroom teacher in the elementary school is in a strategic position to influence attitudes. This is true partly because children acquire attitudes from these adults whose word they respect. Another reason it is true is that pupils often delve somewhat deeply into a subject in school that has only been touched upon at home or has possibly never occurred to them before. To a child who had previously acquired little knowledge of Mexico, his teacher's method of handling such a unit would greatly affect his attitude toward Mexicans.

The media through which the teacher can develop wholesome attitudes are innumerable. Social studies (with special reference to races, creeds and nationalities), science, matters of health and safety, the very atmosphere of the classroom... these are a few of the fertile fields for the inculcation of proper emotional reactions.

However, when children come to school with undesirable attitudes, it is unwise for the teacher to attempt to change their feelings by cajoling or scolding them. She can achieve the proper effect by helping them obtain constructive experiences. To illustrate, firstgrade pupils afraid of policemen will probably alter their attitudes after a classroom chat with the neighborhood officer in which he explains how he protects them. In the same way, a class of older children can develop attitudes through discussion, research, outside reading and all-day trips.

Finally, a teacher must constantly evaluate her own attitude because her influence can be deleterious if she has personal prejudices. This is especially true in respect to controversial issues and questions on which children should be encouraged to reach their own decisions as a result of objective analysis of all the facts.

1. The central idea conveyed in the above passage is that

    A. attitudes affect our actions
    B. teachers play a significant role in developing or changing pupils' attitudes
    C. by their attitudes, teachers inadvertently affect pupils' attitudes
    D. attitudes can be changed by some classroom experiences
    E. attitudes are affected by experience

1.___

2. The author implies that

A. children's attitudes often come from those of other children
B. in some aspects of social studies a greater variety of methods can be used in the upper grades than in the lower grades
C. the teacher should guide all discussions by revealing her own attitude
D. people usually act on the basis of reasoning rather than on emotion
E. parents' and teachers' attitudes are more often in harmony than in conflict

3. A statement NOT made or implied in the passage is that

A. attitudes cannot easily be changed by rewards and lectures
B. a child can develop in the classroom an attitude about the importance of brushing his teeth
C. attitudes can be based on the learning of falsehoods
D. the attitudes of children are influenced by all the adults in their environment
E. the children should accept the teacher's judgment in controversial matters

4. The passage SPECIFICALLY states that

A. teachers should always conceal their own attitudes
B. whatever attitudes a child learns in school have already been introduced at home
C. direct experiences are more valuable than indirect ones
D. teachers can sometimes have an unwholesome influence on children
E. it is unwise for the teacher to attempt to change children's attitudes

5. The first and fourth paragraphs have all the following points in common EXCEPT

A. how reading affects attitudes
B. the importance of experience in building attitudes
C. how attitudes can be changed in the classroom
D. how fear sometimes governs attitudes
E. how differences in approach change attitudes

KEY (CORRECT ANSWERS)

1. B
2. B
3. D
4. D
5. C

TEST 7

DIRECTIONS: Each question or incomplete statement is followed by several suggested answers or completions. Select the one that BEST answers the question or completes the statement. *PRINT THE LETTER OF THE CORRECT ANSWER IN THE SPACE AT THE RIGHT.*

PASSAGE

The word geology refers to the study of the composition, structure, and history of the earth. The term is derived from the Latin, geologia. coined by Bishop Richard de Bury in 1473 to distinguish lawyers who study "earthy things" from theologians. It was first consistently used in its present sense in the latter part of the 17th century. The great mass of detail that constitutes geology is classified under a number of subdivisions which, in turn, depend upon the fundamental sciences, physics, chemistry and biology.

The principal subdivisions of geology are: mineralogy, petrology, structural geology, physiography (geomorphology), usually grouped under physical or dynamical geology; and paleontology, stratigraphy and paleogeography, grouped under historical geology. The term economic geology usually refers to the study of valuable mineral "ore" deposits, including coal and oil. The economic aspects of geology are, however, much more embracive, including many subjects associated with civil engineering, economic geography, and conservation. Some of the more important of these subjects are: meteorology, hydrology, agriculture, and seismology. Subjects which are also distinctly allied to geology are geophysics, geochemistry, and cosmogony.

1. The statement that geology treats of the history of the earth and its life, especially as recorded in the rocks, is

    A. contrary to the paragraph
    B. made in the paragraph
    C. neither made nor implied in the paragraph
    D. not made, but implied in the paragraph
    E. unclear from the passage

    1.___

2. The statement that the principal branches or phases of geology are dynamical geology and historical geology are

    A. contrary to the paragraph
    B. made in the paragraph
    C. neither made nor implied in the paragraph
    D. not made, but implied in the paragraph
    E. unclear from the passage

    2.___

3. The statement that mining geology is a subdivision of geophysics is

    A. contrary to the paragraph
    B. made in the paragraph
    C. neither made nor implied in the paragraph
    D. not made, but implied in the paragraph
    E. unclear from the passage

    3.___

4. The statement that the study of both the exterior of the earth and its inner constitution constitutes the fundamental subject matter of geology is

   A. contrary to the paragraph
   B. made in the paragraph
   C. neither made nor implied in the paragraph
   D. not made, but implied in the paragraph
   E. unclear from the passage

5. The statement that geology utilizes the principles of astronomy, zoology, and botany is

   A. contrary to the paragraph
   B. made in the paragraph
   C. neither made nor implied in the paragraph
   D. not made, but implied in the paragraph
   E. unclear from the passage

6. The statement that geology is synonymous with the study of the attributes of rocks, rock formation, or rock attributes is

   A. contrary to the paragraph
   B. made in the paragraph
   C. neither made nor implied in the paragraph
   D. not made, but implied in the paragraph
   E. unclear from the passage

KEY (CORRECT ANSWERS)

1. D 4. D
2. B 5. D
3. C 6. A

TEST 8

DIRECTIONS: Each question or incomplete statement is followed by several suggested answers or completions. Select the one that *BEST* answers the question or completes the statement. *PRINT THE LETTER OF THE CORRECT ANSWER IN THE SPACE AT THE RIGHT.*

PASSAGE

1 Schiller was the first to ring a change on this state of things
2 by addressing himself courageously to the entire population of his
3 country in all its social strata at one time. He was the great popularizer of our
4 theatre, and remained for almost a century the guiding
5 spirit of the German drama of which Schiller's matchless tragedies
6 are still by many people regarded as the surpassing manifestoes.
7 Schiller's position, while it demonstrates a whole people's gratitude
8 to those who respond to its desires, does not however furnish a
9 weapon of self-defense to the "popularizers" of drama, or rather its
10 diluters. Schiller's case rather proves that the power of popular
11 influence wrought upon a poet may be vastly inferior to the strength
12 that radiates from his own personality. Indeed, whereas the secret
13 of ephemeral power is only too often found in paltriness or mediocrity,
14 an influence of enduring force such as Schiller exerts on the Germans
15 can only emanate from a strong and self-assertive character. No poet
16 lives beyond his day who does not exceed the average in mental stature
17 or who, through a selfish sense of fear of the general, allows
18 himself to be ground down to the conventional size and shape.
19 Schiller, no less than Ibsen, forced his moral demands tyrannically
20 upon his contemporaries. And in the long run your moral despot, pro-
21 vided he be high-minded, vigorous, and able, has a better chance of
22 fame than the pliant time-server. However, there is a great difference
23 between the two cases. For quite apart from the striking dissimilarities
24 between the poets themselves, the public, through the
25 gradual growth of social organization, has become greatly altered.

1. Schiller's lasting popularity may be attributed to

   A. his meeting the desires of a whole people, not just a segment of the people
   B. his abiding by his inmost convictions
   C. his mediocrity and paltriness
   D. his courageous facing up to the problems of his day
   E. his ability to popularize the unknown

2. In the first line, "on this state of things" refers to

   A. romantic drama
   B. the French play of contrived construction
   C. drama directed to the rich and well-born
   D. the popularizers of the theatre of today
   E. the ruling class

3. In the second sentence from the last, "the two cases" refer to

    A. pliant time-server and moral despot
    B. the one who exceeds the average In mental stature and the one who allows himself to be ground down to conventional size
    C. the popularizer and the poet of enduring fame
    D. Ibsen and Schiller
    E. the man of character and the man of wealth

4. We may assume that the author

    A. is no believer in the democratic processes
    B. has no high opinions of the "compact majority"
    C. regards popularity with the people as a measure of enduring success
    D. is opposed to the aristocracy
    E. has no fixed opinions

5. A word used in an ambiguous sense (having two or more possible meanings) in this passage is

    A. "poet" (lines 11, 15, 24)
    B. "power" (lines 10, 13)
    C. "people" (lines 6, 7)
    D. "popularizer" (lines 3, 9)
    E. "moral" (lines 19, 20)

KEY (CORRECT ANSWERS)

1. B
2. C
3. D
4. B
5. D

TEST 9

DIRECTIONS: Each question or incomplete statement is followed by several suggested answers or completions. Select the one that BEST answers the question or completes the statement. PRINT THE LETTER OF THE CORRECT ANSWER IN THE SPACE AT THE RIGHT.

PASSAGE

In one sense, of course, this is not a new insight: all our great social and philosophical thinkers have been keenly aware of the fact of individual differences. It has remained, however, for psychologists to give the insight scientific precision.

What all this adds up to is more than just a working body of information about this and that skill. It adds up to a basic recognition of one important factor in the maturing of the individual. If each individual has a certain uniqueness of power, his maturing will best be accomplished along the line of that power. To try to develop him along lines that go in directions contrary to that of his major strength is to condition him to defeat. Thus, the non-mechanical person who is arbitrarily thrust into a mechanical occupation cannot help but do his work poorly and reluctantly, with some deep part of himself in conscious or unconscious rebellion.

He may blame himself for the low level of his accomplishment or for his persistent discontent; but not all his self-berating, nor even all his efforts to become more competent by further training, can make up for the original aptitude-lack. Unless he discovers his aptitude-lack, he may be doomed to a lifetime of self-blame, with a consequent loss of self-confidence and a halting of his psychological growth.

Or he may take refuge in self-pity – finding reason to believe that his failure is due to one or another bad break, to the jealousy of a superior, to lack of sympathy and help at home, to an initial bad start, to a lack of appreciation of what he does. If he thus goes the way of self-pity, he is doomed to a lifetime of self-commiseration that makes sound growth impossible.

The characteristic of the mature person is that he affirms life. To affirm life he must be involved, heart and soul, in the process of living. Neither the person who feels himself a failure nor the person who consciously or unconsciously resents what life has done to him can feel his heart and soul engaged in the process of living. That experience is reserved for the person whose full powers are enlisted. This, then, is what this fourth insight signifies: to mature, the individual must know what his powers are and must make them competent for life.

1. It is the author's view that

   A. "all men are created equal"
   B. "each man in his life plays many parts"
   C. "all comes to him who waits"
   D. "no kernel of nourishing corn can come to one but through his toil bestowed on that plot of ground given to him to till...."
   E. "that is what it is not to be alive. To move about in a cloud of ignorance... to live with envy... in quiet despair... to feel oneself sunk into a common grey mass..."

1.___

2. Ignorance of this fourth insight

   A. may very likely cause one to take refuge in self pity or conscious or unconscious rebellion
   B. constitutes a failure to understand that each individual is different and must cultivate his special powers in socially rewarding ways
   C. is a major deterrent to a growth to maturity
   D. means unawareness of the fact that each must use all his energy and powers to the best of his ability to make him competent for life
   E. may becloud the use of scientific precision

3. Two possible maladjustments of a man thrust into a position he is unfitted for may be summed up in the phrase,

   A. conscious and unconscious rebellion
   B. guilt-feelings and scapegoating
   C. halting of psychological growth and blaming the "breaks"
   D. "Peccavi – I have sinned" and "all the world is made except thee and me and I am not so sure of thee"
   E. light and darkness

4. We will expect a person placed in a job he is unequal to, to

   A. strike out for himself as an entrepreneur
   B. display quick angers and fixed prejudices
   C. show a great love of life outside of his work
   D. engage in labor union activities
   E. join political and social movements

KEY (CORRECT ANSWERS)

1. D   3. B
2. B   4. B

TEST 10

DIRECTIONS: Each question or incomplete statement is followed by several suggested answers or completions. Select the one that BEST answers the question or completes the statement. *PRINT THE LETTER OF THE CORRECT ANSWER IN THE SPACE AT THE RIGHT.*

PASSAGE

1   "For the ease and pleasure of treading the old road, accepting
2 the fashions, the education, the religion of society, he takes the
3 cross of making his own, and, of course, the self-accusation, the
4 faint heart, the frequent uncertainty and loss of time, which are the
5 nettles and tangling vines in the way of the self-relying and self-
6 directed; and the state of virtual hositility in which he seems to
7 stand to society, and especially to educated society. For all this
8 loss and scorn, what offset? He is to find consolation in exercising
9 the highest functions of human nature. He is one who raises himself
10 from private consideration and breathes and lives on public and
11 illustrious thoughts. He is the world's eye. He is the world's
12 heart. He is to resist the vulgar prosperity that retrogrades ever
13 to barbarism, by preserving and communicating heroic sentiments,
14 noble biographies, melodious verse, and the conclusions of history.
15 Whatsoever oracles the human heart, in all emergencies, in all solemn
16 hours, has uttered as its commentary on the world of actions – these
17 he shall receive and impart. And whatsoever new verdict Reason from
18 her inviolable seat pronounces on the passing men and events of
19 today – this he shall hear and promulgate.
20   "These being his functions, it becomes him to feel all confidence
21 in himself, and to defer never to the popular cry. He and he only
22 knows the world. The world of any moment is the merest appearance.
23 Some great decorum, some fetish of a government, some ephemeral
24 trade, or war, or man, is cried up by half mankind and cried down by
25 the other half, as if all depended on this particular up or down.
26 The odds are that the whole question is not worth the poorest thought
27 which the scholar has lost in listening to the controversy. Let him
28 not quit his belief that a popgun is a popgun, though the ancient and
29 honorable of the earth affirm it to be the crack of doom. In silence,
30 in steadiness, in severe abstraction, let him hold by himself; add
31 observation to observation, patient of neglect, patient of reproach,
32 and bide his own time – happy enough if he can satisfy himself alone
33 that this day he has seen something truly. Success treads on every
34 right step. For the instinct is sure, that prompts him to tell his
35 brother what he thinks. He then learns that in going down into the
36 secrets of his own mind he has descended into the secrets of all
37 minds. He learns that he who has mastered any law in his private
38 thoughts, is master to the extent of all translated. The poet, in
39 utter solitude remembering his spontaneous thoughts and recording
40 them, is found to have recorded that which men in crowded cities
41 find true for them also. The orator distrusts at first the fitness

42 of his frank confessions, his want of knowledge of the persons he
43 addresses, until he finds that he is the complement of his hearers—
44 that they drink his words because he fulfills for them their own
45 nature; the deeper he delves into his privatest, secretest presentiment,
46 to his wonder he finds this is the most acceptable, most public, and
47 universally true. The people delight in it; the better part of every
48 man feels. This is my music; this is myself."

1. It is a frequent criticism of the scholar that he lives by himself, in an "ivory tower," remote from the problems and business of the world. Which of these below constitutes the *BEST* refutation by the writer of the passage to the criticism here noted?   1.____

   A. The world's concern being ephemeral, the scholar does well to renounce them and the world.
   B. The scholar lives in the past to interpret the present.
   C. The scholar at his truest is the spokesman of the people.
   D. The scholar is not concerned with the world's doing because he is not selfish and therefore not engrossed in matters of importance to himself and neighbors.
   E. The scholar's academic researches of today are the businessman's practical products of tomorrow.

2. The scholar's road is rough, according to the passage. Which of these is his GREATEST difficulty?   2.____

   A. He must renounce religion.
   B. He must pioneer new approaches.
   C. He must express scorn for, and hostility to, society.
   D. He is uncertain of his course.
   E. There is a pleasure in the main-traveled roads in education, religion, and all social fashions.

3. When the writer speaks of the "world's eye" and the "world's heart" he means   3.____

   A. the same thing
   B. culture and conscience
   C. culture and wisdom
   D. a scanning of all the world's geography and a deep sympathy for every living thing
   E. mind and love

4. By the phrase, "nettles and tangling vines," the author PROBABLY refers to   4.____

   A. "self-accusation" and "loss of time"
   B. "faint heart" and "self accusation"
   C. "the slings and arrows of outrageous fortune"
   D. a general term for the difficulties of a scholar's life
   E. "self-accusation" and "uncertainty"

3 (#10)

5. The various ideas in the passage are BEST summarized in which of these groups? 5.___
    1. (a) truth versus society
       (b) the scholar and books
       (c) the world and the scholar
    2. (a) the ease of living traditionally
       (b) the glory of a scholar's life
       (c) true knowledge versus trivia
    3. (a) the hardships of the scholar
       (b) the scholar's function
       (c) the scholar's justifications for disregarding the world's business

   A. 1 and 3 together
   B. 3 only
   C. 1 and 2 together
   D. 1 only
   E. 1, 2, and 3 together

6. "seems to stand" (lines 6 and 7) means 6.___

   A. is
   B. gives the false impression of being
   C. ends probably in becoming
   D. is seen to be
   E. the quicksands of time

7. "public and illustrious thoughts" (lines 10 and 11) means 7.___

   A. what the people think
   B. thoughts for the good of mankind
   C. thoughts in the open
   D. thoughts transmitted by the people
   E. the conclusions of history

KEY (CORRECT ANSWERS)

1.	C	5.	B
2.	B	6.	B
3.	C	7.	B
4.	E		

READING COMPREHENSION
UNDERSTANDING AND INTERPRETING
WRITTEN MATERIAL

EXAMINATION SECTION

TEST 1

DIRECTIONS: Each question or incomplete statement is followed by several suggested answers or completions. Select the one that BEST answers the question or completes the statement. *PRINT THE LETTER OF THE CORRECT ANSWER IN THE SPACE AT THE RIGHT.*

In its current application to art, the term *"primitive"* is as vague and unspecific as the term "heathen" is in its application to religion. A heathen sect is simply one which is not affiliated with one or another of three or four organized systems of theology. Similarly, a primitive art is one which flourishes outside the small number of cultures which we have chosen to designate as civilizations. Such arts differ vastly and it is correspondingly difficult to generalize about them. Any statements which will hold true for such diverse aesthetic experiences as the pictographs of the Australians, the woven designs of the Peruvians, and the abstract sculptures of the African tribes must be of the broadest and simplest sort. Moreover, the problem is complicated by the meaning attached to the term "primitive" in its other uses. It stands for something simple, undeveloped, and, by implication, ancestral to more evolved forms. Its application to arts and cultures other than our own is an unfortunate heritage from the nineteenth-century scientists who laid the foundations of anthropology. Elated by the newly enunciated doctrines of evolution, these students saw all cultures as stages in a single line of development and assigned them to places in this series on the simple basis of the degree to which they differed from European culture, which was blandly assumed to be the final and perfect flower of the evolutionary process. This idea has long since been abandoned by anthropologists, but before its demise it diffused to other social sciences and became a part of the general body of popular misinformation. It still tinges a great deal of the thought and writing about the arts of non-European peoples and has been responsible for many misunderstandings.

1. The MAIN purpose of the passage is to 1.____
   A. explain the various definitions of the term "primitive"
   B. show that the term "primitive" can be applied validly to art
   C. compare the use of the term "primitive" to the use of the term "heathen"
   D. deprecate the use of the term "primitive" as applied to art
   E. show that "primitive" arts vary greatly among themselves

2. The nineteenth-century scientists believed that the theory of evolution 2.____
   A. could be applied to the development of culture
   B. was demonstrated in all social sciences
   C. was substantiated by the diversity of "primitive" art
   D. could be applied only to European culture
   E. disproved the idea that some arts are more "primitive" than others

25

2 (#1)

3. With which of the following would the author agree? 3.____
   A. The term "primitive" is used only by the misinformed.
   B. "Primitive" arts may be as highly developed as "civilized" arts.
   C. The arts of a culture often indicated how advanced that culture was.
   D. Australian, Peruvian, and African tribal arts are much like the ancestral forms from which European art evolved.
   E. A simple culture is likely to have a simple art.

4. According to the author, many misunderstandings have been caused by the belief that 4.____
   A. most cultures are fundamentally different
   B. inferior works of art in any culture are "primitive" art
   C. "primitive" arts are diverse
   D. non-European arts are diverse
   E. European civilization is the final product of the evolutionary process

KEY (CORRECT ANSWERS)

1. D
2. A
3. B
4. E

TEST 2

DIRECTIONS: Each question or incomplete statement is followed by several suggested answers or completions. Select the one that BEST answers the question or completes the statement. *PRINT THE LETTER OF THE CORRECT ANSWER IN THE SPACE AT THE RIGHT.*

One of the ways the intellectual *avant-garde* affects the technical intelligentsia is through the medium of art, and art is, if only implicitly, a critique of experience. The turning upon itself of modern culture in the forms of the new visual art, the utilization of the detritus of daily experience to mock that experience, constitutes a mode of social criticism. Pop art, it is true, does not go beyond the surface of the visual and tactile experience of an industrial (and a commercialized) culture. Dwelling on the surface, it allows its consumers to mock the elements of their daily life, without abandoning it. Indeed, the consumption of art in the organized market for leisure serves at times to encapsulate the social criticism of the *avant-garde*. However, the recent engagement of writers, artists, and theater people in contemporary issues suggests that this sort of containment may have begun to reach its limits.

In an atmosphere in which the intellectually dominant group insists on the contradictions inherent in daily experience, the technical intelligentsia will find it difficult to remain unconscious of those contradictions. The technical intelligentsia have until now avoided contradictions by accepting large rewards for their expertise. As expertise becomes increasingly difficult to distinguish from ordinary service on the one hand, and merges on the other with the change of the social environment, the technical intelligentsia's psychic security may be jeopardized. Rendering of labor services casts it back into spiritual proletarianization; a challenge to the social control exercised by elites, who use the technical intelligentsia's labor power, pushes it forward to social criticism and revolutionary politics. That these are matters, for the moment, of primarily spiritual import does not diminish their ultimate political significance. A psychological precondition for radical action is usually far more important than an "objectively" revolutionary situation—whatever that may be.

The chances for a radicalization of the technical intelligentsia, thus extending the student revolt cannot be even approximated. I believe I have shown there is a chance.

1. It may be *inferred* that the technical intelligentsia are
   I. The executives and employers in society
   II. Critics of *avant-garde* art
   III. Highly skilled technical workers
   The CORRECT answer is:
   A. I only   B. I and III   C. I, II, and III
   D. III only   E. I and II

2. The engagement of the intellectual *avant-garde* in contemporary issues
   A. indicates that people tire of questioning the contradictions inherent in day-to-day living
   B. indicates that the technical intelligentsia are close to the point where they will rebel against the *avant-garde*
   C. could cause a challenge to the social control of the elites
   D. could cause the public to become more leisure-oriented
   E. could cause an increase in the consumption of art in the organized market for leisure services

3. The *possible* effect of the intellectual *avant-garde* on the technical intelligentsia is that
   A. the intellectual *avant-garde* makes the technical intelligentsia conscious of society's contradictions
   B. rapid curtailment of large rewards for expertise will result
   C. it may cause a strong likelihood of a radicalization of the technical intelligentsia
   D. the *avant-garde* will replace the employment of the technical intelligentsia in contemporary issues
   E. the rendering of labor services will be eliminated

4. If it is assumed that the technical intelligentsia becomes fully aware of the contradictions of modern life, it is the author's position that
   A. revolution will result
   B. the technical intelligentsia may refuse to perform manual labor
   C. the technical intelligentsia will be pushed forward to social criticism and revolutionary politics
   D. the technical intelligentsia will experience some psychic dislocation
   E. ordinary service will replace technical expertise

5. According to the author,
   A. the state of mind of a particular group may have more influence on its action than the effect of environmental factors
   B. the influence of art will often cause social upheaval
   C. matters of primarily spiritual import necessarily lack political significance
   D. the detritus of day-to-day living should be mocked by the intellectual *avant-garde*
   E. the technical intelligentsia can only protect their psychic security by self-expression through art

6. With which of the following would the author agree?
   I. As contradictions are less contained, the psychic security of all members of the working class would be jeopardized.
   II. The expertise of the technical intelligentsia evolved from the ownership and management of property.
   III. The technical intelligentsia is not accustomed to rendering labor services.
   The CORRECT answer is:
   A. I only   B. III only   C. I and III
   D. II only   E. None of the above

7. The MAIN purpose of the passage is to
   A. discuss the influence of the *avant-garde* art form on the expertise of the technical intelligentsia
   B. discuss the effect of the intellectual *avant-garde* on the working classes
   C. discuss the social significance of the technical intelligentsia
   D. discuss the possible effects of the de-encapsulation of *avant-garde* social criticism
   E. point out that before a change psychological preconditions are first established

KEY (CORRECT ANSWERS)

1. D   5. A
2. C   6. B
3. A   7. D
4. D

TEST 3

DIRECTIONS: Each question or incomplete statement is followed by several suggested answers or completions. Select the one that BEST answers the question or completes the statement. *PRINT THE LETTER OF THE CORRECT ANSWER IN THE SPACE AT THE RIGHT.*

Turbulent flow over a boundary is a complex phenomenon for which there is no really complete theory even in simple laboratory cases. Nevertheless, a great deal of experimental data has been collected on flows over solid surfaces, both in the laboratory and in nature, so that, from an engineering point of view at least, the situation is fairly well understood. The force exerted on a surface varies with the roughness of that surface and approximately with the square of the wind speed at some fixed height above it. A wind of 10 meters per second (about 20 knots, or 22 miles per hour) measured at a height of 10 meters will produce a force of some 30 tons per square kilometer on a field of mown grass or of about 70 tons per square kilometer on a ripe wheat field. On a really smooth surface, such as glass, the force is only about 10 tons per square kilometer.

When the wind blows over water, the whole thing is much more complicated. The roughness of the water is not a given characteristic of the surface but depends on the wind itself. Not only that, the elements that constitute the roughness—the waves—themselves move more or less in the direction of the wind. Recent evidence indicates that a large portion of the momentum transferred from the air into the water goes into waves rather than directly into making currents in the water; only as the waves break, or otherwise lose energy, does their momentum become available to generate currents, or produce Ekman layers. Waves carry a substantial amount of both energy and momentum (typically about as much as is carried by the wind in a layer about one wavelength thick), and so the wave-generation process is far from negligible. A violently wavy surface belies its appearance by acting, as far as the wind is concerned, as though it were very smooth. At 10 meters per second, recent measurements seem to agree, the force on the surface is quite a lot less than the force over mown grass and scarcely more than it is over glass; some observations in light winds of two or three meters per second indicate that the force on the wavy surface is less than it is on a surface as smooth as glass. In some way the motion of the waves seems to modify the airflow so that air slips over the surface even more freely than it would without the waves. This seems not to be the case at higher wind speeds, above about five meters per second, but the force remains strikingly low compared with that over other natural surfaces.

One serious deficiency is the fact that there are no direct observations at all in those important cases in which the wind speed is greater than about 12 meters per second and has had time and fetch (the distance over water) enough to raise substantial waves. The few indirect studies indicate that the apparent roughness of the surface increases somewhat under high-wind conditions, so that the force on the surface increases rather more rapidly than as the square of the wind speed.

Assuming that the force increases at least as the square of the wind speed, it is evident that high-wind conditions produce effects far more important than their frequency of occurrence would suggest. Five hours of 60-knot storm winds will put more momentum into the water than a week of 10-knot breezes. If it should be shown that, for high winds, the force on the surface increases appreciably more rapidly than as the square of the wind speed, then the transfer of momentum to the ocean will turn out to be dominated by what happens during the occasional storm rather than by the long-term average winds.

1. According to the passage, several hours of storm winds (60 miles per hour) over the ocean would
   A. be similar to the force exerted by light winds for several hours over glass
   B. create an ocean roughness which reduces the force exerted by the high winds
   C. have proved to be more significant in creating ocean momentum than light winds
   D. create a force not greater than 6 times the force of a 10-mile-per-hour wind
   E. eventually affect ocean current

2. According to the passage, a rough-like ocean surface
   A. is independent of the force of the wind
   B. has the same force exerted against it by high and light winds
   C. is more likely to have been caused by a storm than by continuous light winds
   D. nearly always allows airflow to be modified so as to cause the force of the wind to be less than on glass
   E. is a condition under which the approximate square of wind speed can never be an accurate figure in measuring the wind force

3. The author indicates that, where a hurricane is followed by light winds of 10 meters per second or less,
   I. ocean current will be unaffected by the light winds
   II. ocean current will be more affected by the hurricane winds than the following light winds
   III. the force of the light winds on the ocean would be less than that exerted on a wheat field.
   The CORRECT combination is:
   A. I only   B. III only   C. II and III   D. I and III   E. II only

4. The MAIN purpose of the passage is to discuss
   A. oceanic momentum and current
   B. turbulent flow of wind over water
   C. wind blowing over water as related to causing tidal flow
   D. the significance of high wind conditions on ocean momentum
   E. experiments in wind force

5. The author would be incorrect in concluding that the transfer of momentum to the ocean is dominated by the occasional storm if
   A. air momentum went directly into making ocean current
   B. high speed winds slipped over waves as easily as low speed winds
   C. waves did not move in the direction of wind
   D. the force exerted on a wheat field was the same as on mown grass
   E. the force of wind under normal conditions increased as the square of wind speed

3 (#3)

6. A wind of 10 meters per second measured at a height of 10 meters will produce a force close to 30 tons per square mile on which of the following? 6._____
   A. Unmown grass   B. Mown grass   C. Glass
   D. Water   E. A football field

KEY (CORRECT ANSWERS)

1. E
2. C
3. C
4. B
5. B
6. A

TEST 4

DIRECTIONS: Each question or incomplete statement is followed by several suggested answers or completions. Select the one that BEST answers the question or completes the statement. *PRINT THE LETTER OF THE CORRECT ANSWER IN THE SPACE AT THE RIGHT.*

Political scientists, as practitioners of a negligibly formalized discipline, tend to be accommodating to formulations and suggested techniques developed in related behavioral sciences. They even tend, on occasion, to speak of psychology, sociology, and anthropology as "hard core sciences." Such a characterization seems hardly justified. The disposition to uncritically adopt into political science non-indigenous sociological and general systems concepts tends, at times, to involve little more than the adoption of a specific, and sometimes barbarous, academic vocabulary which is used to redescribe reasonably well-confirmed or intuitively-grasped low-order empirical generalizations.

At its worst, what results in such instances is a runic explanation, a redescription in a singular language style, i.e., no explanation at all. At their best, functional accounts as they are found in the contemporary literature provide explanation sketches, the type of elliptical explanation characteristic of historical and psychoanalytic accounts. For each such account there is an indeterminate number of equally plausible ones, the consequence of either the complexity of the subject matter, differing perspectives, conceptual vagueness, the variety of sometimes mutually exclusive empirical or quasi-empirical generalizations employed, or syntactical obscurity, or all of them together.

Functional explanations have been most reliable in biology and physiology (where they originated) and in the analysis of servo mechanical and cybernetic systems (to which they have been effectively extended). In these areas we possess a well-standardized body of lawlike generalizations. Neither sociology nor political science has as yet the same resource of well-confirmed lawlike statements. Certainly sociology has few more than political science. What passes for functional explanation in sociology is all too frequently parasitic upon suggestive analogy and metaphor, trafficking on our familiarity with goal-directed systems.

What is advanced as "theory" in sociology is frequently a non-theoretic effort at classification or "codification," the search for an analytic conceptual schema which provides a typology or a classificatory system serviceable for convenient storage and ready retrieval of independently established empirical regularities. That such a schema takes on a hierarchic and deductive character, imparting to the collection of propositions a *prima facie* theoretical appearance, may mean no more than that the terms employed in the high-order propositions are so vague that they can accommodate almost any inference and consequently can be made to any conceivable state of affairs.

1. The author *implies* that, when the political scientist is at his best, his explanations 1.____
    A. are essentially a retelling of events
    B. only then form the basis of an organized discipline
    C. plausibly account for past occurrences
    D. are prophetic of future events
    E. are confirmed principles forming part of the political scientist's theory

2. With which of the following would the author probably agree?
   I. Because of an abundance of reasonable explanations for past conduct, there is the possibility of contending schools within the field of political science developing.
   II. Political science is largely devoid of predictive power.
   III. Political science has very few verified axioms.
   The CORRECT answer is:
   A. III only   B. I and III   C. I and II   D. I, II, III   E. I only

3. The passage *implies* that many sociological theories
   A. are capable of being widely applied to various situations
   B. do not even appear to be superficially theoretical in appearance
   C. contrast with those of political science in that there are many more confirmed lawlike statements
   D. are derived from deep analysis and exhaustive research
   E. appear theoretical but are really very well proved

4. The author's thesis would be UNSUPPORTABLE if
   A. the theories of the political scientist possessed predictive power
   B. political science did not consist of redescription
   C. political scientists were not restricted to "hard core sciences"
   D. political science consisted of a body of theories capable of application to any situation
   E. none of the above

5. The author believe that sociology as a "hard core science," contains reliable and functional explanations
   A. is never more than a compilation of conceptual schema
   B. is in nearly every respect unlike political science
   C. is a discipline which allows for varied inferences to be drawn from its general propositions
   D. is a science indigenous *prima facie* theoretical appearance containing very little codification posing as theory

KEY (CORRECT ANSWERS)

1. C
2. D
3. A
4. A
5. D

TEST 5

DIRECTIONS: Each question or incomplete statement is followed by several suggested answers or completions. Select the one that BEST answers the question or completes the statement. *PRINT THE LETTER OF THE CORRECT ANSWER IN THE SPACE AT THE RIGHT.*

James' own prefaces to his works were devoted to structural composition and analytics and his approach in those prefaces has only recently begun to be understood. One of his contemporary critics, with the purest intention to blame, wrote what might be recognized today as sophisticated praise when he spoke of the later James as "an impassioned geometer" and remarked that "what interested him was not the figures but their relations, the relations which alone make pawns significant." James's explanations of his works often are so bereft of interpretation as to make some of our own austere defenses against interpretation seem almost embarrassingly rich with psychological meanings. They offer, with a kind of brazen unselfconsciousness, an astonishingly artificial, even mechanical view of novelistic invention. It's not merely that James asserts the importance of technique; more radically, he tends to discuss character and situation almost entirely as functions of technical ingenuities. The very elements in a Jamesian story which may strike us as requiring the most explanation are presented by James either as a *solution* to a problem of compositional harmony or else as the *donnee* about which it would be irrelevant to ask any questions at all.

James should constantly be referred to as a model of structuralist criticism. He consistently redirects our attention from the referential aspect of a work of art (its extensions into "reality") to its own structural coherence as the principal source of inspiration.

What is most interesting about James's structurally functional view of character is that a certain devaluation of what we ordinarily think of as psychological interest is perfectly consistent with an attempt to portray reality. It's as if he came to feel that a kind of autonomous geometric pattern, in which the parts appeal for their value to nothing but their contributive place in the essentially abstract pattern, is the artist's most successful representation of life. Thus, he could perhaps even think that verisimilitude—a word he liked—has less to do with the probability of the events the novelist describes than with those processes, deeply characteristic of life, by which he creates sense and coherence from any event. The only faithful picture of life in art is not in the choice of a significant subject (James always argues against the pseudo realistic prejudice), but rather in the illustration of sense- or design-making processes. James proves the novel's connection with life by deprecating its derivation from life; and it's when he is most abstractly articulating the growth of a structure that James is almost most successfully defending the mimetic function of art (and of criticism). His deceptively banal position that only execution matters means most profoundly that verisimilitude, properly considered, is the grace and the truth of a formal unity.

1. The author suggests that James, in explanations of his own art, 1._____
   A. was not bound by formalistic strictures but concentrated on verisimilitude
   B. was deeply psychological and concentrated on personal insight
   C. felt that his art had a one-to-one connection with reality
   D. was basically mechanical and concentrated on geometrical form
   E. was event-and-character-oriented rather than technique-oriented

2. The passage indicates that James's method of approaching reality was
   A. that objective reality did not exist and was patterned only by the mind
   B. that formalism and pattern were excellent means of approaching reality
   C. not to concentrate on specific events but rather on character development
   D. that the only objective reality is the psychological processes of the mind
   E. that in reality events occur which are not structured but rather as random occurrences

3. The MAIN purpose of the paragraph is to
   A. indicate that James's own approach to his work is only now beginning to be understood
   B. deprecate the geometrical approach towards the novel
   C. question whether James's novels were related to reality
   D. indicate that James felt that society itself could be seen as a geometric structure
   E. discuss James's explanation of his works

4. In discussing his own works, James
   I. talks of people and events as a function of technique to the exclusion of all else
   II. is quick to emphasize the referential aspect of the work
   III. felt that verisimilitude could be derived not from character but rather from the ordering of event
   The CORRECT answer is:
   A. I only   B. II only   C. III only   D. I and III   E. I and II

5. The author
   A. *approves* of James's explanations of his work but *disapproves* his lack of discussion into the psychological makings of his characters
   B. *disapproves* of James's explanation of his own work and his lack of discussion into the psychological makings of his characters
   C. *approves* of James's explanations of his works in terms of structure as being well-rated to life
   D. *disapproves* of James's explanation of his works in terms of structure as lacking verisimilitude
   E. *approves* of James's explanation of his works because of the significance of the subjects chosen

6. The following is NOT true of James's explanation of his own works: He
   A. did not explain intriguing elements of a story except as part of a geometric whole
   B. felt the artist could represent life by its patterns rather than its events
   C. defended the imitative function of art by detailing the growth of a structure
   D. attempted to give the reader insight into the psychology of his characters by insuring that his explanation followed a strict geometrical pattern
   E. was able to devalue psychological interest and yet be consistent with an attempt to truly represent life

3 (#5)

7. James believed it to be *essential* to 7._____
   A. carefully choose a subject which would lend itself to processes by which sense and cohesion is achieved
   B. defend the mimetic function of art by emphasizing verisimilitude
   C. emphasize the manner in which different facets of a story could fit together
   D. explain character in order to achieve literary harmony
   E. be artificial and unconcerned with representing life

KEY (CORRECT ANSWERS)

1.	D	5.	C
2.	B	6.	D
3.	E	7.	C
4.	C		

TEST 6

DIRECTIONS: Each question or incomplete statement is followed by several suggested answers or completions. Select the one that BEST answers the question or completes the statement. *PRINT THE LETTER OF THE CORRECT ANSWER IN THE SPACE AT THE RIGHT.*

    The popular image of the city as it is now is a place of decay, crime, of fouled streets, and of people who are poor or foreign or odd. But what is the image of the city of the future? In the plans for the huge redevelopment projects to come, we are being shown a new image of the city. Gone are the dirt and the noise—and the variety and the excitement and the spirit. That it is an ideal makes it all the worse; these bleak new utopias are not bleak because they have to be; they are the concrete manifestation—and how literally—of a deep, and at times arrogant, misunderstanding of the function of the city.
    Being made up of human beings, the city is, of course, a wonderfully resilient institution. Already it has reasserted itself as an industrial and business center. Not so many years ago, there was much talk of decentralizing to campus-like offices, and a wholesale exodus of business to the countryside seemed imminent. But a business pastoral is something of a contradiction in terms, and for the simple reason that the city is the center of things because it is a center, the suburban heresy never came off. Many industrial campuses have been built, but the overwhelming proportion of new office building has been taking place in the big cities. But the rebuilding of downtown is not enough; a city deserted at night by its leading citizens is only half a city. If it is to continue as the dominant cultural force in American life, the city must have a core of people to support its theatres and museums, its shops and its restaurants—even a Bohemia of sorts can be of help. For it is the people who like living in the city who make it an attraction to the visitors who don't. It is the city dwellers who support its style; without them there is nothing to come downtown to.
    The cities have a magnificent opportunity. There are definite signs of a small but significant move back from suburbia. There is also evidence that many people who will be moving to suburbia would prefer to stay in the city—and it would not take too much more in amenities to make them stay. But the cities seem on the verge of muffing their opportunity and muffing it for generations to come. In a striking failure to apply marketing principles and an even more striking failure of aesthetics, the cities are freezing on a design for living ideally calculated to keep everybody in suburbia. These vast, barracks-like superblocks are not designed for people who like cities, but for people who have no other choice. A few imaginative architects and planners have shown that redeveloped blocks don't have to be repellent to make money, but so far their ideas have had little effect. The institutional approach is dominant, and, unless the assumptions embalmed in it are re-examined, the city is going to be turned into a gigantic bore.

1.   The author would NOT be pleased with   1.____
    A. a crowded, varied, stimulating city
    B. the dedication of new funds to the reconstruction of the cities
    C. a more detailed understanding of the poor
    D. the elimination of assumptions which do not reflect the function of the city
    E. the adoption of a laissez-faire attitude by those in charge of redevelopment

2. "The rebuilding of downtown" (1st sentence, 3rd paragraph) refers to
   A. huge redevelopment projects to come
   B. the application of marketing and aesthetic principles to rejuvenating the city
   C. keeping the city as the center of business
   D. attracting a core of people to support the city's functions
   E. the doing away with barracks-like structures

3. According to the author the city, in order to better itself, *must*
   A. increase its downtown population
   B. attract an interested core of people to support its cultural institutions
   C. adhere to an institutional approach rather than be satisfied with the status quo
   D. erect campus-like business complexes
   E. establish an ideal for orderly future growth

4. The MAIN purpose of the passage is to
   A. show that the present people inhabiting the city do not make the city viable
   B. discuss the types of construction which should and should not take place in the city's future
   C. indicate that imaginative architects and planners have shown that redeveloped areas don't have to be ugly to make money
   D. discuss the human element in the city
   E. point out the lack of understanding by many city planners of the city's functions

5. The author's thesis would be LESS supportable if
   I. city planners presently understood that stereotyped reconstruction is doomed to ultimate failure
   II. the institutional approach referred to in the passage was based upon assumptions which took into account the function of the city
   III. there were signs that a shift back to the city from suburbia were occurring
   The CORRECT answer is:
   A. II only   B. II and III   C. I and II   D. I only   E. III only

KEY (CORRECT ANSWERS)

1. D
2. C
3. B
4. E
5. C

TEST 7

DIRECTIONS: Each question or incomplete statement is followed by several suggested answers or completions. Select the one that BEST answers the question or completes the statement. *PRINT THE LETTER OF THE CORRECT ANSWER IN THE SPACE AT THE RIGHT.*

In estimating the child's conceptions of the world, the first question is to decide whether external reality is as external and objective for the child as it is for adults. In other words, can the child distinguish the self from the external world? So long as the child supposes that everyone necessarily thinks like himself, he will not spontaneously seek to convince others, nor to accept common truths, nor, above all, to prove or test his opinions. If his logic lacks exactitude and objectivity, it is because the social impulses of mature years are counteracted by an innate egocentricity. In studying the child's thought, not in this case in relation to others but to things, one is faced at the outset with the analogous problem of the child's capacity to dissociate thought from self in order to form an objective conception of reality.

The child, like the uncultured adult, appears exclusively concerned with things. He is indifferent to the life of thought and the originality of individual points of view escape him. His earliest interests, his first games, his drawings are all concerned solely with the imitation of what is. In short, the child's thought has every appearance of being exclusively realistic.

But realism is of two types, or, rather, objectivity must be distinguished from realism. Objectivity consists in so fully realizing the countless intrusions of the self in everyday thought and the countless illusions which result—illusions of sense, language, point of view, value, etc.—that the preliminary step to every judgment is the effort to exclude the intrusive self. Realism, on the contrary, consists in ignoring the existence of self and thence regarding one's own perspective as immediately objective and absolute. Realism is thus anthropocentric illusion, finality—in short, all those illusions which teem in the history of science. So long as thought has not become conscious of self, it is a prey to perpetual confusions between objective and subjective, between the real and the ostensible; it values the entire content of consciousness on a single lane in which ostensible realities and the unconscious interventions of the self are inextricably mixed. It is thus not futile, but, on the contrary, indispensable to establish clearly and before all else the boundary the child draws between the self and the external world.

1. The result of a child's not learning that others think differently than he does is that
    A. the child will not be able to function as an adult
    B. when the child has matured, he will be innately egocentric
    C. when the child has matured, his reasoning will be poor
    D. upon maturity, the child will not be able to distinguish thought from objects
    E. upon maturity, the child will not be able to make non-ego-influenced value

2. Objectivity is the ability to
    A. distinguish ego from the external world
    B. dissociate oneself from others
    C. realize that others have a different point of view
    D. dissociate ego from thought

3. When thought is not conscious of self,
   A. one is able to draw the correct conclusions from his perceptions
   B. the apparent may not be distinguishable from the actual
   C. conscious thought may not be distinguishable from the unconscious
   D. the ego may influence the actual
   E. ontogeny recapitulates phylogony

4. The MAIN purpose of the passage is to
   A. argue that the child should be made to realize that others may not think like he does
   B. estimate the child's conception of the world
   C. explain the importance of distinguishing the mind from external objects
   D. emphasize the importance of non-ego-influenced perspective
   E. show how the child establishes the boundary between himself and the external world

5. The author *implies* that, if an adult is to think logically,
   A. his reasoning, as he matures, must be tempered by other viewpoints
   B. he must be able to distinguish one physical object from another
   C. he must be exclusively concerned with thought instead of things
   D. he must be able to perceive reality without the intrusions of the self
   E. he must not value the content of consciousness on a single plain

6. Realism, according to the passage, is
   A. the realization of the countless intrusions of the self
   B. final and complete objectivity
   C. a desire to be truly objective and absolute
   D. the ability to be perceptive and discerning
   E. none of the above

7. The child who is exclusively concerned with things
   A. thinks only objectivity
   B. is concerned with imitating the things he sees
   C. must learn to distinguish between realism and anthropomorphism
   D. has no innate ability
   E. will, through interaction with others, often prove his opinions

KEY (CORRECT ANSWERS)

1. C   5. A
2. E   6. E
3. B   7. B
4. D

TEST 8

DIRECTIONS: Each question or incomplete statement is followed by several suggested answers or completions. Select the one that BEST answers the question or completes the statement. *PRINT THE LETTER OF THE CORRECT ANSWER IN THE SPACE AT THE RIGHT.*

Democracy is not logically antipathetic to most doctrines of natural rights, fundamental or higher law, individual rights, or any similar ideals—but merely asks citizens to take note of the fact that the preservation of these rights rests with the majority, in political processes, and does not depend upon a legal or constitutional Maginot line. Democracy may, then, be supported by believers in individual rights providing they believe that rights—or any transcendental ends—are likely to be better safeguarded under such a system. Support for democracy on such instrumental ground may, of course, lead to the dilemma of loyalty to the system vs. loyalty to a natural right—but the same kind of dilemma may arise for anyone, over any prized value, and in any political system, and is insoluble in advance.

There is unanimous agreement that—as a matter of fact and law, not of conjecture—no single right can be realized, except at the expense of other rights and claims. For that reason their absolute status, in some philosophic sense, is of little political relevance. Political policies involve much more than very generable principles or rights. The main error of the older natural rights school was not that it had an absolute right, but that it had too many absolute rights. There must be compromise, and, as any compromise destroys the claim to absoluteness, the natural outcome of experience was the repudiation of all of them. And now the name of "natural right" can only creep into sight with the reassuring placard, "changing content guaranteed." Nor is it at all easy to see how many doctrine of inalienable, natural, individual rights can be reconciled with a political doctrine of common consent—except in an anarchist society, or one of saints. Every natural right ever put forward, and the lists are elusive and capricious, is every day invaded by governments, in the public interest and with widespread public approval.

To talk of relatively attainable justice or rights in politics is not to plump for a moral relativism—in the sense that all values are equally good. But while values may be objective, the specific value judgments and policies are inevitably relative to a context, and is only when a judgment divorces context from general principle that it looks like moral relativism. Neither, of course, does the fact of moral diversity invalidate all moral rules.

Any political system, then, deals only with relatively attainable rights, as with relative justice and freedoms. Hence, we may differ in given instances on specific policies, despite agreement on broad basic principles such as a right or a moral "ought"; and, per contra, we may agree on specific policies while differing on fundamental principles or long-range objectives or natural rights. Politics and through politics, law and policies, give these rights—and moral principles—their substance and limits. There is no getting away from the political nature of this or any other prescriptive ideal in a free society.

1. With which of the following would the author *agree*?   1.____
    A. Natural and individual rights can exist at all only under a democracy.
    B. While natural rights may exist, they are only relatively attainable.
    C. Civil disobedience has no place in a democracy where natural rights have no philosophic relevance.
    D. Utilitarianism, which draws its criteria from the happiness and welfare of individuals, cannot logically be a goal of a democratic state.
    E. Some natural rights should never be compromised for the sake of political policy.

2. It can be *inferred* that a democratic form of government
   A. can be supported by natural rightists as the best pragmatic method of achieving their aims
   B. is a form of government wherein fundamental or higher law is irrelevant
   C. will inn time repudiate all inalienable rights
   D. forces a rejection of moral absolutism
   E. will soon exist in undeveloped areas of the world

3. The MAIN purpose of the passage is to
   A. discuss natural rights doctrine
   B. compare and contrast democracy to individual rights
   C. discuss the reconciliation of a doctrine of inalienable natural rights with a political system
   D. discuss the safeguarding of natural rights in a democratic society
   E. indicate that moral relativism is antipathetic to democracy

4. The author indicates that natural rights
   I. are sometimes difficult to define
   II. are easily definable but at times unreconcilable with a system of government predicated upon majority rule
   III. form a basis for moral relativism
   The CORRECT answer is:
   A. I only   B. II only   C. I and II   D. III only   E. II and III

5. The fact that any political system deals with relatively attainable rights
   A. shows that all values are equally good or bad
   B. is cause for divorcing political reality from moral rules
   C. shows that the list of natural rights is elusive and capricious
   D. is inconsistent with the author's thesis
   E. does not necessarily mean that natural rights do not exist

6. The passage indicates that an important conflict which can exist in a democracy is the rights of competing groups, i.e., labor versus management
   A. adherence to the democratic process versus non-democratic actions by government
   B. difficulty in choosing between two effective compromises
   C. adherence to the democratic process versus the desire to support a specific right
   D. difficulty in reconciling conflict by natural rights

KEY (CORRECT ANSWERS)

1. B   4. A
2. A   5. E
3. C   6. D

READING COMPREHENSION
UNDERSTANDING AND INTERPRETING WRITTEN MATERIAL
EXAMINATION SECTION
TEST 1

DIRECTIONS: Each question or incomplete statement is followed by several suggested answers or completions. Select the one that BEST answers the question or completes the statement. *PRINT THE LETTER OF THE CORRECT ANSWER IN THE SPACE AT THE RIGHT.*

1. Most managers make the mistake of using absolutes as signals of trouble or its absence. A quality problem emerges—that means trouble; a test is passed—we have no problems. Outside of routine organizations, there are always going to be such signals of trouble or success, but they are not very meaningful. Many times everything looks good, but the roof is about to cave in because something no one thought about and for which there is no rule, procedure, or test has been neglected. The specifics of such problems cannot be predicted, but they are often signaled in advance by changes in the organizational system: Managers spend less time on the project; minor problems proliferate; friction in the relationships between adjacent work groups or departments increases; verbal progress reports become overly glib, or overly reticent; change occur in the rate at which certain events happen, not in whether or not they happen. And they are monitored by random probes into the organization—seeing how things are going.
   According to the above paragraph,
   A. managers do not spend enough time managing
   B. managers have a tendency to become overly glib when writing reports
   C. managers should be aware that problems that exist in the organization may not exhibit predictable signals of trouble
   D. managers should attempt to alleviate friction in the relationship between adjacent work groups by monitoring random probes into the organization's problems

   1.____

2. *Lack of challenge* and *excessive zeal* are opposite villains. You cannot do your best on a problem unless you are motivated. Professional problem solvers learn to be motivated somewhat by money and future work that may come their way if they succeed. However, challenge must be present for at least some of the time, or the process ceases to be rewarding. On the other hand, an excessive motivation to succeed, especially to succeed quickly, can inhibit the creative process. The tortoise-and-the-hare phenomenon is often apparent in problem solving. The person who thinks up the simple elegant solution, although he or she may take longer in doing so, often wins. As in the race, the tortoise depends upon an inconsistent performance from the rabbit. And if the rabbit spends so little time on conceptualization that the rabbit merely chooses the first answers that occur, such inconsistency is almost guaranteed.

   2.____

According to the above paragraph,
- A. excessive motivation to succeed can be harmful in problem solving
- B. it is best to spend a long time on solving problems
- C. motivation is the most important component in problem solving
- D. choosing the first solution that occurs is a valid method of problem solving

3. Virginia Woolf's approach to the question of women and fiction, about which she wrote extensively, polemically, and in a profoundly feminist way, was grounded in a general theory of literature. She argued that the writer was the product of her or his historical circumstances and that material conditions were of crucial importance. Secondly, she claimed that these material circumstances had a profound effect on the psychological aspects of writing, and that they could be seen to influence the nature of the creative work itself.
According to this paragraph,
- A. the material conditions and historical circumstances in which male and female writers find themselves greatly influence their work
- B. a woman must have an independent income to succeed as a writer
- C. Virginia Woolf preferred the writings of female authors, as their experiences more clearly reflected hers
- D. male writers are less likely than women writers to be influenced by material circumstances

3.____

4. A young person's first manager is likely to be the most influential person in his or her career. If this manager is unable or unwilling to develop the skills the young employee needs to perform effectively, the latter will set lower personal standards than he or she is capable of achieving, that person's self-image will be impaired, and he or she will develop negative attitudes toward the job, the employer—in all probability—his or her career. Since the chances of building a successful career with the employer will decline rapidly, he or she will leave, if that person has high aspirations, in hope of finding a better opportunity. If, on the other hand, the manager helps the employee to achieve maximum potential, he or she will build a foundation for a successful career.
According to the above paragraph,
- A. If an employee has negative attitudes towards his or her job, the manager is to blame
- B. managers of young people often have a great influence upon their careers
- C. good employees will leave a job they like if they are not given a chance to develop their skills
- D. managers should develop the full potential of their young employees

4.____

5. The reason for these difference is not that the Greeks had a superior sense of form or an inferior imagination or joy in life, but that they thought differently. Perhaps an illustration will make this clear. With the historical plays of Shakespeare in mind, let the reader contemplate the only extant Greek play on a historical subject, the Persians of Aeschylus, a play written less than ten years after the event which it deals with, and performed before the Athenian people who had played so notable a part in the struggle—incidentally,

5.____

immediately below the Acropolis which the Persians had sacked and defiled. Any Elizabethan dramatist would have given us a panorama of the whole war, its moments of despair, hope, and triumph; we should see on the stage the leaders who planned and some of the soldiers who won the victory. In the Persians we see nothing of the sort. The scene is laid in the Persian capital, one action is seen only through Persian eyes, the course of the war is simplified so much that the naval battle of Artemisium is not mentioned, nor even the heroic defense of Thermopylae, and not a single Greek is mentioned by name. The contrast could hardly be more complete.
Which sentence is BEST supported by the above paragraph?
   A. Greek plays are more interesting than Elizabethan plays.
   B. Elizabethan dramatists were more talented than Greek dramatists.
   C. If early Greek dramatists had the same historical material as Shakespeare had, the final form the Greek work would take would be very different from the Elizabethan work.
   D. Greeks were historically more inaccurate than Elizabethans.

6. The problem with present planning systems, public or private, is that accountability is weak. Private planning systems in the global corporations operate on a set of narrow incentives that frustrate sensible public policies such as full employment, environmental protection, and price stability. Public planning is Olympian and confused because there is neither a clear consensus on social values nor political priorities. To accomplish anything, explicit choices must be made, but these choices can be made effectively only with the active participation of the people most directly involved. This, not nostalgia for small-town times gone forever, is the reason that devolution of political power to local communities is a political necessity. The power to plan locally is a precondition for sensible integration of cities, regions, and countries into the world economy.
According to the author,
   A. people most directly affected by issues should participate in deciding those issues
   B. private planning systems are preferable to public planning systems
   C. there is no good system of government
   D. county governments are more effective than state governments

6.____

Questions 7-11.

DIRECTIONS: Questions 7 through 11 are to be answered SOLELY on the basis of the following passage.

    The ideal relationship for the interview is one of mutual confidence. To try to pretend, to put on a front of cordiality and friendship is extremely unwise for the interviewer because he will certainly convey, by subtle means, his real feelings. It is the interviewer's responsibility to take the lead in establishing a relationship of mutual confidence.
    As the interviewer, you should help the interviewee to feel at ease and ready to talk. One of the best ways to do this is to be at ease yourself. If you are, it will probably be evident; if you are not, it will almost certainly be apparent to the interviewee. Begin the interview with topics for discussion which are easy to talk about and non-menacing. This interchange can be like the

conversation of people when they are waiting for a bus, at the ballgame, or discussing the weather. However, do not prolong this warm-up too long since the interviewee knows as well as you do that these are not the things he came to discuss. Delaying too long in betting down too business may suggest to him that you are reluctant to deal with the topic.

Once you get onto the main topics, do all that you can to get the interviewee to talk freely with a little prodding from you as possible. This will probably require that you give him some idea of the area and of ways of looking at it. Avoid, however, prejudicing or coloring his remarks by what you say; especially, do not in any way indicate that there are certain things you want to hear, others which you do not want to hear. It is essential that he feel free to express his own ideas unhampered by your ideas, your values and preconceptions.

Do not appear to dominate the interview, nor have even the suggestion of a patronizing attitude. Ask some questions which will enable the interviewee to take pride in his knowledge. Take the attitude that the interviewee sincerely wants the interview to achieve its purpose. This creates a warm, permissive atmosphere that is most important in all interviews.

7. Of the following, the BEST title for the above passage is
   A. PERMISSIVENESS IN INTERVIEWING
   B. INTERVIEW TECHNIQUES
   C. THE FACTOR OF PRETENSE IN THE INTERVIEW
   D. THE CORDIAL INTERVIEW

8. Which of the following recommendations on the conduct of an interview is made by the above passage?
   A. Conduct the interview as if it were an interchange between people discussing the weather.
   B. The interview should be conducted in a highly impersonal manner.
   C. Allow enough time for the interview so that the interviewee does not feel rushed.
   D. Start the interview with topics which are not threatening to the interviewee.

9. The above passage indicates that the interviewer should
   A. feel free to express his opinions
   B. patronize the interviewee and display a permissive attitude
   C. permit the interviewee to give the needed information in his own fashion
   D. provide for privacy when conducting the interview

10. The meaning of the word *unhampered*, as it is used in the last sentence of the fourth paragraph of the above passage, is MOST NEARLY
    A. unheeded   B. unobstructed   C. hindered   D. aided

11. It can be INFERRED from the above passage that
    A. interviewers, while generally mature, lack confidence
    B. certain methods in interviewing are more successful than others in obtaining information
    C. there is usually a reluctance on the part of interviewers to deal with unpleasant topics
    D. it is best for the interviewer not to waiver from the use of hard and fast rules when dealing with clients

Questions 12-19.

DIRECTIONS: Questions 12 through 19 are to be answered SOLELY on the basis of the following passage.

Disabled cars pose a great danger to bridge traffic at any time, but during rush hours it is especially important that such vehicles be promptly detected and removed. The term *disable car* is an all-inclusive label referring to cars stalled due to a flat tire, mechanical failure, an accident, or locked bumpers. Flat tires are the most common reason why cars become disabled. The presence of disabled vehicles caused 68% of all traffic accidents last year. Of these, 75% were serious enough to require hospitalization of at least one of the vehicle's occupants.

The basic problem in the removal of disabled vehicles is detection of the car. Several methods have been proposed to aid detection. At a 1980 meeting of traffic experts and engineers, the idea of sinking electronic eyes into roadways was first suggested. Such *eyes* let officers know when traffic falls below normal speed and becomes congested. The basic argument against this approach is the high cost of installation of these eyes. One Midwestern state has, since 1978, employed closed circuit television to detect the existence and locations of stalled vehicles. When stalled vehicles are seen on the closed circuit television screen, the information is immediately communicated by radio to units stationed along the roadway, thus enabling the prompt removal of these obstructions to traffic. However, many cities lack the necessary manpower and equipment to use this approach. For the past five years, several east-coast cities have used the method known as *safety chains*, consisting of mobile units which represent the links at the *safety chain*. These mobile units are stationed as posts one or two miles apart along roadways to detect disabled cars. Standard procedure is for the units in the *safety chain* to have roof blinker lights turned on to full rotation. The officer, upon spotting a disabled car, at once assumes a post that gives him the most control in directing traffic around the obstruction. Only after gaining such control does he investigate and decide what action should be taken.

12. From the above passage, The PERCENTAGE of accidents caused by disabled cars in which hospitalization was required by at least one of the occupants of a vehicle last year was
    A. 17%   B. 51%   C. 68%   D. 75%

    12.____

13. According to the above passage, vehicles are MOST frequently disabled because of
    A. flat tires
    B. locked bumpers
    C. brake failure
    D. overheated motors

    13.____

14. According to the above passage, in the electronic eye method of detection, the *eyes* are placed
    A. on lights along the roadway
    B. on patrol cars stationed along the roadway
    C. in booths spaced two miles apart
    D. into the roadway

    14.____

15. According to the above passage, the factor COMMON to both the *safety chain* method and the *closed circuit television* method of detecting disabled vehicles is that both
    A. require the use of *electronic eyes*
    B. may be used where there is a shortage of officers
    C. employ units that are stationed along the highway
    D. require the use of trucks to move the heavy equipment used

    15.____

16. The one of the following which is NOT discussed in the above passage as a method that may be used to detect disabled vehicles is
    A. closed circuit television   B. radar
    C. electronic eyes   D. safety chains

    16.____

17. One DRAWBACK mentioned by the above passage to the use of the closed circuit television method for detection of disabled cars is that this technique
    A. cannot be used during bad weather
    B. does not provide for actual removal of the cars
    C. must be operated by a highly skilled staff of traffic engineers
    D. requires a large amount of manpower and equipment

    17.____

18. The NEWEST of the methods discussed in the above passage for detection of disabled vehicles is
    A. electronic eyes   B. the mobile unit
    C. the safety chain   D. closed circuit television

    18.____

19. When the *safety chain* method is being used, an officer who spots a disabled vehicle should FIRST
    A. turn off his roof blinker lights
    B. direct traffic around the disabled vehicle
    C. send a ratio message to the nearest mobile unit
    D. conduct an investigation

    19.____

20. The universe is 15 billion years old, and the geological underpinnings of the earth were formed long before the first sea creature slithered out of the slime. But it is only in the last 6,000 years or so that men have descended into mines to chop and scratch at the earth's crust. Human history is, as Carl Sagan has put it, the equivalent of a few seconds in the 15 billion year life of the earth. What alarms those who keep track of the earth's crust is that since 1950 human beings have managed to consume more minerals than were mined in all previous history, a splurge of a millisecond in geologic time that cannot be long repeated without using up the finite riches of the earth.
    Of the following, the MAIN idea of this paragraph is:
    A. There is true cause for concern at the escalating consumption of the earth's minerals in recent years.
    B. Human history is the equivalent of a few seconds in the 15 billion year life of the earth
    C. The earth will soon run out of vital mineral resources

    20.____

50

21. The authors of the Economic Report of the President are collectively aware, despite their vision of the asset-rich household, of the real economy in which millions of Americans live. There are glimpses, throughout the Report, of the underworld in which about 23 million people do not have public or private health insurance; in which the number of people receiving unemployment compensation was 41 percent of the total unemployed, in which the average dole for the compensated unemployed is about one-half of take-home pay. The authors understand, for example, that a worker may become physically disabled and that individuals generally do not like the risk of losing their ability to earn income. But such realities justify no more than the most limited interference in the (imperfect) market for disability insurance. There is only, as far as I can tell, one moment of genuine emotion in the entire Report when the authors' passions are stirred beyond market principles. They are discussing the leasing provisions of the 1981 Tax Act (conditions which so reduce tax revenues that they are apparently opposed in their present form by the Business Roundtable, the American Business Conference, and the National Association of Manufacturers).

    In the dark days before the 1981 ACT, according to the Report, (*firms with temporary tax losses* (a condition especially characteristic of new enterprises) were often unable to take advantage of investment tax incentives. The reason was that temporarily unprofitable companies had no taxable income against which to apply the investment tax deduction. It was a piteous contingency for the truly needy entrepreneur. But all was made right with the Tax Act. Social Security for the disabled incompetent corporation: the compassionate soul of Reagan's new economy.

    According to the above passage,
    A. the National Association of Manufacturers and those companies that are temporarily unprofitable oppose the leasing provisions of the 1981 Tax Act
    B. the authors of the Report are willing to ignore market principles in order to assist corporations unable to take advantage of tax incentives
    C. the authors of the Report feel the National Association of Manufacturers and the Business Roundtable are wrong in opposing the leasing provisions of the 1981 Tax Act
    D. the authors of the Report have more compassion for incompetent corporations than for disabled workers

22. Much of the lore of management in the West regards ambiguity as a symptom of a variety of organizational ills whose cure is larger doses of rationality, specificity, and decisiveness. But is ambiguity sometimes desirable? Ambiguity may be thought of as a shroud of the unknown surrounding certain events. The Japanese have a word for it, *ma*, for which there is no English translation. The word is valuable because it gives an explicit place to the unknowable aspect of things. In English, we may refer to an empty space between the chair and the table; the Japanese don't say the space is empty but *full of nothing*. However amusing the illustration, it goes to the core of the issue. Westerners speak of what is unknown primarily in reference to what is known (like the space between the chair and the table, while most eastern languages give honor to the unknown in its own right.

Of course, there are many situations that a manager finds himself in where being explicit and decisive is not only helpful but necessary. There is considerable advantage, however, in having a dual frame of reference—recognizing the value of both the clear and the ambiguous. The point to bear in mind is that in certain situations, ambiguity may serve better than absolute clarity.

Which sentence is BEST supported by the above passage?
- A. We should cultivate the art of being ambiguous.
- B. Ambiguity may sometimes be an effective managerial tool,
- C. Westerners do not have a dual frame of reference.
- D. It is important to recognize the ambiguous aspects of all situations.

23. Everyone ought to accustom himself to grasp in his thought at the same time facts that are at once so few and so simple, that he shall never believe that he has knowledge of anything which he does not mentally behold with a distinctiveness equal to that of the objects which he knows most distinctly of all. It is true that some people are born with a much greater aptitude for such discernment than others, but the mind can be made much more expert at such work by art and exercise. But there is one fact which I should here emphasize above all others; and that is everyone should firmly persuade himself that none of the sciences, however abstruse, is to be deduced from lofty and obscure matters, but that they all proceed only from what is easy and more readily understood.

    According to the author,
    - A. people should concentrate primarily on simple facts
    - B. intellectually gifted people have a great advantage over others
    - C. even difficult material and theories proceed from what is readily understood
    - D. if a scientist cannot grasp a simple theory, he or she is destined to fail

24. Goethe's casual observations about language contain a profound truth. Every word in every language is a part of a system of thinking unlike any other. Speakers of different languages live in different worlds; or rather, they live in the same world but can't help looking at it in different ways. Words stand for patterns of experience. As one generation hand its language down to the next, it also hands down a fixed pattern of thinking, seeing, and feeling. When we go from one language to another, nothing stays put; different peoples carry different nerve patterns in their brains, and there's no point where they fully match.

    According to the above passage,
    - A. language differences and their ramifications are a major cause of tensions between nations
    - B. it is not a good use of one's time to read novels that have been translated from another language because of the tremendous differences in interpretation
    - C. differences in languages reflect the different experiences of people the world over
    - D. language students should be especially careful to retain awareness of the subtleties of their native language

Questions 25-27.

DIRECTIONS: Questions 25 through 27 are to be answered SOLELY on the basis of the following passage.

The context of all education is twofold—individual and social. Its business is to make us more and more ourselves, too cultivate in each of us our own distinctive genius, however modest it may be, while showing us how this genius may be reconciled with the needs and claims of the society of which we are a part. Thought it is not education's aim to cultivate eccentrics, that society is richest, most flexible, and most humane that best uses and most tolerates eccentricity. Conformity beyond a point breeds sterile minds and, therefore, a sterile society.

The function of secondary—and still more of higher education is to affect the environment. Teachers are not, and should not be, social reformers. But they should be the catalytic agents by means of which young minds are influenced to desire and execute reform. To aspire to better things is a logical and desirable part of mental and spiritual growth.

25. Of the following, the MOST suitable title for the above passage is 25.____
   A. EDUCATION'S FUNCTION IN CREATING INDIVIDUAL DIFFERENCES
   B. THE NEED FOR EDUCATION TO ACQUAINT US WITH OUR SOCIAL ENVIRONMENT
   C. THE RESPONSIBILITY OF EDUCATION TOWARD THE INDIVIDUAL AND SOCIETY
   D. THE ROLE OF EDUCATION IN EXPLAINIING THE NEEDS OF SOCIETY

26. On the basis of the above passage, it may be inferred that 26.____
   A. conformity is one of the forerunners of totalitarianism
   B. education should be designed to create at least a modest amount of genius in everyone
   C. tolerance of individual differences tends to give society opportunities for improvement
   D. reforms are usually initiated by people who are somewhat eccentric

27. On the basis of the above passage, it may be inferred that 27.____
   A. genius is likely to be accompanied by a desire for social reform
   B. nonconformity is an indication of the inquiring mind
   C. people who are not high school or college graduates are not able to affect the environment
   D. teachers may or may not be social reformers

Questions 28-30.

DIRECTIONS: Questions 28 through 30 are to be answered SOLELY on the basis of the following passage.

Disregard for odds and complete confidence in one's self have produced many of our great successes. But every young man who wants to go into business for himself should appraise himself as a candidate for the one percent to survive. What has he to offer that is new or better? Has he special talents, special know-how, a new invention or service, or more capital than the average competitor? Has he the most important qualification of all, a willingness to work harder than anyone else? A man who is working for himself without limitation of hours or personal sacrifice can run circles around any operation that relies on paid help. But he must forget the eight-hour day, the forty-hour week, and the annual vacation. When he stops work, his income stops unless he hires a substitute. Most small operations have their busiest day on Saturday, and the owner uses Sunday to catch up on his correspondence, bookkeeping, inventorying, and maintenance chores. The successful self-employed man invariably works harder and worries more than the man on a salary. His wife and children make corresponding sacrifices of family unity and continuity; they never know whether their man will be home or in a mood to enjoy family activities.

28. The title that BEST expresses the ideas of the above passage is   28.____
    A. OVERCOMING OBSTACLES
    B. RUNNING ONE'S OWN BUSINESS
    C. HOW TO BECOME A SUCCESS
    D. WHY SMALL BUSINESSES FAIL

29. The above passage suggests that   29.____
    A. small businesses are the ones that last
    B. salaried workers are untrustworthy
    C. a willingness to work will overcome loss of income
    D. working for one's self may lead to success

30. The author of the above passage would MOST likely believe in   30.____
    A. individual initiative   B. socialism
    C. corporations   D. government aid to small business

KEY (CORRECT ANSWERS)

1.	C	11.	B	21.	D
2.	A	12.	B	22.	B
3.	A	13.	A	23.	C
4.	B	14.	D	24.	C
5.	C	15.	C	25.	C
6.	A	16.	B	26.	D
7.	B	17.	D	27.	D
8.	D	18.	A	28.	B
9.	C	19.	B	29.	D
10.	B	20.	A	30.	A

READING COMPREHENSION
UNDERSTANDING AND INTERPRETING WRITTEN MATERIAL
EXAMINATION SECTION
TEST 1

DIRECTIONS: Each question or incomplete statement is followed by several suggested answers or completions. Select the one that BEST answers the question or completes the statement. *PRINT THE LETTER OF THE CORRECT ANSWER IN THE SPACE AT THE RIGHT.*

1. The question *Who shall now teach Hegel?* is shorthand for the question *Who is going to teach this genre—all the so-called Continental philosophers?* The obvious answer to this question is *Whoever cares to study them.* This is also the right answer, but we can only accept it whole heartedly if we clear away a set of factitious questions. On such question is: *Are these Continental philosophers really philosophers?* Analytic philosophers, because they identify philosophical ability with argumentative skill and notice that there is nothing they would consider an argument in the bulk of Heidegger or Foucault, suggest that these must be people who tried to be philosophers and failed-incompetent philosophers. This is as silly as saying that Plato was an incompetent sophist, or that a hedgehog is an incompetent fox. Hegel knew what he thought about philosophers who imitated the method and style of mathematics. He thought they were incompetent. These reciprocal charges of incompetence do nobody any good. We should just drop the questions of what philosophy really is or who really counts as a philosopher.
Which sentence is BEST supported by the above paragraph?
   A. The study of Hegel's philosophy is less popular now than in the past.
   B. Philosophers must stop questioning the competence of other philosophers.
   C. Philosophers should try to be as tolerant as Foucault and Heidegger.
   D. Analytic philosophers tend to be more argumentative than other philosophers.

1.____

2. It is an interesting question: the ease with which organizations of different kinds at different stages in their history can continue to function with ineffectual leadership at the top, or even function without a clear system of authority. Certainly, the success of some experiments in worker self-management shows that bosses are not always necessary, as some contemporary Marxists argue. Indeed, sometimes the function of those at the top is merely to symbolize organizational accountability, especially in dealing with outside authorities, but not to guide the actions of those within the organization. A vice president of a large insurance company remarked to us that *Presidents are powerless; no one needs them. They should all be sent off to do public relations for the company.* While this is clearly a self-serving statement from someone next in line to command, it does give meaning to the expression being kicked upstairs. According to the author,

2.____

A. organizations function very smoothly without bosses
B. the function of those at the top is sometimes only to symbolize organizational accountability
C. company presidents are often inept at guiding the actions of those within the organization
D. presidents of companies have less power than one might assume they have

3. The goal of a problem is a terminal expression one wishes to cause to exist in the world of the problem. There are two types of goals: specified goal expressions in proof problems and incompletely specified goal expressions in find problems. For example, consider the problem of finding the value of X, given the expression 4X+5 = 17. In this problem, one can regard the goal expression as being of the form X = _____, the goal expression. The goal expression in a find problem of this type is incompletely specified. If the goal expression were specified completely—for example, X = 3—then the problem would be a proof problem, with only the sequence of operations to be determined in order to solve the problem. Of course, if one were not guaranteed that the goal expression X = 3 was true, then the terminal goal expression should really be considered to be incompletely specified—something like the statement X = 3 (true or false).
According to the preceding paragraph,
A. the goal of the equation 4X+5 = 17 is true, not false
B. if the goal expression was specified as being equal to 3, the problem 4X+5 = 17 would be a proof problem
C. if the sequence of operations of the problem given in the paragraph is predetermined, the goal of the problem becomes one of terminal expression, or the number 17
D. X cannot be found unless X is converted into a proof problem

4. We have human psychology and animal psychology, but no plant psychology. Why? Because we believe that plants have no perceptions or intentions. Some plants exhibit *behavior* and have been credited with *habits*. If you stroke the midrib of the compound leaf of a sensitive plant, the leaflets close. The sunflower changes with the diurnal changes in the source of light. The lowest animals have not much more complicated forms of behavior. The sea anemone traps and digests the small creatures that the water brings to it; the pitcher plant does the same thing and even more, for it presents a cup of liquid that attracts insects, instead of letting the surrounding medium drift them into its trap. Here as everywhere in nature where the great, general classes of living things diverge, the lines between them are not perfectly clear. A sponge is an animal; the pitcher plant is a flowering plant, but it comes nearer to *feeding itself* than the animal. Yet the fact is that we credit all animals, and only the animals, with some degree of feeling.
Of the following, the MAIN idea expressed in the above paragraph is:
A. The classification of plants has been based on beliefs about their capacity to perceive and feel
B. Many plants are more evolved than species considered animals

C. The lines that divide the classes of living things are never clear.
D. The abilities and qualities of plants are undervalued.

5. Quantitative indexes are not necessarily adequate measures of true economic significance or influence. But even the raw quantitative data speak loudly of the importance of the new transnationalized economy. The United Nations estimated value added in this new sector of the world economy at $500 billion in 2001, mounting to one-fifth of total GNP of the non-socialist world and exceeding the GNP of any one other country except the United States. Furthermore, all observers agree that the share of this sector in the world economy is growing rapidly. At least since 1980, its annual rate of growth has been high and remarkably steady at 10 percent compared to 4 percent for noninternationalized output in the Western developed countries.
One spokesman for the new system franklin envisages that within a generation some 400 to 500 multinational corporations will own close to two-thirds of the world's fixed assets.
According to the author, all of the following are true EXCEPT
   A. Quantitative indexes are not necessarily adequate measures of actual economic influence.
   B. The transnational sector of the world economy is growing rapidly.
   C. Since 1980, the rate of growth of transnationals has been 10% compared to 4% for internationalized output in the Western developed countries.
   D. Continued growth for multinational corporations is likely.

5.____

6. A bill may be sent to the Governor when it has passed both houses. During the session, he is given ten days to act on bills that reach his desk. Bills sent to him within ten days of the end of the session must be acted on within 30 days after the last day of the session. If the Governor takes no action on a ten day bill, it automatically becomes a law. If he disapproves or vetoes a ten day bill, it can become law only if it is re-passed by two-thirds vote in each house. If he fails to act on a 30 day bill, the bill is said to have received a *pocket veto*. It is customary for the Governor to act, however, on all bills submitted to him, and give his reason in writing for approving or disapproving important legislation.
According to the above paragraph, all of the following are true EXCEPT:
   A. Bills sent to the Governor in the last ten days of the session must be acted on within thirty days after the last day of the session,
   B. If the Governor takes no action on a 10 day bill, it is said to have received a *pocket veto*.
   C. It is customary for the Governor to act on all bills submitted to him.
   D. If the Governor vetoes a ten day bill, it can become law only if passed by a two-thirds vote of the Legislature.

6.____

7. It is particularly when I see a child going through the mechanical process of manipulating numbers without any intuitive sense of what it is all about that I recall the lines of Lewis Carroll: *Reeling and Writhing, of course, to begin with...and then the different branches of Arithmetic-Ambition, Distraction, Uglification, and Derision.* Or, as Max Beberman has put it, much more gently: *Somewhat related to the notion of discovery in teaching is our insistence that*

7.____

the student become aware of a concept before a name has been assigned to the concept. I am quite aware that the issue of intuitive understanding is a very live one among teachers of mathematics, and even a casual reading of the yearbook of the National Council of Teachers of Mathematics makes it clear that they are also very mindful of the gap that exists between proclaiming the importance of such understanding and actually producing it in the classroom.
The MAIN idea expressed in the above paragraph is:
   A. Math teachers are concerned about the difficulties inherent in producing an understanding of mathematics in their students.
   B. It is important that an intuitive sense in approaching math problems be developed, rather than relying on rote, mechanical learning.
   C. Mathematics, by its very nature, encourages rote, mechanical learning.
   D. Lewis Carroll was absolutely correct in his assessment of the true nature of mathematics.

8. Heisenberg's *Principle of Uncertainty*, which states that events at the atomic level cannot be observed with certainty, can be compared to this: In the world of everyday experience, we can observe any phenomenon and measure its properties without influencing the phenomenon in question to any significant extent. To be sure, if we try to measure the temperature of a demitasse with a bathtub thermometer, the instrument will absorb so much heat from the coffee that it will change the coffee's temperature substantially. But with a small chemical thermometer, we may get a sufficiently accurate reading. We can measure the temperature of a living cell with a miniature thermometer, which has almost negligible heat capacity. But in the atomic world, we can never overlook the disturbance caused by the introduction of the measuring apparatus.
Which sentence is BEST supported by the above paragraph?
   A. There is little we do not alter by the mere act of observation.
   B. It is always a good idea to use the smallest measuring device possible.
   C. Chemical thermometers are more accurate than bathtub thermometers.
   D. It is not possible to observe events at the atomic level and be sure that the same events would occur if we were not observing them.

9. It is a myth that American workers are pricing themselves out of the market, relative to workers in other industrialized countries of the world. The wages of American manufacturing workers increased at a slower rate in the 1990s than those of workers in other major western countries. In terms of American dollars, between 1990 and 2000, hourly compensation increased 489 percent in Japan and 464 percent in Germany, compared to 128 percent in the United States. Even though these countries experienced faster productivity growth, their unit labor costs still rose faster than in the United States, according to the Bureau of Labor Statistics. During the 1990s, unit labor costs rose 192 percent in Japan, 252 percent in Germany, and only 78 percent in the United States.
According to the above passage,
   A. unit labor costs in the 1990s were higher in Japan than they were in Germany or the United States
   B. the wages of American workers need to be increased to be consistent with other countries

C. American worker are more productive than Japanese or German workers
D. the wages of American workers in manufacturing increased at a slower rate in the 1990s than the wages of workers in Japan or Germany

10. No people have invented more ways to enjoy life than the Chinese, perhaps to balance floods, famines, warlords, and other ills of fate. The clang of gongs, clashing cymbals, and beating of drums sound through their long history. No month is without fairs and theatricals when streets are hung with fantasies of painted lanterns and crowded with *carriages that flow like water, horses like roaming dragons.* Night skies are illumined by firecrackers—a Chinese invention—bursting in the form of flowerpots, peonies, fiery devils. The ways of pleasure are myriad. Music plays in the air through bamboo whistles of different pitch tied to the wings of circling pigeons. To skim a frozen lake in an ice sleigh with a group of friends on a day when the sun is warm is rapture, like *moving in a cup of jade.* What more delightful than the ancient festival called *Half an Immortal*, when everyone from palace officials to the common man took a ride on a swing? When high in the air, one felt like an Immortal, when back to earth once again human—no more than to be for an instant a god.
According to the above passage,
    A. if the Chinese hadn't had so many misfortunes, they wouldn't have created so many pleasurable past times
    B. the Chinese invented flowerpots
    C. every month the Chinese have fairs and theatricals
    D. pigeons are required to play the game *Half an Immortal*

10.____

11. In our century, instead, poor Diphilus is lost in the crowd of his peers. We flood one another. No one recognizes him as he loads his basket in the supermarket. What grievous fits of melancholy have I not suffered in one of our larger urban bookstores, gazing at the hundreds, thousands, tens of thousands of books on shelve and tables? And what are they to the hundreds of thousands, the millions that stand in our research libraries? More books than Noah saw raindrops. How many readers will read a given one of them—mine, yours—in their lifetimes? And how will it be in the distant future? Incomprehensible masses of books, Pelion upon Ossa, hordes of books, each piteously calling for attention, respect, love, in competition with the vast disgorgements of the past and with one another in the present. Neither is it at all helpful that books can even now be reduced to the size of a postage stamp. Avanti! Place the Bible on a pinhead! Crowding more books into small spaces does not cram more books into our heads. Here I come to the sticking point that unnerves the modern Diphilus. The number of books a person can read in a given time is, roughly speaking, a historical constant. It does not change significantly even when the number of books available for reading does. Constants are pitted against variables to confound both writer and reader.
Of the following, the MAIN idea in this passage is:
    A. It is difficult to attain immortality because so many books are being published.
    B. Too many books are being published, so fewer people are reading them.

11.____

C. Because so many books are being published, the quality of the writing is poorer.
D. Because so many books are available, but only a fixed amount of time to read them, frustration results for both the reader and the writer.

12. Until recently, consciousness of sexual harassment has been low. But workers have become aware of it as more women have arrived at levels of authority in the workplace, feminist groups have focused attention on rape and other violence against women, and students have felt freer to report perceived abuse by professors. In the last 5 years, studies have shown that sexual misconduct at the workplace is a big problem. For example, in a recently published survey of federal employees, 42% of 694,000 women and 15% of 1,168,000 men said they had experienced some form of harassment.
According to the author,
    A. the awareness of sexual harassment at the workplace is increasing
    B. the incidence of harassment is higher in universities than workplaces
    C. sexual harassment is much more commonly experienced by women than men
    D. it is rare for men to experience sexual harassment

12.____

Questions 13-17.

DIRECTIONS: Questions 13 through 17 are to be answered SOLELY on the basis of the following paragraph.

Since discounts are in common use in the commercial world and apply to purchases made by government agencies as well as business firms, it is essential that individuals in both public and private employment who prepare bills, check invoices, prepare payment vouchers, or write checks to pay bills have an understanding of the terms used. These include cash or time discount, trade discount, and discount series. A cash or time discount offers a reduction in price to the buyer for the prompt payment of the bill and is usually expressed as a percentage with a time requirement, stated in days, within which the bill must be paid in order to earn the discount. An example would be 3/10, meaning a 3% discount may be applied to the bill if the payment is forwarded to the vendor within 10 days. On an invoice, the cash discount terms are usually followed by the net terms, which is the time in days allowed for ordinary payment of the bill. Thus, 3/10, Net 30 means that full payment is expected in thirty days if the cash discount of 3% is not taken for having paid the bill within ten days. When the expression Terms Net Cash is listed on a bill, it means that no deduction for early payment is allowed. A trade discount is normally applied to list prices by a manufacturer to show the actual price to retailers so that they may know their cost and determine markups that will allow them to operate competitively and at a profit. A trade discount is applied by the seller to the list price and is independent of a cash or time discount. Discounts may also be used by manufacturers to adjust prices charged to retailers without changing list prices. This is usually done by series discounting and is expressed as a series of percentages. To compute a series discount, such as 40%, 20%, 10%, first apply the 40% discount to the list price, then apply the 20% discount to the remainder, and finally apply the 10% discount to the second remainder.

13. According to the above paragraph, trade discounts are
    A. applied by the buyer
    B. independent of cash discounts
    C. restricted to cash sales
    D. used to secure rapid payment of bills

14. According to the above paragraph, if the sales terms 5/10, Net 60 appear on a bill in the amount of $100 dated December 5 and the buyer submits his payment on December 15, his PROPER payment should be
    A. $60   B. $90   C. $95   D. $100

15. According to the above paragraph, if a manufacturer gives a trade discount of 40% for an item with a list price of $250 and the terms are Net Cash, the price a retail merchant is required to pay for this item is
    A. $250   B. $210   C. $150   D. $100

16. According to the above paragraph, a series discount of 25%, 20%, 10% applied to a list price of $200 results in an ACTUAL price to the buyer of
    A. $88   B. $90   C. $108   D. $110

17. According to the above paragraph, if a manufacturer gives a trade discount of 50% and the terms are 6/10, Net 30, the cost to a retail merchant of an item with a list price of $500 and for which he takes the time discount, is
    A. $220   B. $235   C. $240   D. $250

Questions 18-22.

DIRECTIONS: Questions 18 through 22 are to be answered SOLELY on the basis of the following paragraph.

The city may issue its own bonds or it may purchase bonds as an investment. Bonds may be issued in various denominations, and the face value of the bond is its par value. Before purchasing a bond, the investor desires to know the rate of income that the investment will yield. In computing the yield on a bond, it is assumed that the investor will keep the bond until the date of maturity, except for callable bonds which are not considered in this paragraph. To compute exact yield is a complicated mathematical problem, and scientifically prepared tables are generally used to avoid such computation. However, the approximate yield can be computed much more easily. In computing approximate yield, the accrued interest on the date of purchase should be ignored, because the buyer who pays accrued interest to the seller receives it again at the next interest date. Bonds bought at a premium (which cost more) yield a lower rate of income than the same bonds bought at par (face value), and bonds bought at a discount (which cost less) yield a higher rate of income than the same bonds bought at par.

18. An investor bought a $10,000 city bond paying 6% interest. Which of the following purchase prices would indicate that the bond was bought at a PREMIUM?
    A. $9,000   B. $9,400   C. $10,000   D. $10,600

19. During the year, a particular $10,000 bond paying 74% sold at fluctuating prices.
Which of the following prices would indicate that the bond was bought at a DISCOUNT?
   A. $9,800   B. $10,000   C. $10,200   D. $10,750

20. A certain group of bonds was sold in denominations of $5,000, $10,000, $20,000 and $50,000.
In the following list of four purchase prices, which one is MOST likely to represent a bond sold at par value?
   A. $10,500   B. $20,000   C. $22,000   D. $49,000

21. When computing the approximate yield on a bond, it is DESIRABLE to
   A. assume the bond was purchased at par
   B. consult scientifically prepared tables
   C. ignore accrued interest on the date of purchase
   D. wait until the bond reaches maturity

22. Which of the following is MOST likely to be an exception to the information provided in the above paragraph? Bonds
   A. purchased at a premium   B. sold at par
   C. sold before maturity   D. which are callable

Questions 23-25

DIRECTIONS: Questions 23 through 25 are to be answered SOLELY on the basis of the following paragraph.

There is one bad habit of drivers that often causes chain collisions at traffic lights. It is the habit of keeping one foot poised over the accelerator pedal, ready to step on the gas the instant the light turns green. A driver who is watching the light, instead of watching the cars in front of him, may *jump the gun* and bump the car in front of him, and this car in turn may bump the next car. If a driver is resting his foot on the accelerator, his foot will be slammed down when he bumps into the car ahead. This makes the collision worse and makes it very likely that cars further ahead in the line are going to get involved in a series of violent bumps.

23. Which of the following conclusions can MOST reasonably drawn from the information given in the above paragraph?
   A. American drivers have a great many bad driving habits.
   B. Drivers should step on the gas as soon as the light turns green.
   C. A driver with poor driving habits should be arrested and fined.
   D. A driver should not rest his foot on the accelerator when the car is stopped for a traffic light.

24. From the information given in the above paragraph, a reader should be able to tell that a chain collision may be defined as a collision
   A. caused by bad driving habits at traffic lights
   B. in which one car hits another, this second car hits a third car, and so on

C. caused by drivers who fail to use their accelerators
D. that takes place at an intersection where there is a traffic light

25. The above passage states that a driver who watches the light instead of paying attention to traffic may 25._____
    A. be involved in an accident
    B. end up in jail
    C. lose his license
    D. develop bad driving habits

KEY (CORRECT ANSWERS)

1. B	11. D
2. B	12. A
3. B	13. B
4. A	14. C
5. C	15. C
6. B	16. C
7. B	17. B
8. D	18. D
9. D	19. A
10. C	20. B

21. C
22. D
23. D
24. B
25. A

TEST 2

DIRECTIONS: Each question or incomplete statement is followed by several suggested answers or completions. Select the one that BEST answers the question or completes the statement. *PRINT THE LETTER OF THE CORRECT ANSWER IN THE SPACE AT THE RIGHT.*

Questions 1-4.

DIRECTIONS: Each of the statements in this section is followed by several labeled choices. In the space at the right, write the letter of the sentence which means MOST NEARLY what is stated or implied in the passage.

1. It may be said that the problem in adult education seems to be not the piling up of facts but practice in thinking.
   This statement means MOST NEARLY that
   A. educational methods for adults and young people should differ
   B. adults seem to think more than young people
   C. a well-educated adult is one who thinks but does not have a store of information
   D. adult education should stress ability to think

   1.____

2. Last year approximately 19,000 fatal accidents were sustained in industry. There were approximately 130 non-fatal injuries to each fatal injury.
   According to the above statement, the number of non-fatal accidents was
     A. 146,000   B. 190,000   C. 1,150,000   D. 2,500,000

   2.____

3. No employer expects his stenographer to be a walking encyclopedia, but it is not unreasonable for him to expect her to know where to look for necessary information on a variety of topics.
   The above statement means MOST NEARLY that the stenographer should
   A. be a college graduate
   B. be familiar with standard office reference books
   C. keep a scrapbook of all interesting happenings
   D. go to the library regularly

   3.____

4. For the United States, Canada has become the most important country in the world, yet there are few countries about which Americans know less. Canada is the third largest country in the world; only Russia and China are larger. The area of Canada is more than a quarter of the whole British Empire.
   According to the above statement, the
   A. British Empire is smaller than Russia or China
   B. territory of China is greater than that of Canada
   C. Americans know more about Canada than they do about China or Russia
   D. Canadian population is more than one-quarter the population of the British Empire

   4.____

Questions 5-8.

DIRECTIONS: Questions 5 through 8 are to be answered SOLELY on the basis of the following paragraph.

A few people who live in old tenements have had the bad habit of throwing garbage out of their windows, especially if there is an empty lot near their building. Sometimes the garbage is food; sometimes the garbage is half-empty soda cans. Sometimes the garbage is a little bit of both mixed together. These people just don't care about keeping the lot clean.

5. The above paragraph states that throwing garbage out of windows is a 5.____
   A. bad habit B. dangerous thing to do
   C. good thing to do D. good way to feed rats

6. According to the above paragraph, an empty lot next to an old tenement is sometimes used as a place to 6.____
   A. hold local gang meetings B. play ball
   C. throw garbage D. walk dogs

7. According to the above paragraph, which of the following throw garbage out of their windows? 7.____
   A. Nobody B. Everybody
   C. Most people D. Some people

8. According to the above paragraph, the kinds of garbage thrown out of windows are 8.____
   A. candy and cigarette butts B. food and half-empty soda cans
   C. fruit and vegetables D. rice and bread

Questions 9-12.

DIRECTIONS: Questions 9 through 12 are to be answered SOLELY on the basis of the following paragraph.

The game that is recognized all over the world as an all-American game is the game of baseball. As a matter of fact, baseball heroes like Joe DiMaggio, Willie Mays, and Babe Ruth were as famous in their day as movie stars Robert Redford, Paul Newman, and Clint Eastwood are now. All these men have had the experience of being mobbed by fans whenever they put in an appearance anywhere in the world. Such unusual popularity makes it possible for stars like these to earn at least as much money off the job as on the job. It didn't take manufacturers and advertising men long to discover that their sales of shaving lotion, for instance, increased when they got famous stars to advertise their product for them on radio and television.

9. According to the above paragraph, baseball is known everywhere as a(n) _____ game. 9.____
   A. all-American B. fast C. unusual D. tough

10. According to the above paragraph, being so well known means that it is possible for people like Willie Mays and Babe Ruth to
    A. ask for anything and get it
    B. make as much money off the job as on it
    C. travel anywhere free of charge
    D. watch any game free of charge

10._____

11. According to the above paragraph, which of the following are known all over the world?
    A. Baseball heroes
    B. Advertising men
    C. Manufacturers
    D. Basketball heroes

11._____

12. According to the above paragraph, it is possible to sell much more shaving lotion on television and radio if
    A. the commercials are in color instead of black and white
    B. you can get a prize with each bottle of shaving lotion
    C. the shaving lotion makes you smell nicer than usual
    D. the shaving lotion is advertised by famous stars

12._____

Questions 13-15.

DIRECTIONS: Questions 13 through 15 are to be answered SOLELY on the basis of the following passage.

That music gives pleasure is axiomatic. Because this is so, the pleasures of music may seem a rather elementary subject for discussion. Yet the source of that pleasure, our musical instinct, is not at all elementary. It is, in fact, one of the prime puzzles of consciousness. Why is it that we are able to make sense out of these nerve signals so that we emerge from engulfment in the orderly presentation of sound stimuli as if we had lived through an image of life?

If music has impact for the mere listener, it follows that it will have much greater impact for those who sing it or play it themselves with proficiency. Any educated person in Elizabethan times was expected to read musical notation and take part in a madrigalsing. Passive listeners, numbered in the millions, are a comparatively recent innovation.

Everyone is aware that so-called serious music has made great strikes in general public acceptance in recent years, but the term itself still connotes something forbidding and hermetic to the mass audience. They attribute to the professional musician a kind of initiation into secrets that are forever hidden from the outsider. Nothing could be more misleading. We all listen to music, professionals, and non-professionals alike in the same sort of way, in a dumb sort of way, really, because simple or sophisticated music attracts all of us in the first instance, on the primordial level of sheer rhythmic and sonic appeal. Musicians are flattered, no doubt, by the deferential attitude of the layman in regard to what he imagines to be our secret understanding of music. But in all honesty, we musicians know that in the main we listen basically as others do, because music hits us with an immediacy that we recognize in the reactions of the most simple minded of music listeners.

13. A suitable title for the above passage would be
    A. HOW TO LISTEN TO MUSIC
    B. LEARNING MUSIC APPRECIATION
    C. THE PLEASURES OF MUSIC
    D. THE WORLD OF THE MUSICIAN

    13.____

14. The author implies that the passive listener is one who
    A. cannot read or play music
    B. does not appreciate serious music
    C. does not keep time to the music by hand or toe tapping
    D. will not attend a concert if he has to pay for the privilege

    14.____

15. The author of the above passage is apparently inconsistent when he discusses
    A. the distinction between the listener who pays for the privilege and the one who does not
    B. the historical development of musical forms
    C. the pleasures derived from music by the musician
    D. why it is that we listen to music

    15.____

Questions 16-18.

DIRECTIONS: Questions 16 through 18 are to be answered SOLELY on the basis of the following passage.

Who are the clerisy? They are people who like to read books. The use of a word so unusual, so out of fashion, can only be excused on the ground that it has no familiar synonym. The word is little known because what it describes has disappeared, though I do not believe is gone forever. The clerisy are those who read for pleasure, but not for idleness; who read for pastime, but not to kill time; who love books, but do not live by books.

Let us consider the actual business of reading—the interpretive act of getting the words off the age and into your head in the most effective way. The most effective way is not the quickest way of reading; and for those who think that speed is the greatest good, there are plenty of manuals on how to read a book which profess to tell how to strip off the husk and guzzle the milk, like a chimp attacking a coconut. Who among today's readers would whisk through a poem, eyes aflicker, and say that he had read it? The answer to that last question must unfortunately be: far too many. For reading is not respected for the art it is.

Doubtless there are philosophical terms for the attitude of mind of which nasty reading is one manifestation, but here let us call it end-gaining, for its victims put ends before means; they value not reading, but having read. In this, the end-gainers make mischief and spoil all they do; end-gaining is one of the curses of our nervously tense, intellectually flabby civilization. In reading, as in all arts, it is the means, and not the end, which gives delight and brings the true reward. Not straining forward toward the completion, but the pleasure of every page as it comes, is the secret of reading. We must desire to read a book, rather than to have read it. This change in attitude, so simple to describe, is by no means simple to achieve,, if one has lived the life of an end-gainer.

16. A suitable title for the above passage would be
    A. READING FOR ENLIGHTENMENT
    B. THE ART OF RAPID READING
    C. THE WELL-EDUCATED READER
    D. VALUES IN READING

16.____

17. The author does NOT believe that most people read because they
    A. are bored
    B. have nothing better to do
    C. love books
    D. wish to say that they have read certain books

17.____

18. The change in attitude to which the author refers in the last sentence of the above passage implies a change from
    A. dawdling while reading so that the reader can read a greater number of books
    B. reading light fiction to reading serious fiction and non-fiction
    C. reading works which do not amuse the reader
    D. skimming through a book to reading it with care

18.____

Questions 19-22.

DIRECTIONS: Questions 19 through 22 are to be answered SOLELY on the basis of the following passage.

Violence is not new to literature. The writings of Shakespeare and Cervantes are full of it. But those classic writers did not condone violence. They viewed it as a just retribution for sins against the divine order or as a sacrifice sanctioned by heroism. What is peculiar to the modern literature is violence for the sake of violence. Perhaps our reverence for life has been dulled by mass slaughter, though mass slaughter has not been exceptional in the history of mankind. What is exceptional is the boredom that now alternates with war. The basic emotion in peacetime has become a horror of emptiness: a fear of being alone, of having nothing to do, a neurosis whose symptoms are restlessness, an unmotivated and undirected rage, sinking at times into vapid listlessness. This neurotic syndrome is intensified by the prevailing sense of insecurity. The threat of atomic war has corrupted our faith in life itself.

This universal neurosis has developed with the progress of technology. It is the neurosis of men whose chief expenditure of energy is to pull a lever or push a button, of men who have ceased to make things with their hands. Such inactivity applies not only to muscles and nerves but to the creative processes that once engaged the mind. If one could contrast visually, by time-and-motion studies, the daily actions of an eighteenth-century carpenter with a twentieth-century machinist, the latter would appear as a <u>confined, repetitive clot</u>, the former as a free and even fantastic pattern. But the most significant contrast could not be visualized—the contrast between a mind suspended aimlessly above an autonomous movement and a mind consciously bent on the shaping of a material substance according to the persistent evidence of the senses.

19. A suitable title for the above passage would be
    A. INCREASING PRODUCTION BY MEANS OF SYSTEMATIZATION
    B. LACK OF A SENSE OF CREATIVENESS AND ITS CONSEQUENCE
    C. TECHNOLOGICAL ACHIEVEMENT IN MODERN SOCIETY
    D. WHAT CAN BE DONE ABOUT SENSELESS VIOLENCE

20. According to the author, Shakespeare treated violence as a
    A. basically sinful act not in keeping with religious thinking
    B. just punishment of transgressors against moral law
    C. means of achieving dramatic excitement
    D. solution to a problem provided no other solution was available

21. According to the author, boredom may lead to
    A. a greater interest in leisure-time activities
    B. chronic fatigue
    C. senseless anger
    D. the acceptance of a job which does not provide a sense of creativity

22. The underlined phrase refers to the
    A. hand movements made by the carpenter
    B. hand movements made by the machinist
    C. relative ignorance of the carpenter
    D. relative ignorance of the machinist

23. The concentration of women and female-headed families in the city is both cause and consequence of the city's fiscal woes. Women live in cities because it is easier and cheaper for them to do so, but because fewer women are employed, and those that are receive lower pay than men, they do not make the same contribution to the tax base that an equivalent population of men would. Concomitantly, they are more dependent on public resources, such as transportation and housing. For these reasons alone, urban finances would be improved by increasing women's employment opportunities and pay. Yet nothing in our current urban policy is specifically geared to improving women's financial resources. There are some proposed incentives to create more jobs, but not necessarily ones that would utilize the skills women currently have. The most innovative proposal was a tax credit for new hires from certain groups with particularly high unemployment rates. None of the seven targeted groups were women.
    Which sentence is BEST supported by the above paragraph?
    A. Innovative programs are rapidly improving conditions for seven targeted groups with traditionally high unemployment rates.
    B. The contribution of women to a city's tax base reflects their superior economic position.
    C. Improving the economic position of women who live in cities would help the financial conditions of the cities themselves.
    D. Most women in this country live in large cities.

24. None of this would be worth saying if Descartes had been right in positing a one-to-one correspondence between stimuli and sensations. But we know that nothing of the sort exists. The perception of a given color can be evoked by an infinite number of differently combined wavelengths. Conversely, a given stimulus can evoke a variety of sensations, the image of a duck in one recipient, the image of a rabbit in another. Nor are responses like these entirely innate. One can learn to discriminate colors or patterns which were indistinguishable prior to training. To an extent still unknown, the production of data from stimuli is a learned procedure. After the learning process, the same stimulus evokes a different datum. I conclude that, though data are the minimal elements of our individual experience, they need be shared responses to a given stimulus only within the membership of a relatively homogeneous community: educational, scientific, or linguistic.
Which sentence is BEST supported by the above paragraph?
   A. One stimulus can give rise to a number of different sensations.
   B. There is a one-to-one correspondence between stimuli and sensations.
   C. It is not possible to produce data from stimuli by using a learned procedure.
   D. It is not necessary for a group to be relatively homogeneous in order to share responses to stimuli.

25. Workers who want to move in the direction of participative structures will need to confront the issues of power and control. The process of change needs to be mutually shared by all involved, or the outcome will not be a really participative model. The demand for a structural redistribution of power is not sufficient to address the problem of change toward a humanistic, as against a technological, workplace. If we are to change our institutional arrangements from hierarchy to participation, particularly in our workplaces, we will need to look to transformations in ourselves as well. As long as we are imbued with the legitimacy of hierarchical authority, with the sovereignty of the status quo, we will never be able to generate the new and original forms that we seek. This means if we are to be equal to the task of reorganizing our workplaces, we need to think about how we can reeducate ourselves and become aware of our assumptions about the nature of our social life together. Unless the issue is approached in terms of these complexities, I fear that all the worker participation and quality of work life efforts will fail.
According to the above paragraph, which of the following is NOT true?
   A. Self-education concerning social roles must go hand in hand with workplace reorganization.
   B. The structural changing of the workplace, alone, will not bring about the necessary changes in the quality of work life.
   C. Individuals can easily overcome their attitudes towards hierarchical authority.
   D. Changing the quality of work life will require the participation of all involved.

KEY (CORRECT ANSWERS)

1.	D	11.	A
2.	D	12.	D
3.	B	13.	C
4.	B	14.	A
5.	A	15.	C
6.	C	16.	D
7.	D	17.	C
8.	B	18.	D
9.	A	19.	B
10.	B	20.	B

21. C
22. B
23. C
24. A
25. C

INTERPRETATION OF READING MATERIALS IN THE SOCIAL STUDIES

SAMPLE QUESTION

DIRECTIONS: In the passage that follows, each question or incomplete statement below is followed by several suggested answers or completions. Select the one that BEST answers the question or completes the statement. Base your choice in each case on the materials given and on your own understanding of the subject matter.

PASSAGE

Well, easily the most obvious badge of class in Britain is the accent of spoken language. Sociologists used to predict that the influence of radio would iron out regional accents and pronunciations and convert everyone into a passable imitation of a B.B.C. announcer. They have been proved wrong. In some strange ways, the standard London voices emerging from the wireless set have stiffened the resolution of the regions to maintain their regionalism. The old accents, the broad vowels of Yorkshire and Lancashire, the rich brogues of the West Country and the tortured staccato tones of the Cockney are heard as often as ever they were - and what's more they have more or less ousted spoken B.B.C. from the influential "telly." Most of our TV commercials use lower-middle class inflexions and strong regional accents to put across their message.

Quality and more value for money are clearly associated in the LMC mind with rugged, down-to-earth, nonsense language. During the war, the most effective broadcasters were Winston Churchill and J.B. Priestley, neither of whom used public-school accents. Churchill went out of his way to mispronounce such words as Nazi and Montevideo and spoke simply even when at his most rhetorical. Priestley employed a strong "Bruddersford" accent, as he has always done, and once again the message was strongly reinforced by the mode of delivery. The voice of authority is still that of John Citizen, the Man in the Street.

1. The advent of the B.B.C.

    A. standardized speech
    B. made people aware of the differences in accents
    C. revised the standards of English speech
    D. converted regional accents
    E. encouraged predictions from sociologists

1.____

In paragraph 1, it is mentioned that sociologists used to predict that regional accents would be influenced by the speech of the B.B.C. Therefore, Item E is correct. The paragraph further states that these predictions were proven wrong; therefore, Items A, B, and C must be incorrect. It is stated throughout the passage that regional accents were rather reinforced by the B.B.C. standard. Item B is not mentioned in the passage; however, it is safe to assume that people were always aware of the differences in accents.

2. The regional accent called Yorkshire

    A. stiffened the resolution of this region to change its speech habits
    B. is a kind of brogue
    C. has disappeared

2.____

D. contains broad vowels
E. is staccato

Item A is false because the passage states that the resolution was stiffened to MAINTAIN their speech habits. Item B refers to the West Country accent. Item E refers to Cockney. Item C is false because ...*Yorkshire..., Lancashire...the West Country ...the Cockney are heard as often as ever they were*. The passage also mentions the *broad vowels of Yorkshire*. Therefore, Item D is correct.

3. Most B.B.C. commercials are

   A. prohibited by the government
   B. considered contrary to the principles of B.B.C. broadcasting
   C. referred to as *telly*
   D. using upper-middle class accents
   E. using lower-middle class inflexions

The passage states (end of paragraph one), *Most of our TV commercials use lower-middle class inflexions....* Therefore, Item E is correct. Items A and B are not mentioned in the passage. Item C refers to an English colloquialism for television. Item D is false.

4. Why did Churchill occasionally mispronounce words?
   Because

   A. he rose from the lower classes
   B. he didn't have an extensive education
   C. he wanted the majority of the people to heed him
   D. English pronunciation is often unlike American
   E. he used a public-school accent

Items A and B are false, aside from not being mentioned in the passage. The last paragraph of the passage explains why Item C is the correct one. It states that the voice of authority is the man in the street, that is, a voice which would use simple speech, a regional accent, and occasionally mispronounce words. Item D has nothing to do with the question. Item E is false: a public-school accent, in England, designates a higher standard of speech.

5. J.B. Priestley was

   A. a prominent member of Parliament
   B. a prominent industrialist
   C. the head of the B.B.C.
   D. a novelist
   E. an ambassador

J.B. Priestley was a prominent English playwright and novelist. Therefore, Item D is correct. Items A, B, C, and E are false.

6. The opposite of a *Bruddersford* accent (the combining of the names of two Yorkshire mill towns) might be called

   A. Oxford   B. Cockney   C. Exeter   D. Oxbridge   E. Cambridge

There is an *Oxbridge* accent, also a portmanteau word (PORTMANTEAU WORD, a word made by telescoping or blending two other words, as BRUNCH for BREAKFAST and LUNCH), signifying the accents of Oxford and Cambridge. It is upper-class and, therefore, the opposite of the accent which derives its name from the two mill towns. Therefore, Item D is correct. Items A, B, C, and E are false.

EXAMINATION SECTION
TEST 1

PASSAGE

Secretary of State Richard Olney in 1895 was only stating the truth when he insisted that all basic political power in the Caribbean was in the hands of the United States, but in asserting this view, he used the infuriating word "fiat" - which annoyed both the British and the Latin Americans. Theodore Roosevelt, in creating the Republic of Panama, behaved no worse than the great W.E. Gladstone did in occupying Egypt; but Gladstone occupied Egypt with ostensible reluctance. (Henry Labouchere, the Liberal wit, said that what he objected to in the Grand Old Man was not his having the ace of trumps up his sleeve, but his assertion that God had put it there.) Theodore Roosevelt boasted of what he had done "to take the Canal," and his unfortunate candor was very expensive in cash and credit.

Then there is the question of the Senate. An examination of Molloy's great collection of treaties will show how late the British Foreign Office was in learning that a treaty with the Unites States is valid only if the Senate gives its consent. Again and again, European powers have made what they thought were hard bargains with the executive branch of the United States, only to have them rejected by the Senate. A great deal can be said in favor of many, if not all, of the Senate's actions, but the view expressed by John Hay that a treaty sent to the Senate has as much chance as a bull sent into the bull ring still survives in Europe if it no longer survives in the same form in the United States.

QUESTIONS

1. The author seems to be citing examples of

    A. successful U.S. diplomacy
    B. the need for better statesmen
    C. how certain U.S. statesmen have been diplomatically clumsy
    D. why Europe does not like the U.S.
    E. how the U.S. consistently mishandles foreign relations

2. In John Hay's view,

    A. treaties should not be made with foreign powers
    B. treaties should not be made by the executive branch of the government
    C. treaties should not have to be sent to the Senate
    D. all treaties made with other governments should be rejected by the Senate
    E. a treaty sent to the Senate has little chance of survival

3. Theodore Roosevelt, at one time,

    A. sent W.E. Gladstone to occupy Egypt
    B. stated that all political power in the Caribbean was in the hands of the U.S.
    C. was the Grand Old Man of the Democratic Party
    D. boasted of taking the Panama Canal
    E. infuriated both the British and the Latin Americans by his use of the word *fiat*

4. The author of this passage might be said to be writing in a vein

    A. of acceptance regarding past American blunders
    B. of criticism tempered with humor
    C. which is extremely unflattering to Europe

D. of ridicule
E. of malice

5. The author seems to be suggesting that

   A. European and Latin American countries are in disagreement with the U.S.
   B. the U.S. could be more diplomatically astute
   C. treaties should not be subject to both Senate and Executive approval
   D. Europe does not understand the U.S. system of ratifying treaties
   E. Theodore Roosevelt was not one of the best Presidents of the U.S.

6. Theodore Roosevelt was famous for having said

   A. *"The business of America is business"*
   B. (In reference to isolationism) *"River, stay, 'way from my door"*
   C. *"Speak softly and carry a big stick"*
   D. *"The only thing we have to fear is fear itself"*
   E. *"This generation has a rendezvous with destiny"*

KEY (CORRECT ANSWERS)

1. C   4. B
2. E   5. B
3. D   6. C

EXPLANATION OF ANSWERS

1. The CORRECT ANSWER IS C. The author is not making any general statement, but citing certain cases. Therefore, B, D, and E must be considered too general. And since the author is citing cases of an unsuccessful nature, A is, of course, false.

2. In the last sentence of the last paragraph occurs John Hay's comparison of the Senate and the bull ring. This view indicates that E MUST BE THE CORRECT ANSWER. He did not comment on the treatment of treaties by either branch of the government.

3. The CORRECT ANSWER IS D, as shown in the last sentence of Paragraph 1. Items B and E refer to Richard Olney. While he is referred to in the passage as the Grand Old Man, he was not a Democrat..

4. Closer to the tone of the passage than the possibilities of A, D, or E is the answer stated in B. D and E are rather strong as descriptions of the passage, while A is too weak. C is completely false. The CORRECT ANSWER, THEN, IS B.

5. Items C and E are not stated or suggested at all in the passage. Items A and D are too extreme in their conclusions. B, THEN, WOULD SEEM TO BE THE MOST FITTING ANSWER.   5._____

6. A was said by President Coolidge; D and E by Franklin Delano Roosevelt; C WAS SAID BY THEODORE ROOSEVELT AND IS THE CORRECT ANSWER.   6._____

TEST 2
PASSAGE

　　The position Makarios holds in Cyprus is the result of his own skillful maneuvers. It is a position which he has built up by Byzantine wiliness, by clever use of other personalities, of the press, of the emotions of the people he knows so well. When other governments, driven to desperation by the Cyprus problem, drop hints that were Makarios to be overthrown the problem could quickly be solved, they are talking dangerous nonsense. Makarios is a man of his people, with their strengths and their weaknesses. If the Cyprus problem is to be solved, he is the man who must be convinced that the solution is just, he is the man whose confidence must be gained, for in Cyprus he alone will be able to convince and retain the confidence of his people.

　　Makarios explains the relationship between himself and his people this way: "The Archbishop of Cyprus is elected by the whole people. Ours is the only church in the world where this happens. He is elected to be the religious and national leader. I, therefore, enjoy the confidence of the vast majority of my people. I can convince the people. I am not a party leader; I have no army to force them to follow me: I express the will of the people and the people follow me. I just do what I think right."

　　Makarios does not himself dismiss the thesis that were he removed, the Cyprus problem could be more quickly solved. He admits that he is a stubborn man and that this stubbornness has already thwarted both the Americans and the British in imposing their ideas of a settlement. "I am stubborn. I cannot do what I do not believe in."

QUESTIONS

1. Makarios, President and Archbishop of Cyprus, gained his position

    A. by a Byzantine coup
    B. by consent of the populace
    C. through the press
    D. by playing upon emotionalism
    E. through strategic use of his armies

2. The author of the passage indicated a belief that Makarios

    A. was in danger of being overthrown
    B. was actually a dictator
    C. should not head both church and state
    D. was representative of the average Cypriote
    E. did not enjoy the confidence of his people

3. The British had been thwarted in imposing their ideas by

    A. the Americans　　　　　　B. the Cypriote army
    C. party leadership　　　　　D. Makarios
    E. NATO

4. The Cypriote Orthodox Church is unique in that it(s)

    A. has its own army
    B. is not wholly separate from affairs of state

C. head is appointed
D. Archbishop is elected by the whole people
E. religious leader is not its national leader

5. Cyprus is an island which belongs to (the)

   A. Greece
   B. Turkey
   C. Malta
   D. British Commonwealth
   E. Enosis

6. Corcyra, an adjacent Grecian island, is acknowledged to be immortalized in the literary work of

   A. THE TEMPEST
   B. ELECTRA
   C. MEDEA
   D. ETRUSCAN PLACES
   E. OEDIPUS REX

KEY (CORRECT ANSWERS)

1. B   4. D
2. D   5. D
3. D   6. A

EXPLANATION OF ANSWERS

1. The passage states Makarios is a *man of his people* and retains the confidence of his people. The passage further states, *"The Archbishop of Cyprus is elected by the whole people."* Therefore, though C and D may have influenced their decision, he holds his office by consent of the people. THE CORRECT ANSWER, THEN, IS B.

2. Towards the end of the first paragraph, Makarios is deemed to be *a man of his people.....with their strengths and weaknesses,* WHICH WOULD MAKE ITEM D CORRECT. The writer refers to the talk of his being overthrown as *dangerous nonsense.* He does not express any opinion on Items B and C, and refutes Item E.

3. The passage states that both the Americans and the British have been thwarted in imposing their ideas, and, we must presume, have been so thwarted by Makarios. THEREFORE, THE ANSWER IS D. He says, in the passage, *"I am not a party leader...,"* discounting C as a possible answer. B and E are not mentioned.

3 (#2)

4. D IS THE CORRECT ANSWER and is stated in the quotation in Paragraph 2, where Makarios says, *"...Ours is the only church in the world where this happens."* Item B is a correct statement regarding the Church, but is not a unique fact; Items A, C, and E are false.

   4.____

5. The Cypriotes elected in 1961 to become members of the British Commonwealth of Nations. It has rejected its political ties with Greece; THEREFORE, THE CORRECT ANSWER WOULD BE D. (Enosis, Item E, is the Greek word for *union,* referring, in this case, to the union of Greece and Cyprus.)

   5.____

6. Shakespeare's THE TEMPEST is said to have derived its locale from Corcyra, WHICH RENDERS ITEM A CORRECT. (And there exists in THE TEMPEST a name which is an anagram for Corcyra.) D is a travelogue about Greece written by D.H. Lawrence but is not specifically related to Corcyra; nor are answers B, C, and E.

   6.____

TEST 3

PASSAGE

The old argument about the respective merits of career and non-career appointments has little relevance. Today and in the future, most ambassadors will come from the career service - the proportion is now about two out of three - but there will still be room for candidates with special qualifications brought in from outside - as witness General Taylor. There is no place, however, as Ambassador Samuel Berger, recent envoy to Korea, has said, for a "non-career man who brings neither interest, nor aptitude, nor professional skills" to the job.

Over the years, successful ambassadors have come from many different backgrounds and occupations. If any generalization is valid, it may be that a solid foundation in some specialty is an asset, for mastery of a particular field often seems to lend a person added depth and confidence. The Foreign Service has tried to give young officers opportunities to specialize, but, on the whole, too few have been allowed to spend enough time in one place or in one type of work or to take advanced studies. Today, qualifications in the social sciences, in economics or in military affairs are highly desirable.

Yet, when all is said and done, the important thing is that an ambassador be a cultivated man who, in the best sense, is wise in the ways of the world, with the maturity of judgment that comes from varied experience, and with reserves of know-how and courage to call upon in a pinch.

QUESTIONS

1. It is found to be an asset that an ambassador have

    A. interest
    B. depth
    C. some specialization
    D. as many languages as possible
    E. confidence

2. One reason the officers of the foreign service have NOT become proficient in any one field is

    A. the concentration required is incompatible with the temperament of the typical ambassador
    B. they have too much to do
    C. their work demands a general knowledge
    D. they concentrate on one type of work
    E. they move around too much

3. An ambassador should be

    A. highly civilized
    B. well-liked
    C. reliable
    D. a linguist
    E. courageous

4. Successful ambassadors, prior to their appointment, are enlisted from

    A. the best universities
    B. varied backgrounds
    C. men active in Washington
    D. Cabinet members
    E. industry

5. Fundamentally, an ambassador is

A. totally responsible for our *image* abroad
B. responsible for any uprisings that might occur in the country to which he is appointed
C. the President's personal agent
D. guaranteed diplomatic immunity
E. fulfilling a social as well as political role

6. His traditional role is 6.____

   A. that of teacher
   B. to promote industry
   C. to see that people form the best possible impression of the U.S.
   D. that of a negotiator
   E. that of a propagandist

KEY (CORRECT ANSWERS)

1. C   4. B
2. E   5. C
3. A   6. D

EXPLANATION OF ANSWERS

1. *"A solid foundation in some specialization is an asset,"* states the author. Answers B and E are mentioned as beneficial, but they are the by-products of NUMBER C, WHICH IS THE CORRECT ANSWER.

2. The ANSWER IS CONTAINED IN PARAGRAPH 2, SENTENCE 3. B and C might be considered valid answers were it not for the more specific inclusion of Answer E, which is taken directly from the passage.

3. The last paragraph describes a cultivated man: wise, mature, experienced, courageous. It states that this is *the important thing.* Such a man would be termed highly civilized. THUS, THE ANSWER IS A. The other items, particularly E, courageous, are assets but are merely parts of the *whole-cultivated* or civilized.

4. THE OPENING SENTENCE OF PARAGRAPH 2 CONTAINS THE ANSWER: IT IS ITEM B. While any of the other answers presented may count as factors in the selection of an ambassador, no particular one is favored.

5. C IS THE CORRECT ANSWER. For any one man to fulfill the requirements of Answers A and B would be impossible. D and E are true factually regarding ambassadors, but hardly describe their fundamental role.

6. D IS THE ANSWER HERE. He is not a teacher nor is he that which is stated in B. C and E are superficial duties compared to the vital act of negotiator or arbiter.

TEST 4
PASSAGE

Unless all the warning signals are wrong, this year we are really in for it. The mudslinging, the personal attacks, and the smears that always accompany a national election threaten in the next few weeks to submerge completely the voices of reasoned debate. Once again, as Lord Bryce declared, we are going to be treated to "the spectacle of half the honest men supporting for the leadership of the nation a person whom the other half declare to be a knave."

A knave, did he say? No mere knave. A thief, a cheat, a fixer of elections, a fake, a phony, a dodger of military duty, an inciter of riots, a coddler of Communists - and a man who is certain to be the victim of another heart attack.

Or: a crypto-Fascist, a warmonger, an extremist, a nuclear adventurer, a fool, a frustrated dictator, a simpleton, a racist, a fallout fancier, a know-nothing, a menace to little girls eating ice cream cones - and a man subject to recurrent nervous breakdowns.

All these epithets have been hurled at President Johnson or Senator Goldwater already. And the real smear season - the final frenzied few weeks of the campaign - is still to come.

Even before the cannonading began, Bruce L. Felknor, executive director of the Fair Campaign Practices Committee, the 10-year-old private agency that attempts to referee election battles, predicted that this would be an "exceptionally rough" campaign. He said that the "unusual polarization of opinion" - exemplified by Senator Gold-water's determination to provide "a choice, not an echo" - has given this campaign an encompassing emotional intensity rare in national politics.

QUESTIONS

1. The author states that mudslinging

    A. is always accompanied by warning signals
    B. is the worst sort of personal attack
    C. is dishonest
    D. was denounced by Lord Bryce
    E. always accompanies a national election

2. While Lord Bryce uses the word *knave*, the author implies that

    A. he really means a thief
    B. usually half the nation denounces the man running for office
    C. were Lord Bryce living today he would find other words
    D. today such a word would be considered mild
    E. men running for office can inspire riots

3. The *spectacle* referred to in the passage is the

    A. political campaign speeches
    B. election
    C. political parties

85

D. reasoned or unreasoned debate
E. manner in which the people express their choice

4. In which of the following comparisons made by the author is the parallelism of the characteristics MOST satisfactory?

   A. A cheat and an extremist
   B. The victim of a heart attack and a man subject to nervous breakdowns
   C. A phony and a fallout fancier
   D. An inciter of riots and a crypto-Fascist
   E. A fake and a fool

5. Why does the author feel that personal attacks threaten to submerge reasoned debate? Because

   A. they are incompatible with one another
   B. people are swayed by such attacks
   C. a man who will denounce and attack personally is incapable of reason
   D. valid personal attacks may disqualify an otherwise suitable candidate
   E. the persons seeking to defame through personal attack may thereby promote public sympathy for the opposition through vile or illogical defamation

6. What does the author mean by the term *nuclear adventurer?* A man who

   A. would be inclined to experiment in the search for more effective nuclear weapons
   B. would seek to employ nuclear discoveries to maintain the peace
   C. would be adventurous and imaginative in recruiting scientists to better our nuclear position in the arms race
   D. would probably spend too much of the taxpayers' money on the building of unnecessary planes and bombs
   E. might act without sufficient forethought and consultation and possibly plunge the world into a nuclear war

KEY (CORRECT ANSWERS)

1. E   4. B
2. D   5. A
3. E   6. E

EXPLANATION OF ANSWERS

1. This is a common sense question answered directly in the passage. It is also the theme of the article. THE CORRECT ANSWER IS E. While C and D might be considered indirectly correct through deduction, they are not stated in the passage.

2. The author uses the quotation in Paragraph 1 directly to contrast with the stronger terminology of Paragraph 2. The clue to the correct answer is contained in the second sentence of Paragraph 2, THE ONLY POSSIBLE ANSWER THEN BEING D. C is misleading because the author's attention is focused on the changes in the times and in words, not in conjecture on the words Lord Bryce might use today.

3. The *spectacle* referred to in the quotation is concerned with .... *half the honest men....leadership of the nation-.... to be a knave.* Therefore, THE CORRECT ANSWER IS E. While A and C seek to condition the response of the people, they, themselves, are not the *spectacle*.

4. THE ONLY ANSWER WHICH STATES SIMILAR CHARACTERISTICS IS B. The other pairs of epithets bears no relationship to one another.

5. The author implies that the smear personal attack is unreasonable and absurd, thus making it impossible to stem from, or to exist alongside, reasonable argument. A, THEN, IS THE ONLY POSSIBLE CORRECT ANSWER. While B and E may be true, they are not in direct relation to the question.

6. Though this information is not specifically contained in the passage, it should be reasonably surmised that the term stated is an epithet, which disqualifies A, B, and C. The threat contained in E is far stronger and more extreme than the description in D. THEREFORE, E IS THE CORRECT ANSWER.

1.____
2.____
3.____
4.____
5.____
6.____

TEST 5
PASSAGE

The permanent system, which went into force in 1920, includes essentially all the elements of immigration policy that are in our law today. The immigration statutes now establish a system of annual quotas to govern immigration from each country. Under this system, 156,987 quota immigrants are permitted to enter the United States each year. The quotas from each country are based upon the national origins of the population of the United States in 1920.

The use of the year 1920 is arbitrary. It rests upon the fact that this system was introduced in 1924, and the last prior census was in 1920. The use of a national origins system is without basis in either logic or reason. It neither satisfies a national need nor accomplishes an international purpose.

In an age of interdependence among nations, such a system is an anachronism, for it discriminates among applicants for admission into the United States on the basis of accident of birth.

Because of the composition of our population in 1920, the system is heavily weighted in favor of immigration from northern Europe and severely limits immigration from southern and eastern Europe and from other parts of the world.

A qualified person born in England or Ireland who wants to emigrate to the United States can do so at any time. A person born in Italy, Hungary, Poland, or the Baltic states may have to wait many years before his turn is reached.

One writer has listed six motives behind the act of 1924. They were: (1) postwar isolationism; (2) the doctrine of the alleged superiority of Anglo-Saxon and Teutonic "races"; (3) the fear that "pauper labor" would lower wage levels; (4) the belief that people of certain nations were less law-abiding than others; (5) the fear that entrance of many people with different customs and habits would undermine our national and social unity and order.

QUESTIONS

1. The immigration quota in effect then was based upon the

    A. current population of the United States
    B. population of the United States in 1920
    C. act of 1921
    D. population of the United States in 1929
    E. nationalities living at present in the United States

2. The author of the passage seems to feel that our immigration system is

    A. necessary
    B. illogical
    C. understandable
    D. inevitable
    E. though not completely fair, the only one possible at this time

2 (#5)

3. Which of the reasons listed in parentheses at the end of the passage indicates why a person of English birth may (or may not) enter the United States? 3.____

   A. (1)   B. (2)   C. (3)   D. (4)   E. (5)

4. Why is the immigration system an anachronism? Because 4.____

   A. where it was once of value, it no longer is
   B. it dated back to 1920
   C. it favors immigration from southern and eastern Europe
   D. it limits immigration from northern Europe
   E. of our independence of other nations

5. A quota is 5.____

   A. a changing estimate
   B. a proportional part or share
   C. something that is quoted
   D. a number or amount
   E. a bid or offer so named or published

6. An emigrant is one who 6.____

   A. enters one country from another
   B. seeks residence in the United States
   C. migrates
   D. leaves a country for residence elsewhere
   E. enters and settles in another country

KEY (CORRECT ANSWERS)

1. B   4. B
2. B   5. B
3. B   6. D

EXPLANATION OF ANSWERS

1. At the end of Paragraph 1, the passage states, *"The quotas from each country are based upon the population of the United States in 1920."* THEREFORE, THE CORRECT ANSWER IS B. Since Items A, C, D, and E refer to events that have taken place since 1920, they are false. Item D indicates the year the permanent system went into force. Item C is not mentioned. Item A is not mentioned in relation to the immigration quota and what it is based upon; nor is item E.

2. The author states (Paragraph 2), *"The use of a national origins system is without basis in either logic or reason."* THEREFORE, THE CORRECT ANSWER IS B. From the quotation, the reader may assume that Items A, C, and E are false. Nowhere is Item D mentioned.

3. THE CORRECT ANSWER IS B. The passage states: *"(2) the doctrine of the alleged superiority of the Anglo-Saxon and Teutonic 'races'"*; this statement immediately follows the flat declaration that *"A qualified person born in England....who wants to emigrate to the United States can do so at any time."* Items C, D, and E are contradictory to Item B. Item A is contradictory and irrelevant.

4. The author states, in Paragraph 3, that our present system is an anachronism because it is based on what was true of our population in 1920. THEREFORE, B IS THE CORRECT ANSWER. Item A is not correct because the author does not indicate that it was ever of value. Items C and D are false statements. And in Paragraph 3, the author speaks of the *interdependence* among nations, discounting E.

5. Item C refers to a quotation. Item E refers to a quotation of another kind, i.e., the stock market. Item D is incomplete and incorrect. THE CORRECT ANSWER, THEN, IS B. Item A is false because a quota is unchanging in its percentage effect.

TEST 6
PASSAGE

In Stalin's time, a leader removed from the Soviet power pyramid was tried, imprisoned, or executed, or became an "unperson" - disappearing not only physically but from all Soviet history and reference books.

Under Nikita Khrushchev, things changed. When "Khrush" got rid of "Bulge" (Premier Bulganin) and his other rivals in 1957, the worst he did was to accuse them of being "anti-party" and send them into obscurity.

Week before last, when Mr. K's own time came, there was a throwback of sorts to the Russia of Koestler's "Darkness at Noon." Official secrecy on how he was removed remained complete. The new "B and K" team of Leonid Brezhnev, 57, party First Secretary (and hence Number One) and Aleksei Kosygin, 60, Premier, conducted itself at public functions for the three latest Soviet cosmonauts as though the "dearly beloved Nikita Sergeyevitch" of the past seven years no longer existed. Books about him disappeared from bookstores; portraits of him still remaining on store counters, could not be bought.

The rigidly controlled Soviet press rested on its brief announcement of 11 days ago that Mr. Khrushchev had been relieved of his duties at his own request due to advancing age (he was 70) and failing health. And, by early last week, it became clear that this way of disposing of leaders would no longer suffice - not for the foreign Communist parties, with their new and less subservient relationship with Moscow, nor, possibly, for the Russian people, thawed out partially from political terror and less susceptible to myths and mysteries.

QUESTIONS

1. When Khrushchev's position as Soviet leader terminated,

    A. he was imprisoned
    B. he was accused of being *antiparty*
    C. there was complete official secrecy regarding the manner
    D. Brezhnev and Kosygin spoke well of him
    E. he was sent into obscurity

2. He was replaced as First Secretary by

    A. Brezhnev
    B. Kosygin
    C. Nikita Sergeyevitch
    D. Bulganin
    E. Brezhnev and Kosygin

3. Books written about Khrushchev

    A. unlike those in Stalin's period, did not disappear
    B. remained, unsold, on the bookshelves
    C. are currently being rewritten
    D. disappeared from the bookstores
    E. shared the same fate as his portraits

4. The author seems to be of the opinion that, regarding Khrushchev,

   A. his age and health made it impossible for him to maintain his position
   B. the Russian people have accepted his absence without question
   C. foreign branches of the party will cease to ask questions
   D. the party will have to elaborate on its eleven-day-old statement
   E. the people are too susceptible to political terror to demand further information or explanation

5. Stalin, after his death, was replaced by

   A. Mikoyan and Bulganin
   B. Molotov and Khrushchev
   C. Gromyko and Malenkov
   D. Beria, Khrushchev, and Malenkov
   E. Aleksei Adzubei and Marshal Zhukhov

6. In 1962, Khrushchev suffered a defeat when he

   A. withdrew troops from Vietnam
   B. had to abandon his farm programs as disastrous
   C. made a diplomatic break with China
   D. had to answer charges of nepotism
   E. was forced to withdraw missiles from Cuba

KEY (CORRECT ANSWERS)

1. C   4. D
2. A   5. D
3. D   6. E

EXPLANATION OF ANSWERS

1. Item A relates to the Stalinist period, and Items B and E relate to the Khrushchev period. Item D is inaccurate because he was not spoken of by these men. And in Paragraph 3, it is stated that *"official secrecy on how he was removed remained complete."* THE ANSWER, THEN, IS C.

2. Khrushchev held two positions, that of First Secretary and Premier. He was replaced as First Secretary by Brezhnev (Paragraph 3, sentence 3), and as Premier by Kosygin (Item B). THEREFORE, THE CORRECT ANSWER IS A. Item D, Bulganin, was his predecessor, and Item C, Nikita Sergeyevitch, are actually Khrushchev's first two names.

3. In the last sentence of Paragraph 3, the author states: *Books about him disappeared from bookstores...."* THIS INDICATES THAT D IS THE CORRECT ANSWER. Portraits of him (reference to Item E) remained in the stores but could not be bought (last clause of the last sentence of Paragraph 3), thus indicating that Item E is false. Item A is false because the books DID disappear. There is no mention made in the passage of their being rewritten, thus eliminating Item C. And the passage further indicates that they did NOT remain on the bookshelves, thus discounting B.

4. The last portion of the final paragraph makes clear the author's opinion that *this way of disposing of leaders would no longer suffice.* The final paragraph clearly refutes the acceptability of Items A, B, C, and E. THE CORRECT ANSWER HERE IS D.

5. Item E, Adzubei, was Khrushchev's son-in-law and the former editor of IZVESTIA, the official government newspaper. THE CORRECT ANSWER IS D, the *troika* of Beria, Khrushchev, and Malenkov. Beria was soon thereafter put to death, and Malenkov was deposed after approximately two years in power.

6. THE CORRECT ANSWER IS ITEM E. In the *nuclear crisis* of November, 1962, President Kennedy, of the United States, demanded the removal of all missiles from Cuba by the Russians. In a gigantic test of nerves, Khrushchev gave in. One year later, Kennedy was dead, the victim of an assassin's bullet. Tow years later, Khrushchev was out of power, peacefully deposed by the other party leaders. Item A, B, C, and D are not true.

TEST 7
PASSAGE

He is half the size of an American soldier and twice as disciplined. He does not smoke or drink. He shuns fish and meat and shrinks from contact with women.

To many exasperated Westerners, he seems bent on losing in Saigon any advantage the soldier wins on the battlefield. He believes that only his strategy will bring peace to Vietnam, that he will succeed where soldiers are bound to fail. His religion teaches humility and reconciliation, but he is jealous of his new political power and defiant in his demands.

He is a Buddhist priest. Like some Black clergymen in the United States, he has come to the forefront of a struggle that is recasting (1965) the shape of his country. He toppled one government in 1963. This(1965) year, he shook another until its military leader approached his temple as chastened as a novice seeking instruction.

In one sense, each priest exemplifies the movement. Since they united to overthrow President Ngo Dinh Diem, the Buddhists have spoken with a single voice.

QUESTIONS

1. In the passage, the author makes a comparison between

    A. a Black man and a clergyman
    B. a priest and a Buddhist
    C. the battlefield and Saigon
    D. a soldier and a priest
    E. the Buddhists and President Diem

2. The Buddhist priest, on matters of military strategy,

    A. looks to the United States
    B. trusts the Vietnamese soldiers
    C. trusts the American soldiers
    D. belives only in himself
    E. disbelieves in toppling governments

3. In matters of food, he is

    A. a vegetarian
    B. constantly fasting
    C. as disciplined as his countrymen
    D. disinterested
    E. a consumer of fish and meat only

4. The author indicates there is a contradiction between the Buddhists'

    A. religion and their political demands
    B. humility and their belief in reconciliation
    C. desire to recast the shape of their government and their toppling of governments
    D. strategy and their announced political aim
    E. jealousy of their political power and their new demands

5. Until 1963, Vietnam was ruled by

    A. a Buddhist, Thich Tam Chau
    B. a Roman Catholic Archbishop
    C. Nguyen Khanh
    D. *Big Minh*
    E. Ngo Dinh Diem

6. A coup d'etat refers specifically to the overthrow of an existing government by

    A. stuffing the ballot boxes
    B. civil war
    C. dynastic legitimization
    D. a decisive blow
    E. a revolutionary small group

KEY (CORRECT ANSWERS)

1.	D	4.	A
2.	D	5.	E
3.	A	6.	E

EXPLANATION OF ANSWERS

1. The passage begins with a comparison between an American soldier and a Buddhist priest. THUS, D IS THE PROPER COMPLETION OF THE STATEMENT. The battlefield and Saigon (Item C) are not compared but, rather, the soldier and the priest in relation to them. There is a comparison made between a Black clergyman and a Buddhist priest, but not in the vein of Items A and B. There is no comparison such as Item E suggests in the passage.

2. In Paragraph 2 of the passage, the author states, *"He believes that only his strategy will bring peace to Vietnam";* and further that *"he will succeed where soldiers are bound to fail."* In Paragraph 3, the reader finds *"....he toppled one government in 1963."* Therefore, Items A, B, C, and E may be discarded, and D IS THE CORRECT ANSWER.

3. The reader is told (in Paragraph 1) that, *"....he shuns fish and meat."* This means he must be a consumer of such other foods as fruits, vegetables, etc., ESTABLISHING A AS THE CORRECT ANSWER. There is no mention made of the eating habits of his countrymen. And his diet, though disciplined, is not referred to as one of *constantly fasting* (Item B). Items C and D are not mentioned in the passage, and Item E is denied.

4. The last sentence in Paragraph 2 states, *"His religion teaches humility and reconciliation but he is jealous of his new political power and defiant in his demands."* THIS CONTRADICTION WOULD INDICATE THAT A IS THE CORRECT ANSWER. The other combinations of answers (Items B, C. D, and E) are actually consistent with one another, and not contradictory.   4.____

5. The rule of Vietnam by President Ngo Dinh Diem, a Catholic layman, was overthrown in 1963 by a bloody military coup led by General Minh and General Khanh. ITEM E IS, THEREFORE, THE CORRECT ANSWER. Item A refers to the present (1965) Buddhists' chief political spokesman. Items A, B, C, and D are false. Item B refers to President Diem's brother, who was the Roman Catholic Archbishop of Vietnam.   5.____

6. A *coup d'etat* is the violent overthrow of an existing government by a small group. That is, it signifies the overthrow and displacement of the leaders, rather than that of the system of government itself. E IS, THEREFORE, THE CORRECT ANSWER. Item D refers to a *coup de grace,* administering the final blow (or death) to a losing cause (or a dying person). Items A, B, and C are incorrect. General Khanh (Item C), a military leader, was apparently the real power in Vietnam then in 1965. *Big Minh* (Item D) refers to General Minh, who served briefly in a primary role after the deposition of Diem but who has now been relegated to a secondary place by General Khanh.   6.____

TEST 8
PASSAGE

He won his unique place in history by what he did between the ages of 65 and 70. This is a stage of life at which most people have already retired and relaxed their grip. A lifetime's opportunity at 65! How many of us could have taken advantage of this at that age? But, at 65, Churchill was just ready to get going. In his 60's, he was what most of us are in our 40's. He was at the height of his powers.

In the trajectory of a human life, there is a brief span in which the unspent vigor of youth overlaps with the accumulated experience and wisdom of maturity. For most of us, if this brief golden moment comes at all, it comes between 40 and 50. Churchill's golden moment came 20 years farther on in life than usual. This was fortunate for Britain and for the world, and it was fatal for the Nazis and for Germany.

Some people who are famous today were virtually unknown during their lifetime. Mendel, the discoverer of the laws of genetics, had to wait till a whole generation had passed before he suddenly leaped into fame. Churchill's leap into fame was sudden, like Mendel's, but fortunately Churchill did not have to wait so long to receive his due. He had become supremely famous within a few days of taking over the Government of Britain in the dark and desperate situation in which Britain found herself in the summer of 1940. Churchill then became famous immediately, all over the world, and it is noteworthy that he became as famous in the United States as everywhere else.

This is noteworthy considering what Churchill's major achievement was. It was Churchill who foiled Germany's attempt to conquer the world, and the American people - so it seems to a European observer - have not even yet realized how near Germany came, twice within Churchill's lifetime, to accomplishing her evil ambition. Americans seem never to have taken the deadly German menace to human freedom so much to heart as they have taken the less formidable Communist menace.

QUESTIONS

1. Churchill had in common with Mendel

    A. a generation's wait before recognition
    B. a sudden leap into fame
    C. the fact that they both became famous within a few days of their accomplishments
    D. the fact that they both became famous for political reasons
    E. a similar attitude toward fame

2. The MOST unusual thing about Churchill's accomplishments in relation to his age was:

    A. In his 40's, he was what most of us are in our 60's
    B. What he had already accomplished by the time he was 65
    C. What he did between the ages of 65 and 70
    D. What he accomplished after the age of 70
    E. Churchill's *golden moment* came 20 years earlier than usual

3. What was MOST striking about Churchill's career?

    A. He foiled Germany's attempt to conquer the world.
    B. He became as famous in Europe as in America.
    C. Americans never seemed to take the German menace so seriously as the Communist one.
    D. He became as famous in the United States as everywhere else.
    E. He never achieved so much fame in America as he did in Europe.

4. The author feels there is a brief, important span of life which comes

    A. when certain elements of youth and maturity merge
    B. between 40 and 50
    C. with unspent youth
    D. with accumulated experience
    E. with the wisdom of maturity

5. Since the people of America considered Churchill every bit as important as the people of Europe, this was probably because

    A. Germany was as close to domination of America as it was to domination of Europe
    B. America never took the German menace to freedom so seriously as the Europeans
    C. the Americans recognized that their destiny, too, was at stake
    D. he had such emotional impact
    E. Germany had gained control of all Europe except for Britain

6. During the Second World War, Churchill was

    A. a leading member of Parliament
    B. England's Prime Minister
    C. First Lord of the Admiralty
    D. a prominent author of several books
    E. a member of the Cabinet

KEY (CORRECT ANSWERS)

1. B   4. A
2. C   5. C
3. D   6. B

3 (#8)

EXPLANATION OF ANSWERS

1. Paragraph 3 states that *"Churchill's leap into fame was sudden, like Mendel's..."* And this was, apparently, the only thing they had in common. THEREFORE, B IS THE CORRECT ANSWER. Item A applies to Mendel alone, NOT to Churchill. Items C, D, and E are false.

2. *"He won his unique place in history by what he did between the ages of 65 and 70"* begins the passage. THEREFORE, C IS CLEARLY THE CORRECT ANSWER. Item A is incorrect because the reverse is actually stated in the passage. Items B, D, and E are false.

3. The author points out (at the end of Paragraph 3) how noteworthy it was that Churchill became as famous in the United States as he did everywhere else, albeit this was NOT his major achievement. THEREFORE, THE CORRECT ANSWER IS D. Item A is, according to the author, Churchill's major achievement, but it is not the correct answer here because it is not what the question calls for. Item B is incorrect. It is actually a reversal of Item A. Item E is false. Item C is stated in the passage but is not related to the question.

4. THE CORRECT ANSWER IS A and is explained at the beginning of Paragraph 3. This is a better answer than B because it is more specific. Items C, D, and E are only part of the correct answer and so are incomplete.

5. THE CORRECT ANSWER IS C. Item A is incorrect; Germany was not so close to the domination of America. Item E is true but is not the reason for, or the answer to, the statement. Item D is irrelevant. Item B is possibly true but does not satisfactorily complete the statement.

6. During World War II, Churchill was Prime Minister of England. He did hold all the other posts mentioned in Items A, C, and E, but PRIOR to World War II. He was a journalist and writer of books, Item D, but that was not his primary function during the war. THE CORRECT ANSWER, THEN, IS B.

TEST 9
PASSAGE

In the long, fabled history of China, many of her leaders have, like Mao Tse-tung, pushed their way by iron will and shrewdness from humble beginnings to supreme power. In one of his poems, Mao implied that none who has ruled China in the past, not even the pitiless Chin Emperor, Shih Huang Ti, nor the great Han Wu Ti, is his equal. Mao's estimate of himself was an index to the vanity and self-confidence of this one-time country bumpkin who not only wielded more power over China's swarming millions than any of his predecessors but aspired as well to power on a world scale.

The success that was to be his seemed already in Mao's sharp, reflective eyes and assured manner when this writer last saw him in Yenan in the winter of 1945. He received visiting foreign correspondents in the rustic building that was headquarters in bleak, northwest China for the Chinese Communist party. A big man with a round face, high cheekbones, and a shock of black hair combed straight back, he was dressed in a long-sleeved padded gown. Pictures showed him older, a little heavier, but with the same sharp, distant, dreamy look in his eyes that he had in Yenan. Aloofly, politely, he greeted us and then excused himself for more pressing duties, leaving the tedious details of explaining Chinese Communist views to Liu Shao-chi, then, as now, his right-hand man.

QUESTIONS

1. In 1945, Mao Tse-tung gave the impression of

    A. a man from humble beginnings
    B. a poet
    C. realistic self-confidence
    D. a man who had no wish for domination beyond China
    E. self-assurance

2. Mao felt himself to be the equal of

    A. Liu Shao-chi
    B. no one
    C. any of China's past Emperors
    D. Han Wu Ti
    E. Shih Huang Ti

3. The passage was taken from an article containing an interview with Mao. This interview took place in

    A. Cambodia   B. Manchuria   C. Yenan
    D. Canton   E. southwest China

4. A rather surprising disclosure, considering Mao's position, was that he

    A. was not humble
    B. did not feel himself greater than Han Wu Ti
    C. received visitors in a rustic building
    D. had written poems
    E. wore a long-sleeved padded gown

5. A part of China within his jurisdiction was

    A. Macao   B. Kunming   C. Hong Kong
    D. Formosa   E. Laos

5.____

6. Mao's political philosophy of government was

    A. socialistic
    B. capitalistic
    C. that of a representative republic
    D. communistic
    E. democratic

6.____

KEY (CORRECT ANSWERS)

1. E   4. D
2. B   5. B
3. C   6. D

EXPLANATION OF ANSWERS

1. The author seems to feel that Mao had an excess of self-confidence which was not realistic. Also, the reader is told he *"...aspires as well to power on a world scale"* (end of Paragraph 1). The answer is contained in the first sentence of Paragraph 2 where the author speaks of Mao's *self-assured manner.* Obviously, he did not give the impression of a man from humble beginnings (Item A). THE CORRECT ANSWER, THEN, IS E. Item C is incorrect because a wish for such power does not seem realistic. Item D is false because the reverse is true. Item B is neither mentioned nor implied in relation to the impression Mao gave.

2. The passage states, *"In one of his poems, Mao implied that none who has ruled China in the past.....is his equal."* This leads us to discard Item C. THEREFORE, THE CORRECT ANSWER IS B. Liu Shao-chi (Item A) is his right-hand man. The other men (Items D and E) are past Emperors of China.

3. In Paragraph 2, the author states, *"He received visiting foreign correspondents.....in Yenan."* THEREFORE, C IS THE CORRECT ANSWER, and Items A, B, and D are false. Yenan is in northwest China, states the passage, discounting E.

4. The rustic building was headquarters for the Chinese Communist party, and is, therefore, not the correct answer. This discounts Item C. However, the reader is told in the first paragraph that Mao DOES write poems. THEREFORE, THE CORRECT ANSWER IS Items A and B are false statements. Item E is true but hardly a surprising disclosure.

5. THE CORRECT ANSWER TO QUESTION 5 is B. Kunming is a city in China. Item A, Macao, is a Portuguese possession. Item C, Hong Kong, is a British Crown Colony. Laos is an independent country, discounting E. Item D, Formosa, is not within the jurisdiction of Mao, and so is false. 5._____

6. China is now under Communist rule. THEREFORE, THE CORRECT ANSWER IS D. Items A, B, C, and E are false. 6._____

TEST 10
PASSAGE

On Sunday morning, November 24, arrangements were made for Oswald's transfer from the city jail to the Dallas County jail, about 1 mile away. The news media had been informed on Saturday night that the transfer of Oswald would not take place until after 10 A.M. on Sunday. Earlier on Sunday, between 2:30 and 3 A.M., anonymous telephone calls threatening Oswald's life had been received by the Dallas office of the FBI and by the office of the county sheriff. Nevertheless, on Sunday morning, television, radio, and newspaper representatives crowded into the basement to record the transfer. As viewed through television cameras, Oswald would emerge from a door in front of the cameras and proceed to the transfer vehicle. To the right of the cameras was a "down" ramp from Main Street on the north. To the left was an "up" ramp leading to Commerce Street on the south.

The armored truck in which Oswald was to be transferred arrived shortly after 11 A.M. Police officials then decided, however, that an unmarked police car would be preferable for the trip because of its greater speed and maneuverability. At approximately 11:20 A.M., Oswald emerged from the basement jail office flanked by detectives on either side and at his rear. He took a few steps toward the car and was in the glaring light of the television cameras when a man suddenly darted out from an area on the right of the cameras where newsmen had been assembled. The man was carrying a Colt .38 revolver in his right hand and, while millions watched on television, he moved quickly to within a few feet of Oswald and fired one shot into Oswald's abdomen. Oswald groaned with pain as he fell to the ground and quickly lost consciousness. Within 7 minutes, Oswald was at Parkland Hospital where, without having regained consciousness, he was pronounced dead at 1:07 P.M.

QUESTIONS

1. The news media were

    A. not informed of the transfer
    B. given the wrong time
    C. not present
    D. informed of the transfer
    E. informed that the transfer would take place on Saturday

2. To facilitate maneuverability, the police

    A. barred the press
    B. used an unmarked car
    C. used an armored truck
    D. flanked Oswald as he emerged from the basement
    E. announced the time of the transfer

3. Oswald died of

    A. a succession of shots fired
    B. one shot in the head
    C. one shot in the abdomen
    D. one shot from a Colt .32 revolver
    E. one shot fired from a rifle

2 (#10)

4. The armored truck arrived   4._____

   A. at 11:20 A.M.
   B. before Oswald emerged from the basement jail office
   C. about 10:00 A.M.
   D. at exactly 1:07 P.M.
   E. shortly before 2:30 A.M.

5. In relation to the television cameras, Commerce Street was   5._____

   A. to the left of the *up* ramp
   B. leading from Main Street
   C. leading from a *down* ramp
   D. to the left
   E. to the right

6. Oswald was shot when he   6._____

   A. had left the glaring light of the TV cameras
   B. took a few steps toward the car
   C. emerged from the basement
   D. entered the car
   E. emerged from the jail office

7. Oswald was   7._____

   A. an assassin
   B. an alleged assassin
   C. a murderer in the first degree
   D. a murderer in the second degree
   E. insane

8. The report containing the passage is popularly known as the _____ Report.   8._____

   A. Kennedy   B. Dallas   C. Oswald
   D. Warren   E. Presidential

KEY (CORRECT ANSWERS)

1. D   5. D
2. B   6. B
3. C   7. B
4. B   8. D

EXPLANATION OF ANSWERS

1. The news media were informed of the transfer on Saturday, discounting Items A and E. They were given the correct time, discounting B. Also, they were present at the transfer, eliminating Item C. ITEM D IS THE CORRECT ONE, as stated in the second sentence of the first paragraph.

2. The passage states (second sentence, second paragraph), *"Police officials decided... an unmarked car would be preferable...because of its greater speed and maneuverability."* THEREFORE, ITEM B IS CORRECT. Item A is false. Item C indicates a discarded choice. Items D and E are true in themselves but had nothing to do with facilitating maneuverability; therefore, they are incorrect in this context.

3. The passage states that (second paragraph, third sentence from end), *"....he....fired one shot into Oswald's abdomen."* THEREFORE, ITEM C IS CORRECT. Item D is incorrect because, actually, *"The man was carrying a Colt .38 revolver...."* Items A, B, and E are false.

4. *"The armored truck arrived shortly after 11:00..."* states the passage in Paragraph 2, sentence one. Item A is the time Oswald emerged from the basement. Item C was the announced time of the transfer. Item D was the time of his death. Item E is the time the police received anonymous telephone calls. ITEM B IS, THEREFORE, CORRECT.

5. Item A is false because the street was not to the left of the ramp. Item B is false because Main St. and Commerce St. are not mentioned as connecting. Item C is false because the *down* ramp led from the cameras to Main St. ITEM D IS CORRECT as found in the last sentence of Paragraph 1. Item E is false; the right led to Main St.

6. Item A is false because the cameras were still on him. ITEM B IS CORRECT because it is the last moment referred to in the passage before the description of the shooting. Item C is false, as is Item E, because movements are detailed beyond that point. Item D is false because Oswald was shot before he got to the car.

7. Oswald did not live to stand trial. In view of this and because of the absence of complete proof, Oswald must be technically termed the ALLEGED assassin of President Kennedy. THEREFORE, ITEM B IS CORRECT. Items A, C, and D are false. Item E can now neither be proved nor disproved.

8. The report was issued by a commission headed by Earl Warren, Chief Justice of the Supreme Court. ITEM D IS CORRECT. Items A, B, C, and E are incorrect.

EXAMINATION SECTION
TEST 1

PASSAGE

By far, the best-known industry in Steuben County is the manufacture of glass. Just after the Civil War, the Flint Glass Company moved from Brooklyn to Coming, One reason why the company chose to settle in Coming was that the railroad from Pennsylvania to Corning brought coal for fuel at a low cost. In the early days, the company made lantern chimneys, bottles, and such familiar products. Later, it began making electric light bulbs. Now it manufactures all kinds of glass products. It makes Pyrex, a kind of glass that resists heat so well that it is used for cooking and baking. The company also makes glass wool, which is used for insulation and other purposes, and glass bricks, out of which the walls of some modern buildings are built.

1. The Flint Glass Company moved to Corning because it

    A. would be exempt from local taxes
    B. had been promised free land for its buildings
    C. could obtain coal cheaply
    D. could make glass bricks there

2. Glass wool, made in Corning, is used for

    A. insulation
    B. low cost fuel
    C. manufacturing lantern chimneys
    D. making electric blankets

3. Since its early days in Corning, the number and variety of the products of the glass industry have

    A. decreased
    B. remained about the same
    C. increased slightly
    D. increased greatly

4. The county in which Corning is located is

    A. Chautauqua   B. Cortland   C. Seneca   D. Steuben

5. Pyrex is used for

    A. antifreeze
    B. cooking utensils
    C. curtain material
    D. refrigeration

KEY (CORRECT ANSWERS)

1. C
2. A
3. D
4. D
5. B

TEST 2

PASSAGE

While Admiral Dewey was waiting in Manila Bay, exciting events were happening in the Atlantic. Soon after the start of the war, a Spanish fleet under Admiral Pascual Cervera set sail from the coast of Spain. An American fleet under Admiral William T. Sampson set out to give battle to Cervera's fleet. On May 19, Cervera's fleet came to anchor in the Cuban harbor of Santiago. Sampson's fleet quickly took up its position just outside the channel in order to blockade the harbor, which was too well defended by forts for the Americans to sail in. An American army was landed on the coast a few miles south of Santiago. On July 1-2, this force captured the outer defenses of the city at San Juan Hill and began a siege of Santiago. One of the regiments of volunteers that took part in the charge at San Juan Hill had been recruited by Theodore Roosevelt, who was second in command. The victory of the American army caused the Spaniards to give up hope. The Spanish commander in Cuba ordered Admiral Cervera to put to sea and save his fleet if he could. On July 3, Cervera, with his ships under full steam, started out of Santiago Harbor.

1. The paragraph describes a campaign in the

    A. War of 1812
    B. Mexican War
    C. Civil War
    D. Spanish-American War

2. At the time of the Cuban campaign, a new regiment was recruited by

    A. Cervera B. Dewey C. Roosevelt D. Sampson

3. The American victory at San Juan Hill caused the enemy to

    A. lose confidence
    B. surrender unconditionally
    C. retreat to San Juan Hill
    D. enter Santiago

4. The war was fought

    A. only in the Atlantic Ocean
    B. only in the Pacific Ocean
    C. on both land and sea
    D. off the coast of Tripoli

5. Sampson's fleet tried to

    A. keep Cervera's fleet from entering the harbor
    B. blockade Santiago Harbor
    C. attack San Juan Hill
    D. prevent the United States regiment from entering the battle

KEY (CORRECT ANSWERS)

1. D
2. C
3. A
4. C
5. B

TEST 3

PASSAGE

In the generation after Appomattox, the pattern of our present society and economy took shape. Growth - in area, numbers, wealth, power, social complexity, and economic maturity - was the one most arresting fact. The political divisions of the republic were drawn in their final form, a dozen new states were admitted to the Union, and an American empire was established. In a space of forty years, population increased from thirty-one to seventy-six million, fifteen million immigrants - an ever-increasing proportion of them from southern and eastern Europe - poured into the Promised Land, and great cities like New York, Chicago, Pittsburgh, Cleveland, and Detroit doubled and redoubled their size. In swift succession, the Indians were harried out of their ancient haunts on the high plains and in the mountains and valleys beyond and herded into reservations, the mining and cattle kingdoms rose and fell, the West was peopled and farmed, and by the end of the century, the frontier was no more. Vast new finds of iron ore, copper, and oil created scores of great industries; small business grew into big business.

1. Which one of the following terms BEST describes the period discussed?

    A. Expansion B. Conservation C. Regulation D. Isolation

2. The policy of the Federal government toward the Indians was to

    A. break up the tribal governments
    B. disenfranchise the Indians
    C. educate all Indian children in public schools
    D. remove them to reservations

3. An IMPORTANT factor in the industrial development that followed the Civil War was the

    A. diversification of agriculture
    B. development of new mineral resources
    C. rapid transformation of farmers into industrial workers
    D. development of a colonial empire

4. The last stage in the development of the West was accomplished by

    A. Indians B. farmers C. ranchers D. miners

5. Which one of the following statements is made concerning the United States during the period described in the paragraph? The United States

    A. established an empire
    B. secured special interests in the oil wells and copper mines of Mexico
    C. developed a policy of dollar diplomacy
    D. advocated the open-door policy

6. Which one of the following statements concerning the frontier is made in the paragraph?

    A. After the admission of twelve states, expansion ceased.
    B. An outstanding characteristic of the frontier people was their intense nationalism.
    C. At the end of the 19th century, the frontier came to an end.
    D. The frontier was most important in shaping our present society.

KEY (CORRECT ANSWERS)

1. A
2. D
3. B
4. B
5. A
6. C

TEST 4

PASSAGE

If George Washington could have visited the United States in the 1840's, his thoughts might have run somewhat like this:

"I find it hard to believe that over 20,000,000 people now live in the United States, and that towns have been built beyond the Mississippi River. In my day, there were only 4,000,000 people, and most of these lived along the Atlantic Coast. Can this great city be New York, where I took the oath of office as President? The city I knew had 60,000 inhabitants; today, they tell me, it is the largest city in the New World and has a population of 500,000. What is this engine belching smoke and sparks which carries people across the countryside? When I traveled from Mount Vernon to New York in 1789, I depended on horses. I see factories where machines spin thread to weave it into cloth. Who ever heard in my day of a machine that could spin eighty threads at one time? Here is a boat run by steam which travels against the current of a river! In my time, we depended on the wind to drive our boats. Who would have believed that this country could change so greatly in fifty years!"

1. How much GREATER was the population of the United States in 1840 than in 1789?

    A. Twice as great
    B. Five times as great
    C. Twelve times as great
    D. Twenty times as great

2. George Washington was inaugurated in

    A. Boston
    B. Mount Vernon
    C. New York
    D. Philadelphia

3. A method of transportation used in the 1840's but not in Washington's time was the

    A. airplane   B. automobile   C. sailboat   D. railroad

4. The changes described in the paragraph took place within a period of about _____ years.

    A. 10   B. 20   C. 50   D. 70

5. In Washington's time, MOST of the people in the United States lived

    A. beyond the Mississippi
    B. along the eastern seaboard
    C. in the deep South
    D. in the Northwest

KEY (CORRECT ANSWERS)

1. B
2. C
3. D
4. C
5. B

TEST 5

PASSAGE

In philosophy, the New Deal was democratic, in method evolutionary. Because for fifteen years legislative reforms had been dammed up, they now burst upon the country with what seemed like violence but when the waters subsided, it was clear that they ran in familiar channels. The conservation policy of the New Deal had been inaugurated by Theodore Roosevelt; railroad and trust regulation went back to the eighties; banking and currency reforms had been advocated by Bryan and partially achieved by Wilson; the farm-relief program borrowed much from the Populists, labor legislation from the practices of such states as Wisconsin and Oregon. Even judicial reform, which caused such a mighty stir, had been anticipated by Lincoln and Theodore Roosevelt. And in the realm of international relations, the policies of the New Deal were clearly continuations of the traditional policies of strengthening national security, maintaining freedom of the seas, supporting law and peace, and championing democracy in the Western world.

1. All of the following are suitable titles for the selection EXCEPT

   A. The New Deal - an Evolution
   B. The Radical Program of the New Deal
   C. Precedents for the New Deal
   D. Conservatism in the New Deal

2. Many students of history do not agree that legislative reforms had been *dammed up* during the fifteen-year period preceding the New Deal.
   All of the following legislative measures were passed during this fifteen-year period EXCEPT the _____ Act.

   A. Norris-LaGuardia
   B. Reconstruction Finance Corporation
   C. Sherman Antitrust
   D. Agricultural Marketing

3. This selection traces the origin of many of the policies of the New Deal to all of the following EXCEPT

   A. former Presidents
   B. legislation of the Western states
   C. minority parties
   D. the Supreme Court

4. All of the following were indications of isolationism in the New Deal period EXCEPT the

   A. *cash-and-carry* policy
   B. Johnson Debt-Default Act
   C. Lima Conference
   D. *America First* organization

5. Abraham Lincoln, Theodore Roosevelt, and Franklin Roosevelt had all of the following policies in common EXCEPT

   A. trust regulation
   B. expansion of executive powers
   C. land reforms
   D. economic betterment of the common man

6. According to the selection legislative reforms of the 6.____
New Deal are characterized by all of the following adjectives EXCEPT

   A. democratic
   B. evolutionary
   C. reactionary
   D. traditional

7. All of the following Presidents were associated with banking reforms EXCEPT 7.____

   A. Warren Harding
   B. Andrew Jackson
   C. Abraham Lincoln
   D. Woodrow Wilson

8. According to the selection, some legislative precedents for the New Deal were furthered 8.____
in the United States by all of the following Presidents EXCEPT

   A. Abraham Lincoln
   B. Theodore Roosevelt
   C. Calvin Coolidge
   D. Woodrow Wilson

9. The student seeking primary source material on the New Deal farm program should consult 9.____

   A. THE WORLD ALMANAC
   B. the CONGRESSIONAL RECORD
   C. an encyclopedia of the social studies
   D. WHO'S WHO IN AMERICA

KEY (CORRECT ANSWERS)

1. B
2. C
3. D
4. C
5. A
6. C
7. A
8. C
9. B

TEST 6

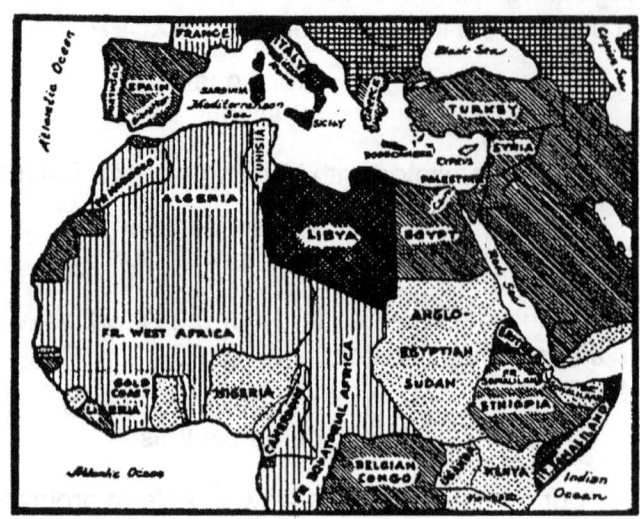

PASSAGE

London, August 14, 1948. A bankrupt empire was put for disposal in London this week. Although the empire, once the property of Italy, has few assets, bidding for the properties was spirited. Italy, despite her present domestic problems, was bidding strongly. Only Italy seemed to want the whole lot; others were angling for bits and pieces and odd parcels of the colonies. On the other hand, Great Britain, which wants the properties almost as badly as Italy, was bidding timidly as if she were afraid of running up the price too fast and too far.

The international auction sale was arranged last year when the winning powers in the recent war settled accounts with Italy. In the Italian peace treaty, Italy renounced all rights to her colonies. The Dodecanese promptly were ceded to Greece. In an annex to the treaty, the Big Four agreed that their Foreign Ministers should decide on the disposal of the other three colonies - Eritrea and Italian Somaliland on the east coast of Africa and Libya in North Africa. Failing a decision within one year, that is, by September 15, 1948, the Big Four agreed that they would hand over the problem to the United Nations General Assembly and abide by its verdict.

That year was nearly out when the deputies of the Big Four Foreign Ministers met, not to decide finally the future of the colonies, but merely to pass on recommendations to the Council of Foreign Minis- ters. When these deputies met last October, they sent out a four-power commission to investigate the situation in the colonies and the wishes of the inhabitants. Reports of that commission were in the hands of the deputies when they met this week.

1. The writer believes that the former Italian colonies   1.____

    A. have many fine resources
    B. are desired by some of the great powers
    C. are financially sound
    D. are strategically important to Russia

2. The Italian colonies in Africa include

   A. Ethiopia, Eritrea, Libya
   B. Italian Somaliland, Eritrea, Libya
   C. Eritrea, Libya, and the Dodecanese
   D. Ethiopia, Tripoli, and the Dodecanese

3. Italy's African colonies bordered on the

   A. Mediterranean Sea
   B. Indian Ocean
   C. Atlantic Ocean and Red Sea
   D. Red Sea, Mediterranean Sea, and Indian Ocean

4. The MOST appropriate title for the article would be

   A. PROBLEMS OF WORLD EMPIRES
   B. FATE OF ITALY'S AFRICAN EMPIRE UNDECIDED
   C. FOUR POWERS INVESTIGATE ITALY'S COLONIES
   D. ITALY'S WEALTH IN AFRICA

5. Libya lies

   A. east of Algeria
   B. east of Egypt
   C. north of Egypt
   D. west of Tunisia

6. The author of the article

   A. thinks that the colonies will be restored to the natives
   B. says the colonies will be given to the Arabs
   C. predicts that the colonies will be returned to Italy
   D. makes no prediction as to the action of the United Nations Assembly

7. MOST of Libya's boundaries bordered on

   A. possessions of the French Empire
   B. possessions of the British Empire
   C. the sea
   D. independent countries

8. If the Big Four cannot agree upon the disposition of the Italian colonies, they will refer the problem to the

   A. International Court of Justice
   B. Trusteeship Council
   C. General Assembly of the United Nations
   D. Security Council of the United Nations

9. The author of the article states that

   A. the colonies were disposed of in the Italian peace treaty
   B. Greece received all the Italian colonies
   C. the Big Four were first assigned disposal of the colonies
   D. the United Nations Assembly would have to approve the disposal of the colonies

10. The author names the following countries as bidders in the disposal of the remaining colonies

    A. France and the Netherlands
    B. Great Britain and France
    C. Italy and Portugal
    D. Great Britain and Italy

11. By a study of this map, a student could determine the

    A. number of air miles from Rome to Cairo
    B. most densely populated areas
    C. notable topographic features of Ethiopia
    D. boundaries and comparative areas

12. Of the following statements selected from the article, the one that is CLEARLY a statement of opinion is that

    A. the Dodecanese were ceded to Greece
    B. the Big Four agreed to hand over the problem to the United Nations under certain conditions
    C. the deputies met in October, 1947
    D. Great Britain was afraid of running the price up too fast and too far

KEYS (CORRECT ANSWERS)

1. B
2. B
3. D
4. B
5. A

6. D
7. A
8. C
9. C
10. D

11. D
12. D

TEST 7

PASSAGE

"We hold these truths to be self-evident: that all men and women are created equal; that they are endowed by their Creator with certain inalienable rights; that among these are life, liberty, and the pursuit of happiness...

"The history of mankind is a history of repeated injuries and usurpations on the part of man toward woman, having in direct object the establishment of an absolute tyranny over her. To prove this, let facts be submitted to a candid world.

"He has never permitted her to exercise her inalienable right to the elective franchise.

"He has compelled her to submit to laws, in the formation of which she had no voice...

"He has so framed the laws of divorce, as to what shall be the proper causes, and in case of separation, to whom the guardianship of the children shall be given, as to be wholly regardless of the happiness of women - the law, in all cases, going upon a false supposition of the supremacy of man, and giving all power into his hands...

"He has monopolized nearly all the profitable employments, and from those she is permitted to follow, she receives but a scanty remuneration. He closes against her all the avenues to wealth and distinction which he considers most honorable to himself. As a teacher of theology, medicine, or law, she is not known.

"He has denied her the facilities for obtaining a thorough education, all colleges being closed against her..."

RESOLUTIONS ADOPTED AT THE SENECA FALLS CONVENTION, 1848

1. This selection appeals for support of the movement for

    A. temperance
    B. women's rights
    C. social security
    D. child labor legislation

2. Which served as a model for this selection?

    A. Federal Bill of Rights
    B. Emancipation Proclamation
    C. Mayflower Compact
    D. Declaration of Independence

3. An *inalienable right* is BEST defined as a right that

    A. cannot be taken away
    B. is granted to women only
    C. is granted to all except aliens
    D. is guaranteed by the preamble to the Federal Constitution

4. Which right did women enjoy at the time of the Seneca Falls Convention?

    A. The right to serve on juries
    B. The right of assembly
    C. Equal vocational opportunities
    D. Equal rights before the law

5. Which problem of the Seneca Falls Convention remains a legal issue in the United States today?

   A. A voice in making laws
   B. College admission
   C. Equal pay for equal work in industry
   D. Exclusion from the practice of medicine

6. About how long after the Seneca Falls Convention was the right to the elective franchise (referred to in the selection) achieved by a constitutional amendment? _____ years.

   A. 5   B. 50   C. 75   D. 100

KEY (CORRECT ANSWERS)

1. B
2. D
3. A
4. B
5. C
6. C

TEST 8

FROM THE FOUR CORNERS OF THE COUNTRY

1. The cartoon suggests that in the 82nd Congress

   A. harmony prevailed
   B. more agreement existed on domestic issues than on foreign policy
   C. only the reactionary Democrats opposed Truman's foreign policy
   D. there was disagreement within both the Democratic and the Republican parties

2. The cartoon specifically refers to division within the Republican party over

   A. foreign policy
   B. inflation
   C. civil rights
   D. taxation

3. Which of the following are leaders of the two Republican groups represented in the cartoon?

   A. Taft and Acheson
   B. Dewey and Hoover
   C. Austin and Dulles
   D. Stassen and Lehman

4. We can conclude from the cartoon that in the 82nd Congress, there was

   A. little prospect that either group in the Democratic party will take a world-minded view
   B. no possibility of any important legislation
   C. no possibility that the President's recommendations will receive favorable consideration
   D. little likelihood of settling significant foreign policy issues on strict party lines

5. Which of the following conclusions drawn from the cartoon can be readily proved?

   A. There was a reaction group in the Democratic party.
   B. All isolationists came from the same part of the country.
   C. The 82nd Congress was evenly divided between Republicans and Democrats.
   D. The Republicans were more interested in foreign policy than in domestic issues.

KEY (CORRECT ANSWERS)

1. D
2. A
3. B
4. D
5. A

TEST 9

FAMILY INCOME BEFORE TAXES
United States, 1946 and 1953

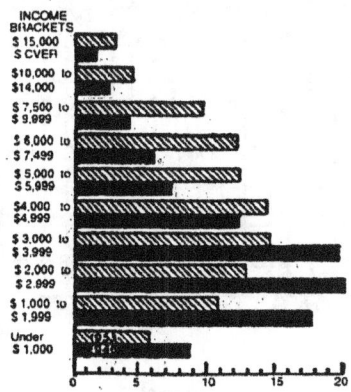

PERCENT OF FAMILIES

1. In 1953, the percent of families with incomes between $3000 and $3,999 was APPROXIMATELY

   A. 5%   B. 10%   C. 15%   D. 20%

2. In 1946, which income bracket included the largest percentage of families?

   A. $1,000 to $1,999
   B. $2,000 to $2,999
   C. $3,000 to $3,999
   D. $4,000 to $4,999

3. Which of these income brackets included a larger percentage of families in 1953 than in 1946?

   A. $1,000 to $1,999
   B. $2,000 to $2,999
   C. $3,000 to $3,999
   D. $4,000 to $4,999

4. In 1953, the percent of families with incomes less than $3,000 was about

   A. 30   B. 45   C. 60   D. 75

5. The average family income in 1953 was CLOSEST TO

   A. $1,500   B. $2,500   C. $4,500   D. $6,000

KEY (CORRECT ANSWERS)

1. C
2. B
3. D
4. A
5. C

TEST 10

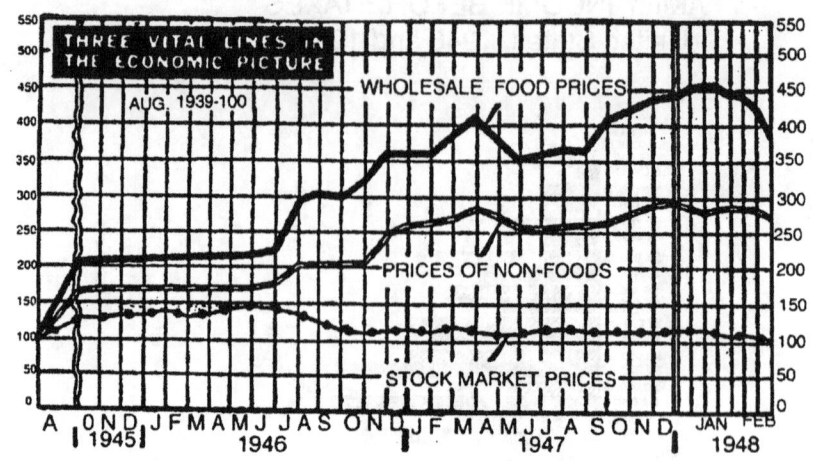

1. For the year 1948, the chart shows a _____ period.

    A. two-month B. six-week C. seven-week D. eight-week

2. Throughout the period from October 1945 to February 1948, stock market prices

    A. rose sharply
    B. declined sharply
    C. remained comparatively steady
    D. fluctuated greatly

3. A comparison of wholesale food prices at the end of the second week in February 1948 with wholesale food prices in October 1945 shows an increase of APPROXIMATELY _____ points.

    A. 50 B. 100 C. 200 D. 300

4. In the period covered by the graph, wholesale food prices declined sharply

    A. once B. twice C. three times D. four times

5. The prices of non-food items reached their highest peak in

    A. March 1946   B. December 1946
    C. March 1947   D. December 1947

6. For the period shown in 1948, all items

    A. rose   B. remained the same
    C. declined   D. fluctuated greatly

7. The month in which the GREATEST increase in wholesale food prices occurred was

    A. July 1946   B. October 1946
    C. September 1947   D. December 1947

8. The same wholesale order of groceries that cost $100 in August 1939 cost approximately $450 in

    A. November 1946   B. March 1947
    C. December 1947   D. January 1948

KEY (CORRECT ANSWERS)

1. C 6. C
2. C 7. A
3. C 8. D
4. B
5. D

INTERPRETATION OF LITERARY MATERIALS
EXAMINATION SECTION
TEST 1

DIRECTIONS: In the passages that follow, each question or incomplete statement that follows each passage is followed by several suggested answers or completions. Select the one that BEST answers the question or completes the statement. Base your choice in each case on the materials given and on your own understanding of the subject matter.

What things there are to write, if one could only write them! My mind is full of gleaming thoughts; gay moods and mysterious, mothlike meditations hover in my imagination, fanning their painted wings. They would make my fortune if I could catch them; but always the rarest, those freaked with azure and the deepest crimson, flutter away beyond my reach. The ever-baffled chase of these filmy nothings often seems, for one of sober years in a sad world, a trifling occupation. But have I not read of the great Kings of Persia who used to ride out to hawk for butterflies, nor deemed this pastime beneath their royal dignity?

1. The author believes that striving to write well is

    A. inappropriate for a mature person
    B. unappreciated
    C. unnecessary
    D. a trifling occupation
    E. a worthy occupation

2. The author finds that

    A. there are few subjects to write about
    B. he cannot capture the pictures of his imagination
    C. he is too old for writing gay trifles
    D. he cannot keep his mind on his writing
    E. it is easy to write

3. The theme of this paragraph is

    A. thoughts about butterflies
    B. the sport of kings
    C. the pursuit of ideas
    D. fortune out of reach
    E. the joy of writing

KEY (CORRECT ANSWERS)

1. E
2. B
3. C

TEST 2

DIRECTIONS: In the passages that follow, each question or incomplete statement that follows each passage is followed by several suggested answers or completions. Select the one that BEST answers the question or completes the statement. Base your choice in each case on the materials given and on your own understanding of the subject matter.

The single business of Henry Thoreau, during forty-odd years of eager activity, was to discover an economy calculated to provide a satisfying life. His one concern, that gave to his ramblings in Concord fields a value of high adventure, was to explore the true meaning of wealth. As he understood the problem of economics, there were three possible solutions open to him: to exploit himself, to exploit his fellows, or to reduce the problem to its lowest denominator. The first was quite impossible—to imprison oneself in a treadmill when the morning called to great adventure. To exploit one's fellows seemed to Thoreau's sensitive social conscience an even greater infidelity. Freedom with abstinence seemed to him better than serfdom with material well-being, and he was content to move to Walden Pond and to set about the high business of living, "to front only the essential facts of life and to see what it had to teach." He did not advocate that other men should build cabins and live isolated. He had no wish to dogmatize concerning the best mode of living—each must settle that for himself. But that a satisfying life should be lived, he was vitally concerned. The story of his emancipation from the lower economics is the one romance of his life, and WALDEN is his great book. It is a book in praise of life rather than of Nature, a record of calculating economies that studied saving in order to spend more largely. But it is a book of social criticism as well, in spite of its explicit denial of such a purpose. In considering the true nature of economy, he concluded, with Ruskin, that the cost of a thing is the amount of life which is required in exchange for it, immediately or in the long run. In WALDEN, Thoreau elaborated the text: "The only wealth is life."

1. In Thoreau's opinion, the price of a thing should always be measured in terms of

   A. time B. effort C. money
   D. romance E. life

2. According to Thoreau, the wealth of an individual is measured by

   A. the money he makes
   B. the experience he gains
   C. the amount he saves
   D. the books he writes
   E. his social standing

3. Thoreau's solution to the problem of living was to

   A. study Nature
   B. make other men work for him
   C. work in a mill
   D. live in a simple way
   E. write for a living

4. Thoreau was very

   A. active B. lazy C. dissatisfied
   D. unsociable E. stingy

5. Thoreau's CHIEF aim in life was to

    A. discover a satisfactory economy
    B. do as little work as possible
    C. convert others to his way of life
    D. write about Nature
    E. live in isolation

6. The theme of this paragraph is

    A. problems of economics
    B. Thoreau's philosophy of life
    C. WALDEN, Thoreau's greatest work
    D. how Thoreau saved money
    E. life at Walden Pond

KEY (CORRECT ANSWERS)

1.	E	4.	A
2.	B	5.	A
3.	D	6.	B

TEST 3

DIRECTIONS: In the passages that follow, each question or incomplete statement that follows each passage is followed by several suggested answers or completions. Select the one that BEST answers the question or completes the statement. Base your choice in each case on the materials given and on your own understanding of the subject matter.

A moment's reflection will make it clear that one can not live a full, free, influential life in America without argument. No doubt, people often argue on insufficient evidence and for insufficient reasons; no doubt, they often argue on points about which they should rather be thinking and studying; no doubt, they sometimes fancy they are arguing when they are merely wrangling and disputing. But this is only proof that argument is employed badly, that it is misused rather than used skillfully. Argument, at the right moment and for the right purpose and in the right way, is undoubtedly one of the most useful instruments in American life; it is an indispensable means of expressing oneself and impressing others.

1. The theme of this paragraph is

    A. the usefulness of argument
    B. principles of argument
    C. how to win arguments
    D. misuses of argument
    E. need for evidence in argument

2. Argument is an important factor in American life because it gives people a chance to

    A. talk about things of which they know little
    B. influence the ideas of others
    C. develop sufficient evidence
    D. have friendly conversations
    E. use argument at the right time and in the right way

3. Argumentation is being used unwisely when it results in

    A. understanding   B. compromise
    C. deliberation   D. bickering
    E. differences of opinion

KEY (CORRECT ANSWERS)

1. A
2. B
3. D

TEST 4

DIRECTIONS: In the passages that follow, each question or incomplete statement that follows each passage is followed by several suggested answers or completions. Select the one that BEST answers the question or completes the statement. Base your choice in each case on the materials given and on your own understanding of the subject matter.

The characteristic American believes, first, in justice as the foundation of civilized government and society, and, next, in freedom for the individual, so far as that freedom is possible without interference with the equal rights of others. He conceives that both justice and freedom are to be secured through popular respect for the laws enacted by the elected representatives of the people and through the faithful observance of those laws. It should be observed, however, that American justice in general keeps in view the present common good of the vast majority, and the restoration rather than the punishment of the exceptional malignant or defective individual. It is essentially democratic; and especially it finds sufferings inflicted on the innocent unintelligible and abhorrent.

Blind obedience and implicit submission to the will of another do not commend themselves to characteristic Americans. The discipline in which they believe is the voluntary cooperation of many persons in the orderly and effective pursuit of common ends. Thus, they submit willingly to any restrictions on individual liberty which can be shown to be necessary to the preservation of the public health, and they are capable of the most effective cooperation at need in business, sports, and war.

1. The American people believe in 1.____

    A. unquestioning obedience to their laws
    B. strict discipline
    C. liberty without restraint
    D. subservience to the President
    E. working together for a necessary purpose

2. American justice emphasizes 2.____

    A. the welfare of the minority
    B. retaliation for disobedience
    C. rehabilitation of wrongdoers
    D. the sufferings of the innocent
    E. punishment of criminals

3. The PRIMARY element in the American way of life is 3.____

    A. the right to vote
    B. freedom
    C. willingness to follow leaders
    D. justice
    E. popular respect for laws

4. The theme of this selection is
   A. American justice
   B. a plea for cooperation
   C. the basis of American democracy
   D. the American government
   E. liberty as the foundation of government

KEY (CORRECT ANSWERS)

1. E
2. C
3. D
4. C

TEST 5

DIRECTIONS: In the passages that follow, each question or incomplete statement that follows each passage is followed by several suggested answers or completions. Select the one that BEST answers the question or completes the statement. Base your choice in each case on the materials given and on your own understanding of the subject matter.

The change in the treatment of his characters is a significant index to Shakespeare's growth as a dramatist. In the earlier plays, his men and women are more engaged with external forces than with internal struggles. In as excellent an early tragedy as ROMEO AND JULIET, the hero fights more with outside obstacles than with himself. In the great later tragedies, the internal conflict is more emphasized, as in the cases of HAMLET and MACBETH. He grew to care less for mere incident, for plots based on mistaken identity, as in the COMEDY OF ERRORS; he became more and more interested in the delineation of character, in showing the effect of evil on Macbeth and his wife, of jealousy on OTHELLO, of indecision on Hamlet, as well as in exploring the ineffectual attempts of many of his characters to escape the consequences of their acts.

1. The development of Shakespeare as a dramatist is MOST clearly revealed in his

    A. improved treatment of complications
    B. increased use of involved plots
    C. handling of emotional conflicts
    D. increased variety of plot
    E. decreased dependency on historical characters

2. In his later plays, Shakespeare became interested in

    A. plots based on mistaken identity
    B. great characters from history
    C. the history of his country
    D. the study of human nature
    E. the struggle of the hero with external forces

3. The theme of this paragraph is

    A. comedies and tragedies of Shakespeare
    B. Shakespeare's best plays
    C. Shakespeare's development as a dramatist
    D. the moral aspects of Shakespeare's later plays
    E. Shakespeare's interest in good and evil

KEY (CORRECT ANSWERS)

1. C
2. D
3. C

TEST 6

DIRECTIONS: In the passages that follow, each question or incomplete statement that follows each passage is followed by several suggested answers or completions. Select the one that BEST answers the question or completes the statement. Base your choice in each case on the materials given and on your own understanding of the subject matter.

Solitude is a great chastener when once you accept it. It quietly eliminates all sorts of traits that were a part of you - among others, the desire to pose, to keep your best foot forever in evidence, to impress people as being something you would like to have them think you are even when you aren't. Some men I know are able to pose even in solitude; had they valets they no doubt would be heroes to them. But I find it the hardest kind of work myself; and as I am lazy, I have stopped trying. To act without an audience is so tiresome and profitless that you gradually give it up and at last forget how to act at all. For you become more interested in making the acquaintance of yourself as you really are, which is a meeting that, in the haunts of men, rarely takes place. It is gratifying, for example, to discover that you prefer to be clean rather than dirty even when there is no one but God to care which you are; just as it is amusing to note, however, that for scrupulous cleanliness, you are not inclined to make superhuman sacrifices, although you used to believe you were. Clothes, you learn, with something of a shock, have for you no interest whatsoever....You learn to regard dress merely as covering, a precaution. For its color and its cut you care nothing.

1. The activities of everyday life seldom give us the chance to

    A. learn our own peculiarities
    B. keep our best foot forward
    C. impress people
    D. dress as we would like
    E. be immaculately clean

2. The desire to appear well-dressed USUALLY depends upon

    A. an audience   B. industriousness
    C. personal pride   D. the need for cleanliness
    E. a fondness for acting

3. In solitude, clothes

    A. constitute one item that pleases the valet
    B. make one careless
    C. are part of acting
    D. are valued for their utility only
    E. are tiresome

4. A desire to appear at your best is a trait that

    A. goes with laziness
    B. may disappear when you are alone
    C. depends primarily on clothes
    D. is inhuman
    E. is evil

5. The theme of this paragraph is 5._____
   A. carelessness in clothes
   B. acting without an audience
   C. discoveries through solitude
   D. showing off to best advantage
   E. being a hero to yourself

KEY (CORRECT ANSWERS)

1. A
2. A
3. D
4. B
5. C

TEST 7

DIRECTIONS: In the passages that follow, each question or incomplete statement that follows each passage is followed by several suggested answers or completions. Select the one that BEST answers the question or completes the statement. Base your choice in each case on the materials given and on your own understanding of the subject matter.

In width of scope, Yeats far exceeds any of his contemporaries. He is the only poet since the 18th century who has been a public man in his own country and the only poet since Milton who has been a public man at a time when his country was involved in a struggle for political liberty. This may not seem an important matter, but it is a question whether the kind of life lived by poets for the last two hundred years or so has not been one great reason for the drift of poetry away from the life of the community as a whole, and the loss of touch with tradition. Once the life of contemplation has been divorced from the life of action, or from real knowledge of men of action, something is lost which it is difficult to define, but which leaves poetry enfeebled and incomplete. Yeats responded with all his heart as a young man to the reality and the romance of Ireland's struggle, but he lived to be completely disillusioned about the value of the Irish rebellion. He saw his dreams of liberty blotted out in horror by "the innumerable clanging wings that have put out the moon." It brought him to the final conclusion of the futility of all discipline that is not of the whole being, and of "how base at moments of excitement are minds without culture"; but he remained a man to whom the life of action always meant something very real.

1. According to the writer of the paragraph, great poetry is MOST often produced by poets who

    A. are involved in the problems of life around them
    B. spend their time in contemplation
    C. drift away from the community
    D. break away from tradition
    E. take part in war

2. The writer implies that, as compared with older poetry, present-day poetry is more

    A. complete   B. romantic   C. alive
    D. ineffectual   E. comprehensive

3. Yeats was PRIMARILY a

    A. soldier   B. man of action
    C. dreamer   D. rigid disciplinarian
    E. politician

4. The theme of this paragraph is

    A. basis of true poetry
    B. the necessity of culture
    C. action versus contemplation
    D. Yeats as a poet and patriot
    E. Yeats' part in the Irish rebellion

KEY (CORRECT ANSWERS)

1. A
2. D
3. B
4. D

TEST 8

DIRECTIONS: In the passages that follow, each question or incomplete statement that follows each passage is followed by several suggested answers or completions. Select the one that BEST answers the question or completes the statement. Base your choice in each case on the materials given and on your own understanding of the subject matter.

Only twice in literary history has there been a great period of tragedy, in the Athens of Pericles and in Elizabethan England. What these two periods had in common, two thousand years and more apart in time, that they expressed themselves in the same fashion, may give us some hint of the nature of tragedy, for far from being periods of darkness and defeat, each was a time when life was seen exalted, a time of thrilling and unfathomable possibilities. They held their heads high, those men who conquered at Marathon and Salamis and those who fought Spain and saw the Great Armada sink. The world was a place of wonder; manking was beauteous; life was lived on the crest of the wave. More than all, the poignant joy of heroism had stirred men's hearts. Not stuff for tragedy, would you say? But on the crest of the wave, one must feel either tragically or joyously; one cannot feel tamely. The temper of mind that sees tragedy in life has not for its opposite the temper that sees joy. The opposite pole to the tragic view of life is the sordid view. When humanity is seen as devoid of dignity and significance, trivial, mean, and sunk in dreary hopelessness, then the spirit of tragedy departs.

1. In an age of glory, one

    A. is not indifferent
    B. usually feels tragic
    C. feels happy
    D. is apathetic
    E. feels mean and hopeless

2. The two periods in which great tragedies were written were periods of

    A. gloom   B. serenity   C. defeat
    D. confusion   E. valor

3. The mental attitude that finds tragedy in life is characterized by

    A. sordidness   B. indifference   C. exaltation
    D. triviality   E. hopelessness

4. The theme of this paragraph is

    A. two thousand years of tragedy
    B. Periclean Athens
    C. the tragedy of war
    D. the psychology of happiness
    E. mainsprings of tragic drama

KEY (CORRECT ANSWERS)

1. A
2. E
3. C
4. E

TEST 9

DIRECTIONS: In the passages that follow, each question or incomplete statement that follows each passage is followed by several suggested answers or completions. Select the one that BEST answers the question or completes the statement. Base your choice in each case on the materials given and on your own understanding of the subject matter.

There are few books which go with midnight, solitude, and a candle. It is much easier to say what does not please us then than what is exactly right. The book must be, anyhow, something benedictory by a sinning fellow man. Cleverness would be repellent at such an hour. Cleverness, anyhow, is the level of mediocrity today, we are all too infernally clever. The first witty and perverse paradox blows out the candle. Only the sick mind craves cleverness, as a morbid body turns to drink. The late candle throws its beams a great distance, and its rays make transparent much that seemed massy and important. The mind at rest beside that light, when the house is asleep, and the consequential affairs of the urgent world have diminished to their right proportions because we seem them distantly from another and a more tranquil place in the heavens, where duty, honor, witty arguments, controversial logic on great questions, appear such as will leave hardly a trace of fossil in the indurated mud which will cover them—the mind then smiles at cleverness. For though at that hour the body may be dog-tired, the mind is white and lucid, like that of a man from whom a fever has abated. It is bare of illusions. It has a sharp focus, small and starlike, as a clear and lonely flame left burning by the altar of a shrine from which all have gone but one. A book which approaches that light in the privacy of that place must come, as it were, with open and honest pages.

1. At midnight in the solitude of one's room, the mind is

   A. tired   B. keen   C. sick
   D. troubled   E. clever

2. The author considers the average book of today

   A. inane   B. sinful   C. benedictory
   D. restful   E. open and honest

3. Naming the qualities of a book suitable for reading when one retires is

   A. logical   B. a clever job
   C. difficult   D. like lighting a candle
   E. tiresome

4. To make good reading at bedtime, a book must be

   A. light   B. witty   C. controversial
   D. historical   E. straightforward

5. The theme of this paragraph is

   A. reading by candlelight
   B. books for convalescents
   C. not a time to read
   D. books for tired minds
   E. books for midnight reading

KEY (CORRECT ANSWERS)

1. B
2. A
3. C
4. E
5. E

TEST 10

DIRECTIONS: In the passages that follow, each question or incomplete statement that follows each passage is followed by several suggested answers or completions. Select the one that BEST answers the question or completes the statement. Base your choice in each case on the materials given and on your own understanding of the subject matter.

Few things are move stimulating than the sight of the forceful wings of large birds cleaving the vagueness of air and making the piled clouds a mere background for their concentrated life. The peregrine falcon, becalmed in the blue depths, cruises across space without a tremor of his wide wings. Wild geese beat up in the sky in a compact wedge. Primeval force is in their strongly moving wings and their beautiful, outstretched necks, in their power of untiring effort, and the eager search of their wild hearts for the free spaces they love. The good fellowship of swift, united action, the joy of ten thousand that move as one, is in the flight of flocks of birds. When seagulls flash up from the water with every wing at full stretch, there is no deliberation; it is as if each bird saw a sweeping arc before it and followed its individual way faithfully. The unerring judgment of the grand curve when the wings are so near and yet never collide, the speed of the descent, are pure poetry.

1. He admires the ability of seagulls to

    A. coordinate their flight
    B. reach great heights
    C. stretch their wings
    D. rise from the water
    E. dive swiftly

2. The flight of the wild goose, as compared with that of the falcon, is MORE

    A. active
    B. beautiful
    C. poetic
    D. deliberate
    E. graceful

3. The author finds the sight of flying birds

    A. inspiring
    B. awesome
    C. joyful
    D. consoling
    E. primitive

4. The author admires the falcon's

    A. wild freedom
    B. effortless flight
    C. united action
    D. primitive force
    E. unerring judgment

5. The theme of this paragraph is

    A. our wild birds
    B. the superb falcon
    C. the beauty of flight
    D. citizens of the sky
    E. the lure of the wild

KEY (CORRECT ANSWERS)

1. A
2. A
3. A
4. B
5. C

TEST 11

DIRECTIONS: In the passages that follow, each question or incomplete statement that follows each passage is followed by several suggested answers or completions. Select the one that BEST answers the question or completes the statement. Base your choice in each case on the materials given and on your own understanding of the subject matter.

As we know the short story today, it is largely a product of the nineteenth and twentieth centuries and its development parallels the rapid development of industrialism in America. We have been a busy people, busy principally in evolving a production system supremely efficient. Railroads and factories have blossomed almost overnight; mines and oil fields have been discovered and exploited; mechanical inventions by the thousand have been made and perfected. Speed has been an essential element in our endeavors, and it has affected our lives, our very natures. Leisurely reading has been, for most Americans, impossible. As with our meals, we have grabbed bits of reading standing up, cafeteria style, and gulped down cups of sentiment on the run. We have had to read while hanging on to a strap in a swaying trolley car or in a rushing subway or while tending to a clamoring telephone switchboard. Our popular magazine has been our literary automat, and its stories have often been no more substantial than sandwiches.

1. From this selection, one would assume that the author's attitude toward short stories is one of

    A. approval   B. indifference   C. contempt
    D. impartiality E. regret

2. The short story has developed because of Americans'

    A. reactions against the classics
    B. need for reassurance
    C. lack of culture
    D. lack of education
    E. taste for speed

3. The short story today owes its popularity to its

    A. settings   B. plots   C. style
    D. length   E. characters

4. The theme of this paragraph is

    A. *quick-lunch* literature
    B. life in the machine age
    C. culture in modern life
    D. reading while traveling
    E. the development of industrialism

KEY (CORRECT ANSWERS)

1. E
2. E
3. D
4. A

TEST 12

DIRECTIONS: In the passages that follow, each question or incomplete statement that follows each passage is followed by several suggested answers or completions. Select the one that BEST answers the question or completes the statement. Base your choice in each case on the materials given and on your own understanding of the subject matter.

If Shakespeare needs any excuse for the exuberance of his language (the high key in which he pitched most of his dramatic dialogue), it should be remembered that he was doing on the plastic stage of his own day what on the pictorial stage of our day is not so much required. Shakespeare's dramatic figures stood out on a platform-stage, without background, with the audience on three sides of it. And the whole of his atmosphere and environment had to come from the gestures and language of the actors. When they spoke, they provided their own scenery, which we now provide for them. They had to do a good deal more (when they spoke) than actors have to do today in order to give the setting. They carried the scenery on their backs, as it were, and spoke it in words.

1. The nature of the stage for which Shakespeare wrote made it necessary for him to   1.____

   A. employ only highly dramatic situations
   B. depend on scenery owned by the actors themselves
   C. have the actors shift the scenery
   D. create atmosphere through the dialogue
   E. restrict backgrounds to familiar types of scenes

2. In comparison with actors of Shakespeare's time, actors of today   2.____

   A. carry the settings in their words
   B. pitch their voices in a lower key
   C. depend more on elaborate settings
   D. have to do more to make the setting clear
   E. use many gestures

3. The theme of this paragraph is   3.____

   A. the scenery of the Elizabethan stage
   B. the importance of actors in the Shakespearean drama
   C. the influence of the Elizabethan stage on Shakespeare's style
   D. the importance of words
   E. suitable gestures for the Elizabethan stage

KEY (CORRECT ANSWERS)

1. D
2. C
3. C

TEST 13

DIRECTIONS: In the passages that follow, each question or incomplete statement that follows each passage is followed by several suggested answers or completions. Select the one that BEST answers the question or completes the statement. Base your choice in each case on the materials given and on your own understanding of the subject matter.

It is no secret that I am not one of those naturalists who suffer from cities, or affect to do so, nor do I find a city unnatural or uninteresting, or a rubbish heap of follies. It has always seemed to me that there is something more than mechanically admirable about a train that arrives on time, a fire department that comes when you call it, a light that leaps into the room at a touch, and a clinic that will fight for the health of a penniless man and mass for him the agencies of mercy, the x-ray, the precious radium, the anesthetics and the surgical skill. For, beyond any pay these services receive, stands out the pride in perfect performance. And above all, I admire the noble impersonality of civilization that does not inquire where the recipient stands on religion or politics or race. I call this beauty, and I call it spirit—not some mystical soulfulness that nobody can define, but the spirit of man, that has been a million years a-growing.

1. The author implies that efficient operation of public utilities is

    A. expensive
    B. of no special interest
    C. admired by most naturalists
    D. mechanically commendable
    E. spiritual in quality

2. The aspect of city life MOST commendable to this author is its

    A. punctuality   B. free benefits
    C. impartial service   D. mechanical improvement
    E. health clinics

3. The author makes a defense of

    A. cities   B. prompt trains
    C. rural life   D. nature
    E. free clinics

4. The services rendered by city agencies are given

    A. only for pay
    B. on time
    C. only to people having a certain political allegiance
    D. to everybody
    E. to the spirit of man

5. The theme of this paragraph is

    A. the spirit of the city
    B. advantages of a city home
    C. disagreement among naturalists
    D. admirable characteristics of cities
    E. tolerance in the city

145

2 (#13)

KEY (CORRECT ANSWERS)

1. E
2. C
3. A
4. D
5. D

———

TEST 14

DIRECTIONS: In the passages that follow, each question or incomplete statement that follows each passage is followed by several suggested answers or completions. Select the one that BEST answers the question or completes the statement. Base your choice in each case on the materials given and on your own understanding of the subject matter.

The annual survey of chemistry published by the American Chemical Society attributes the vast change in warfare to the airplane and, above all, to the motor fuels of today. We never think of gasoline as an explosive, yet it has to some extent taken the place of the artillery propellants of a quarter of a century ago. A bomber is hardly a gun, but it certainly performs the function of one, with a range of many hundred miles.

About fifteen years ago, we began to hear of iso-octane, a fuel used to measure antiknock qualities of high-compression gasoline. It was ideal for airplanes but quantity production was not practical Now we make lakes of it. Its performance is so remarkable that the planes propelled by it can carry loads that would have been inconceivable only ten years ago. As a result, octane numbers and indexes of antiknock properties have lost much of their former significance. It will probably be necessary to adopt some new standard. If we relate size and weight of engine to octane number, a truer picture of what aviation fuels really are is obtained. For each pound of weight, aviation engines of today produce, respectively, 100 percent and 50 percent more power than could those of 1918 and 1930.

1. The writer suggests that gasoline may be considered an explosive because

   A. it produces high compression
   B. modern bombing planes are essentially long-range guns
   C. guns now have greater range
   D. iso-octane is now manufactured in quantity
   E. it has replaced explosives in cannons

2. The proposed standard for measuring the quality of motor fuels is the

   A. ratio of power to weight
   B. antiknock index
   C. iso-octane number
   D. load-carrying ability
   E. relation of engine weight and size to octane number

3. Per pound of weight, the average engine now produces

   A. very much iso-octane
   B. high compression
   C. twice as much power as in 1930
   D. double the power of 1918
   E. 100 percent efficiency

2 (#14)

4. The theme of this selection is   4._____
   A. the chemist speeds the airplane
   B. mass production of iso-octane
   C. improving the gasoline engine
   D. changing methods in warfare
   E. gasoline as an explosive

KEY (CORRECT ANSWERS)

1. B
2. E
3. D
4. A

TEST 15

DIRECTIONS: In the passages that follow, each question or incomplete statement that follows each passage is followed by several suggested answers or completions. Select the one that BEST answers the question or completes the statement. Base your choice in each case on the materials given and on your own understanding of the subject matter.

Once the rivers of America slid undisturbed between their banks, save when a birch canoe, manned by stolid Indians, sewed a narrow seam in the water. Then came a day when our rivers were broad highways filled with packets, lumber rafts, and houseboats. There were years when the rivers languished, deserted by the great commerce they had carried; years, too, of floods and devastation. Today, there is a difference. Efforts are being made to tame the untamed, to yoke the slow-sliding rivers to useful purpose. Dams are being built that will end the tragic flooding of the lowlands. Wasteful torrents are being taught economy, taught to irrigate the lands that lie fallow, needing only water to bring them to fruitfulness. The life-giving fluid to renewed utility is being fed into these rivers of ours, and they are again becoming a vital and integral part of our economy.

1. A MAJOR reason for flood control is

    A. provision of suitable streams for the Indians
    B. profits for the public utilities
    C. conservation of farming areas
    D. relief of unemployment
    E. restoring river commerce

2. America's rivers have

    A. been a steady commercial asset
    B. helped protect us against invasion
    C. brought serious destruction through floods
    D. alternated frequently between periods of usefulness and of destruction or neglect
    E. suffered complete neglect as railroads developed

3. Failing to utilize a country's rivers

    A. is economically wasteful
    B. makes the rivers sluggish
    C. restores their scenic beauty
    D. renews their picturesque traffic
    E. causes wasteful torrents

4. For the safety of property and people, rivers must be

    A. made into highways
    B. used for irrigation
    C. allowed to lie fallow
    D. utilized for commerce
    E. brought under control

5. The theme of this paragraph is
   A. from Indian canoe to modern boat
   B. conservation and our rivers
   C. the utility of water
   D. changing river traffic
   E. rivers, dams, and the public utilities

KEY (CORRECT ANSWERS)

1. C
2. C
3. A
4. E
5. B

Interpretation of Reading Materials in the Natural Sciences
EXAMINATION SECTION
TEST 1
PASSAGE

The higher forms of plants and animals, such as seed plants and vertebrates, are similar or alike in many respects but decidedly different in others. For example, both of these groups of organisms carry on digestion, respiration, reproduction, conduction, growth, and exhibit sensitivity to various stimuli. On the other hand, a number of basic differences are evident. Plants have no excretory systems comparable to those of animals. Plants have no heart or similar pumping organ. Plants are very limited in their movements. Plants have nothing similar to the animal nervous system. In addition, animals cannot synthesize carbohydrates from inorganic substances. Animals do not have special regions of growth, comparable to terminal and lateral meristems in plants, which persist throughout the life span of the organism. And finally, the animal cell wall in only a membrane, while plant cell walls are more rigid, usually thicker, and may be composed of such substances as cellulose, lignin, pectin, cutin, and suberin. These characteristics are important to an understanding of living organisms and their functions and should, consequently, be carefully considered in plant and animal studies.

1. Which of the following do animals lack?

   A. Ability to react to stimuli
   B. Ability to conduct substances from one place to another
   C. Reproduction by gametes
   D. A cell membrane
   E. A terminal growth region

2. Which of the following statements is FALSE?

   A. Animal cell walls are composed of cellulose.
   B. Plants grow as long as they live.
   C. Plants produce sperms and eggs.
   D. All vertebrates have hearts.
   E. Wood is dead at maturity.

3. Respiration in plants take place

   A. only during the day
   B. only in the presence of carbon dioxide
   C. both day and night
   D. only at night
   E. only in the presence of certain stimuli

4. An example of a vertebrate is the

   A. earthworm   B. starfish   C. amoeba
   D. cow   E. insect

1.____

2.____

3.____

4.____

5. Which of the following statements is TRUE?

    A. All animals eat plants as a source of food.
    B. Respiration, in many ways, is the reverse of photosyn-thesis.
    C. Man is an invertebrate animal
    D. Since plants have no hearts, they cannot develop high pressures in their cells.
    E. Plants cannot move.

6. Which of the following do plants lack?

    A. A means of movement
    B. Pumping structures
    C. Special regions of growth
    D. Reproduction by gametes
    E. A digestive process

7. A substance that can be synthesized by green plants but not by animals is

    A. protein   B. cellulose   C. carbon dioxide
    D. uric acid   E. water

KEY (CORRECT ANSWERS)

1. E   5. B
2. A   6. B
3. C   7. B
4. D

TEST 2
PASSAGE

The discovery of antitoxin and its specific antagonistic effect upon toxin furnished an opportunity for the accurate investigation of the relationship of a bacterial antigen and its antibody. Toxin-antitoxin reactions were the first immunological processes to which experimental precision could be applied, and the discovery of principles of great importance resulted from such studies. A great deal of the work was done with diphtheria toxin and antitoxin and the facts elucidated with these materials are in principle applicable to similar substances.

The simplest assumption to account for the manner in which an antitoxin renders a toxin innocuous would be that the antitoxin destroys the toxin. Roux and Buchner, however, advanced the opinion that the antitoxin did not act directly upon the toxin, but affected it indirectly through the mediation of tissue cells. Ehrlich, on the other hand, conceived the reaction of toxin and antitoxin as a direct union, analogous to the chemical neutralization of an acid by a base.

The conception of toxin destruction was conclusively refuted by the experiments of Calmette. This observer, working with snake poison, found that the poison itself (unlike most other toxins) possessed the property of resisting heat to 100° C, while its specific antitoxin, like other antitoxins, was destroyed at or about 70° C. Nontoxic mixtures of the two substances, when subjected to heat, regained their toxic properties. The natural inference from these observations was that the toxin in the original mixture had not been destroyed, but had been merely inactivated by the presence of the antitoxin and again set free after destruction of the antitoxin by heat.

1. Both toxins and antitoxins ordinarily

    A. are completely destroyed at body temperatures
    B. are extremely resistant to heat
    C. can exist only in combination
    D. are destroyed at 180° F
    E. are products of nonliving processes

2. MOST toxins can be destroyed by

    A. bacterial action
    B. salt solutions
    C. boiling
    D. diphtheria antitoxin
    E. other toxins

3. Very few disease organisms release a true toxin into the bloodstream. It would follow, then, that

    A. studies of snake venom reactions have no value
    B. studies of toxin-antitoxin reactions are of little importance
    C. the treatment of most diseases must depend upon information obtained from study of a few
    D. antitoxin plays an important part in the body defense against the great majority of germs
    E. only toxin producers are dangerous

4. A person becomes susceptible to infection again immediately after recovering from

    A. mumps   B. tetanus   C. diphtheria
    D. smallpox   E. tuberculosis

5. City people are more frequently immune to communicable diseases than country people are because

    A. country people eat better food
    B. city doctors are better than country doctors
    C. the air is more healthful in the country
    D. country people have fewer contacts with disease carriers
    E. there are more doctors in the city than in the country

6. The substances that provide us with immunity to disease are found in the body in the

    A. blood serum   B. gastric juice
    C. urine   D. white blood cells
    E. red blood cells

7. A person ill with diphtheria would MOST likely be treated with

    A. diphtheria toxin   B. diphtheria toxoid
    C. dead diphtheria germs   D. diphtheria antitoxin
    E. live diphtheria germs

8. To determine susceptibility to diphtheria, an individual may be given the _____ test.

    A. Wassermann   B. Schick   C. Widal
    D. Dick   E. Kahn

9. Since few babies under six months of age contract diphtheria, young babies PROBABLY

    A. are never exposed to diphtheria germs
    B. have high body temperatures that destroy the toxin if acquired
    C. acquire immunity from their mothers
    D. acquire immunity from their fathers
    E. are too young to become infected

10. Calmette's findings

    A. contradicted both Roux and Buchner's opinion and Ehrlich's conception
    B. contradicted Roux and Buchner, but supported Ehrlich
    C. contradicted Ehrlich, but supported Roux and Buchner
    D. were consistent with both theories
    E. had no bearing on the point at issue

KEY (CORRECT ANSWERS)

1. D   6. A
2. C   7. D
3. C   8. B
4. E   9. C
5. D   10. D

TEST 3
PASSAGE

Sodium chloride, being by far the largest constituent of the mineral matter of the blood, assumes special significance in the regulation of water exchanges in the organism. And, as Cannon has emphasized repeatedly, these latter are more extensive and more important than may at first thought appear. He points out *there are a number of circulations of the fluid out of the body and back again, without loss.* Thus, for example, it is estimated that from a quart and one-half of water daily *leaves the body* when it enters the mouth as saliva, another one or two quarts are passed out as gastric juice, and perhaps the same amount is contained in the bile and the secretions of the pancreas and the intestinal wall. This large volume of water enters the digestive processes; and practically all of it is reabsorbed through the intestinal wall, where it performs the equally important function of carrying in the digestive foodstuffs. These and other instances of what Cannon calls *the conservative use of water in our bodies* involve essentially osmotic pressure relationships in which the concentration of sodium chloride plays an important part.

1. This passage implies that

    A. the contents of the alimentary canal are not to be considered within the body
    B. sodium chloride does not actually enter the body
    C. every particle of water ingested is used over and over again
    D. water cannot be absorbed by the body unless it contains sodium chloride
    E. substances can pass through the intestinal wall in only one direction

2. According to this passage, which of the following processes requires most water? The

    A. absorption of digested foods
    B. secretion of gastric juice
    C. secretion of saliva
    D. production of bile
    E. concentration of sodium chloride solution

3. A body fluid that is NOT saline is

    A. blood   B. urine   C. bile
    D. gastric juice   E. saliva

4. An organ that functions as a storage reservoir from which large quantities of water are reabsorbed into the body is the

    A. kidney   B. liver   C. large intestine
    D. mouth   E. pancreas

5. Water is reabsorbed into the body by the process of

    A. secretion   B. excretion   C. digestion
    D. osmosis   E. oxidation

6. Digested food enters the body PRINCIPALLY through the

    A. mouth   B. liver   C. villi
    D. pancreas   E. stomach

7. The metallic element found in the blood in compound form and present there in larger quantities than any other metallic element is

   A. iron
   B. calcium
   C. magnesium
   D. chlorine
   E. sodium

8. An organ that removes water from the body and prevents its reabsorption for use in the body processes is the

   A. pancreas
   B. liver
   C. small intestine
   D. lungs
   E. large intestine

9. In which of the following processes is sodium chloride removed MOST rapidly from the body?

   A. Digestion
   B. Breathing
   C. Oxidation
   D. Respiration
   E. Perspiration

10. Which of the following liquids would pass from the alimentary canal into the blood MOST rapidly?

    A. A dilute solution of sodium chloride in water
    B. Gastric juice
    C. A concentrated solution of sodium chloride in water
    D. Digested food
    E. Distilled water

11. The reason why it is unsafe to drink ocean water even under conditions of extreme thirst is that it

    A. would reduce the salinity of the blood to a dangerous level
    B. contains dangerous disease germs
    C. contains poisonous salts
    D. would greatly increase the salinity of the blood
    E. would cause salt crystals to form in the bloodstream

KEY (CORRECT ANSWERS)

1. A
2. A
3. D
4. C
5. D
6. C
7. E
8. D
9. E
10. E

TEST 4
PASSAGE

In the days of sailing ships, when voyages were long and uncertain, provisions for many months were stored without refrigeration in the holds of the ships. Naturally, no fresh or perishable foods could be included. Toward the end of particularly long voyages, the crews of such ships became ill and often many died from scurvy. Many men, both scientific and otherwise, tried to devise a cure for scurvy. Among the latter was John Hall, a son-in-law of William Shakespeare, who cured some cases of scurvy by administering a sour brew made from scurvy grass and watercress.

The next step was the suggestion of William Harvey that scurvy could be prevented by giving the men lemon juice. He thought that the beneficial substance was the acid contained in the fruit.

The third step was taken by Dr. James Lind, an English naval surgeon, who performed the following experiment with 12 sailors, all of whom were sick with scurvy: Each was given the same diet, except that four of the men received small amounts of dilute sulfuric acid, four others were given vinegar, and the remaining four were given lemons. Only those who received the fruit recovered.

1. Credit for solving the problem described above belongs to

    A. Hall, because he first devised a cure for scurvy
    B. Harvey, because he first proposed a solution of the problem
    C. Lind, because he proved the solution by means of an experiment
    D. both Harvey and Lind, because they found that lemons are more effective than scurvy grass or watercress
    E. all three men, because each made some contribution

2. A good substitute for lemons in the treatment of scurvy is

    A. fresh eggs   B. tomato juice
    C. cod-liver oil   D. liver
    E. whole-wheat bread

3. The number of control groups that Dr. Lind used in his experiment was

    A. one   B. two   C. three   D. four   E. none

4. A substance that will turn blue litmus red is

    A. aniline   B. lye   C. ice
    D. vinegar   E. table salt

5. The hypothesis tested by Lind was:

    A. Lemons contain some substance not present in vinegar
    B. Citric acid is the most effective treatment for scurvy
    C. Lemons contain some unknown acid that will cure scurvy
    D. Some specific substance, rather than acids in general, is needed to cure scurvy
    E. The substance needed to cure scurvy is found only in lemons

6. A problem that Lind's experiment did NOT solve was: 6.____

   A. Will citric acid alone cure scurvy?
   B. Will lemons cure scurvy?
   C. Will either sulfuric acid or vinegar cure scurvy?
   D. Are all substances that contain acids equally effective as a treatment for scurvy?
   E. Are lemons more effective than either vinegar or sulfuric acid in the treatment of scurvy?

7. The PRIMARY purpose of a controlled scientific experiment is to 7.____

   A. get rid of superstitions
   B. prove a hypothesis is correct
   C. disprove a theory that is false
   D. determine whether a hypothesis is true or false
   E. discover new facts

KEY (CORRECT ANSWERS)

1. E   5. D
2. B   6. A
3. B   7. D
4. D

TEST 5
PASSAGE

Photosynthesis is a complex process with many intermediate steps. Ideas differ greatly as to the details of these steps, but the general nature of the process and its outcome are well established. Water, usually from the soil, is conducted through the xylem of root, stem, and leaf to the chlorophyl-containing cells of a leaf. In consequence of the abundance of water within the latter cells, their walls are saturated with water. Carbon dioxide, diffusing from the air through the stomata and into the intercellular spaces of the leaf, comes into contact with the water in the walls of the cells which adjoin the intercellular spaces. The carbon dioxide becomes dissolved in the water in these walls, and in solution diffuses through the walls and the plasma membranes into the cells. By the agency of chlorophyl in the chloroplasts of the cells, the energy of light is transformed into chemical energy. This chemical energy is used to decompose the carbon dioxide and water, and the products of their decomposition are recombined into a new compound. The compound first formed is successively built up into more and more complex substances until finally a sugar is produced.

1. The union of carbon dioxide and water to form starch results in an excess of

   A. hydrogen
   B. carbon
   C. oxygen
   D. carbon monoxide
   E. hydrogen peroxide

2. Synthesis of carbohydrates takes place

   A. in the stomata
   B. in the intercellular spaces of leaves
   C. in the walls of plant cells
   D. within the plasma membranes of plant cells
   E. within plant cells that contain chloroplasts

3. In the process of photosynthesis, chlorophyl acts as a

   A. carbohydrate
   B. source of carbon dioxide
   C. catalyst
   D. source of chemical energy
   E. plasma membrane

4. In which of the following places are there the GREATEST number of hours in which photosynthesis can take place during the month of December?

   A. Buenos Aires, Argentina
   B. Caracas, Venezuela
   C. Fairbanks, Alaska
   D. Quito, Ecuador
   E. Calcutta, India

5. During photosynthesis, molecules of carbon dioxide enter the stomata of leaves because

   A. the molecules are already in motion
   B. they are forced through the stomata by the sun's rays
   C. chlorophyl attracts them
   D. a chemical change takes place in the stomata
   E. oxygen passes out through the stomata

6. Besides food manufacture, another useful result of photosynthesis is that it

    A. aids in removing poisonous gases from the air
    B. helps to maintain the existing proportion of gases in the air
    C. changes complex compounds into simpler compounds
    D. changes certain waste products into hydrocarbons
    E. changes chlorophyl into useful substances

7. A process that is almost the exact reverse of photosynthesis is the

    A. rusting of iron
    B. burning of wood
    C. digestion of starch
    D. ripening of fruit
    E. storage of food in seeds

8. The leaf of the tomato plant will be unable to carry on photosynthesis if the

    A. upper surface of the leaf is coated with vaseline
    B. upper surface of the leaf is coated with lampblack
    C. lower surface of the leaf is coated with lard
    D. leaf is placed in an atmosphere of pure carbon dioxide
    E. entire leaf is coated with lime

KEY (CORRECT ANSWERS)

1. C   5. A
2. E   6. B
3. C   7. B
4. A   8. C

TEST 6
PASSAGE

The British pressure suit was made in two pieces and joined around the middle in contrast to the other suits, which were one-piece suits with a removable helmet. Oxygen was supplied through a tube, and a container of soda lime absorbed carbon dioxide and water vapor. The pressure was adjusted to a maximum of 2 1/2 pounds per square inch (130 millimeters) higher than the surrounding air. Since pure oxygen was used, this produced a partial pressure of 130 millimeters, which is sufficient to sustain the flier at any altitude.

Using this pressure suit, the British established a world's altitude record of 49,944 feet in 1936 and succeeded in raising it to 53,937 feet the following year. The pressure suit is a compromise solution to the altitude problem. Full sea-level pressure cannot be maintained, as the suit would be so rigid that the flier could not move arms or legs. Hence, a pressure one-third to one-fifth that of sea level has been used. Because of these lower pressures, oxygen has been used to raise the partial pressure of alveolar oxygen to normal.

1. The MAIN constituent of air not admitted to the pressure suit described was   1.____

   A. oxygen   B. nitrogen   C. water vapor
   D. carbon dioxide E. hydrogen

2. The pressure within the suit exceeded that of the surrounding air by an amount equal to   2.____
   130 millimeters of

   A. mercury   B. water   C. air
   D. oxygen   E. carbon dioxide

3. The normal atmospheric pressure at sea level is _____ mm.   3.____

   A. 130   B. 250   C. 760   D. 1000   E. 1300

4. The water vapor that was absorbed by the soda lime came from   4.____

   A. condensation
   B. the union of oxygen with carbon dioxide
   C. body metabolism
   D. the air within the pressure suit
   E. water particles in the upper air

5. The HIGHEST altitude that has been reached with the British pressure suit is about   5.____
   _____ miles.

   A. 130   B. 2 1/2   C. 6   D. 10   E. 5

6. If the pressure suit should develop a leak, the   6.____

   A. oxygen supply would be cut off
   B. suit would fill up with air instead of oxygen
   C. pressure within the suit would drop to zero
   D. pressure within the suit would drop to that of the surrounding air
   E. suit would become so rigid that the flier would be unable to move arms or legs

7. The reason why oxygen helmets are unsatisfactory for use in efforts to set higher altitude records is that

    A. it is impossible to maintain a tight enough fit at the neck
    B. oxygen helmets are too heavy
    C. they do not conserve the heat of the body as pressure suits do
    D. if a parachute jump becomes necessary, it cannot be made while such a helmet is being worn
    E. oxygen helmets are too rigid

8. The pressure suit is termed a compromise solution because

    A. it is not adequate for stratosphere flying
    B. aviators cannot stand sea-level pressure at high altitudes
    C. some suits are made in two pieces, others in one
    D. other factors than maintenance of pressure have to be accommodated
    E. full atmospheric pressure cannot be maintained at high altitudes

9. The passage implies that

    A. the air pressure at 49,944 feet is approximately the same as it is at 53,937 feet
    B. pressure cabin planes are not practical at extremely high altitudes
    C. a flier's oxygen requirement is approximately the same at high altitudes as it is at sea level
    D. one-piece pressure suits with removable helmets are unsafe
    E. a normal alveolar oxygen supply is maintained if the air pressure is between one-third and one-fifth that of sea level

KEY (CORRECT ANSWERS)

1.	B	6.	D
2.	A	7.	D
3.	C	8.	E
4.	C	9.	C
5.	D		

TEST 7
PASSAGE

The formed elements of the blood are the red corpuscles or erythrocytes, the white corpuscles or leucocytes, the blood platelets, and the so-called blood dust or hemoconiae. Together, these constitute 30-40 percent by volume of the whole blood, the remainder being taken up by the plasma. In man, there are normally 5,000,000 red cells per cubic millimeter of blood; the count is somewhat lower in women. Variations occur frequently, especially after exercise or a heavy meal, or at high altitudes. Except in camels, which have elliptical corpuscles, the shape of the mammalian corpuscle is that of a circular, nonnucleated, bi-concave disk. The average diameter usually given is 7.7 microns, a value obtained by examining dried preparations of blood and considered by Ponder to be too low. Ponder's own observations, made on red cells in the fresh state, show the human corpuscle to have an average diameter of 8.8 microns. When circulating in the blood vessels, the red cell does not maintain a fixed shape but changes its form constantly, especially in the small capillaries. The red blood corpuscles are continually undergoing destruction, new corpuscles being formed to replace them. The average life of red corpuscles has been estimated by various investigators to be between three and six weeks. Preceding destruction, changes in the composition of the cells are believed to occur which render them less resistant. In the process of destruction, the lipids of the membrane are dissolved and the hemoglobin which is liberated is the most important, though probably not the only, source of bilirubin. The belief that the liver is the only site of red cell destruction is no longer generally held. The leucocytes, of which there are several forms, usually number between 7000 and 9000 per cubic millimeter of blood. These increase in number in disease, particularly when there is bacterial infection.

1. Leukemia is a disease involving the

   A. red cells B. white cells C. plasma
   D. blood platelets E. blood dust

2. *The erythrocytes in the blood are increased in number after a heavy meal.* The paragraph implies that this

   A. is true
   B. holds only for camels
   C. is not true
   D. may be true
   E. depends on the number of white cells

3. When blood is dried, the red cells

   A. contract B. remain the same size
   C. disintegrate D. expand
   E. become elliptical

4. Ponder is PROBABLY classified as a professional

   A. pharmacist B. physicist C. psychologist
   D. physiologist E. psychiatrist

5. The term *erythema,* when applied to skin conditions, signifies

   A. redness B. swelling C. irritation
   D. pain E. roughness

163

6. Lipids are insoluble in water and soluble in such solvents as ether, chloroform, and benzene.
It may be inferred that the membranes of red cells MOST closely resemble

   A. egg white   B. sugar   C. bone
   D. butter   E. cotton fiber

7. Analysis of a sample of blood yields cell counts of 4,800,000 erythrocytes and 16,000 leucocytes per cubic millimeter.
These data suggest that the patient from whom the blood was taken

   A. is anemic
   B. has been injuriously invaded by germs
   C. has been exposed to high-pressure air
   D. has a normal cell count
   E. has lost a great deal of blood

8. Bilirubin, a bile pigment, is

   A. an end product of several different reactions
   B. formed only in the liver
   C. formed from the remnants of the cell membranes of erythrocytes
   D. derived from hemoglobin exclusively
   E. a precursor of hemoglobin

9. Bancroft found that the blood count of the natives in the Peruvian Andes differed from that usually accepted as normal. The blood PROBABLY differed in respect to

   A. leucocytes   B. blood platelets
   C. cell shapes   D. erythrocytes
   E. hemoconiae

10. Hemoglobin is probably NEVER found

   A. free in the bloodstream
   B. in the red cells
   C. in women's blood
   D. in the blood after exercise
   E. in the leucocytes

KEY (CORRECT ANSWERS)

1. B   6. D
2. D   7. B
3. A   8. A
4. D   9. D
5. A 10. E

TEST 8
PASSAGE

Chemical investigations show that during muscle contraction, the store of organic phosphates in the muscle fibers is altered as energy is released. In doing so, the organic phosphates (chiefly adenosine triphosphate and phospho-creatine) are transformed anaerobically to organic compounds plus phosphates. As soon as the organic phosphates begin to break down in muscle contraction, the glycogen in the muscle fibers also transforms into lactic acid plus free energy; this energy the muscle fiber uses to return the organic compounds plus phosphates into high-energy organic phosphates ready for another contraction. In the presence of oxygen, the lactic acid from the glycogen decomposition is changed also. About one-fifth of it is oxidized to form water and carbon dioxide and to yield another supply of energy. This time the energy is used to transform the remaining four-fifths of the lactic acid into glycogen again.

1. The energy for muscle contraction comes directly from the

    A. breakdown of the organic phosphates
    B. resynthesis of adenosine triphosphate
    C. breakdown of glycogen into lactic acid
    D. oxidation of lactic acid

2. Lactic acid does not accumulate in a muscle that is(has)

    A. in a state of lacking oxygen
    B. an ample supply of oxygen
    C. in a state of fatigue
    D. repeatedly being stimulated

3. The energy for the resynthesis of adenosine triphosphate and phosphocreatine comes from the

    A. oxidation of lactic acid
    B. synthesis of organic phosphates
    C. change from glycogen to lactic acid
    D. resynthesis of glycogen

4. The energy for the resynthesis of glycogen comes from the

    A. breakdown of organic phosphates
    B. resynthesis of organic phosphates
    C. change occurring in one-fifth of the lactic acid
    D. change occurring in four-fifths of the lactic acid

5. The breakdown of the organic phosphates into organic compounds plus phosphates is an _____ reaction.

    A. anabolic   B. aerobic
    C. endothermic   D. anaerobic

KEY (CORRECT ANSWERS)

1. A
2. B
3. C
4. C
5. D

TEST 9

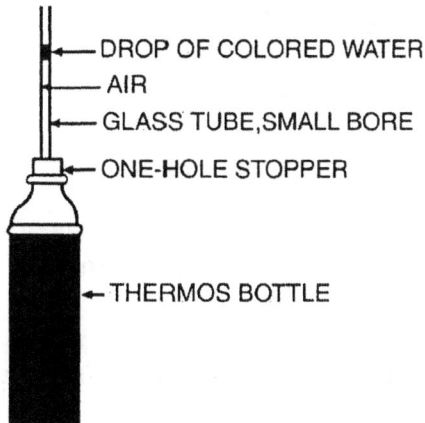

1. The device shown in the diagram above indicates changes that are measured more accurately by a(n)

   A. thermometer B. hygrometer C. anemometer
   D. hydrometer   E. barometer

   1.____

2. If the device is placed in a cold refrigerator for 72 hours, which of the following is MOST likely to happen?

   A. The stopper will be forced out of the bottle.
   B. The drop of water will evaporate.
   C. The drop will move downward.
   D. The drop will move upward.
   E. No change will take place.

   2.____

3. When the device was carried in an elevator from the first floor to the sixth floor of a building, the drop of colored water moved about $\frac{1}{4}$ inch in the tube.
   Which of the following is MOST probably true?
   The drop moved

   A. downward because there was a decrease in the air pressure
   B. upward because there was an increase in the air pressure
   C. downward because there was an increase in the air temperature
   D. upward because there was an increase in the air temperature
   E. downward because there was an increase in the air temperature and a decrease in the pressure

   3.____

4. The part of a thermos bottle into which liquids are poured consists of

   A. a single-walled, metal flask coated with silver
   B. two flasks, one of glass and one of silvered metal
   C. two silvered-glass flasks separated by a vacuum
   D. two silver flasks separated by a vacuum
   E. a single-walled, glass flask with a silver-colored coating

   4.____

167

5. The thermos bottle is MOST similar in principle to

   A. the freezing unit in an electric refrigerator
   B. radiant heaters
   C. solar heating systems
   D. storm windows
   E. a thermostatically controlled heating system

6. In a plane flying at an altitude where the air pressure is only half the normal pressure at sea level, the plane's altimeter should read approximately _____ feet.

   A. 3000   B. 9000   C. 18000   D. 27000   E. 60000

7. Which of the following is the POOREST conductor of heat?

   A. Air under a pressure of 1.5 pounds per square inch
   B. Air under a pressure of 15 pounds per square inch
   C. Unsilvered glass
   D. Silvered glass
   E. Silver

KEY (CORRECT ANSWERS)

1. A   5. D
2. C   6. C
3. B   7. A
4. C

TEST 10

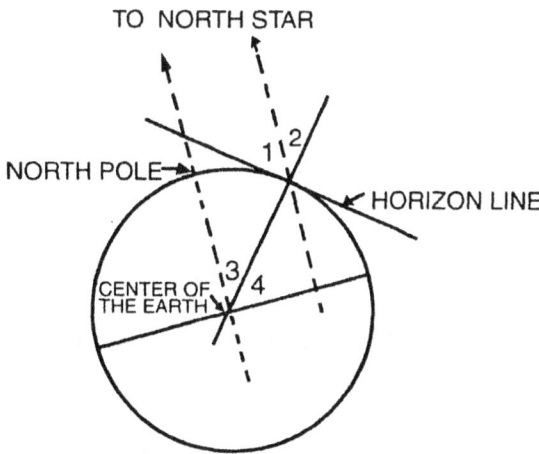

The latitude of any point on the earth's surface is the angle between a plumb line dropped to the center of the earth from that point and the plane of the earth's equator. Since it is impossible to go to the center of the earth to measure latitude, the latitude of any point may be determined indirectly as shown in the accompanying diagram.

It will be recalled that the axis of the earth, if extended outward, passes very near the North Star. Since the North Star is, for all practical purposes, infinitely distant, the line of sight to the North Star of an observer on the surface of the earth is virtually parallel with the earth's axis. Angle 1, then, in the diagram represents the angular distance of the North Star above the horizon.

Angle 2 is equal to angle 3, because when two parallel lines are intersected by a straight line, the corresponding angles are equal. Angle 1 plus angle 2 is a right angle and so is angle 3 plus angle 4. Therefore, angle 1 equals angle 4 because when equals are subtracted from equals, the results are equal.

1. If an observer finds that the angular distance of the North Star above the horizon is 30°, his latitude is _____ ° N.

   A. 15   B. 30   C. 60   D. 90   E. 120

2. To an observer on the equator, the North Star would be _____ the horizon.

   A. 30° above   B. 60° above   C. 90° above
   D. on   E. below

3. To an observer on the Arctic Circle, the North Star would be

   A. directly overhead   B. 23 1/2° above the horizon
   C. 66 1/2° above the horizon   D. on the horizon
   E. below the horizon

4. The distance around the earth along a certain parallel of latitude is 3600 miles. At that latitude, how many miles are there in one degree of longitude? _____ mile(s).

   A. 1   B. 10   C. 30   D. 69   E. 100

5. At which of the following latitudes would the sun be directly overhead at noon on June 21?

   A. 0°   B. 23 1/2°S   C. 23 1/2°N   D. 66 1/2°N   E. 66 1/2°S

6. On March 21, the number of hours of daylight at places on the Arctic Circle is

   A. none   B. 8   C. 12   D. 16   E. 24

7. The distance from the equator to the 45th parallel, measured along a meridian, is APPROXIMATELY _____ miles.

   A. 450   B. 900   C. 1250   D. 3125   E. 6250

8. The difference in time between the meridians that pass through longitude 45° E and longitude 105° W is _____ hours.

   A. 6   B. 2   C. 8   D. 4   E. 10

9. Which of the following is NOT a great circle or part of a great circle?

   A. Arctic Circle
   B. 100th meridian
   C. equator
   D. shortest distance between New York and London
   E. Greenwich meridian

10. At which of the following places does the sun set EARLIEST on June 21?

    A. Montreal, Canada
    B. Santiago, Chile
    C. Mexico City, Mexico
    D. Lima, Peru
    E. Manila, P.I.

KEY (CORRECT ANSWERS)

1. B   6. C
2. D   7. D
3. C   8. E
4. B   9. A
5. C   10. B

INTERPRETATION OF READING MATERIALS IN THE NATURAL SCIENCES
EXAMINATION SECTION
TEST 1
PASSAGE

Less than 100 years ago, a fabulous *new era* of medicine—or so it was supposed to be—was ushered in by the *wonder drugs,* the germkillers extraordinary. Here, it seemed, were the ultimate weapons that could rout hordes of pestilential bugs. Once and for all, there was to be an end to the menace of dozens of infectious diseases. It was a heady dream—but it grossly underestimated the enemy.

The infections are still with us. The bugs have been fighting back. Their counter-attacks, indeed, have sometimes been so vicious that scientists have been forced to go to new lengths to try to repulse them. The battle today seesaws.

One of the latest examples of bug turnabout was noted a few weeks ago when tuberculosis experts met at an isoniazid *reunion* luncheon to take a look at that drug-ten years after it had been hailed as the conqueror of TB and after the first desperately ill patients to receive it got up out of their beds and danced exuberantly in hospital corridors. Currently, as many as 6 percent of TB patients are beyond help by isoniazid—infected with strains of tubercle bacilli impervious to the drug—and resistance to isoniazid is growing.

The trend, not yet calamitous, follows explosive epidemics produced by *hospital staph* bacteria that sneer at penicillin and many other antibiotics. There have been-and continue to be-troubles with numerous other disease organisms despite, and even because of, antibiotics.

As early as 1954, University of Michigan physicians, noting the ability, evident even then, of some germs to live with highly vaunted antibiotics, suggested that *man may be sitting on a time bomb, capable of * * * shattering the illusion of medical miracles* * *.*

1. What is meant by the statement in the passage that *man may be sitting on a time bomb*? 1.____

    A. The *bugs* may progressively develop resistances to the drugs.
    B. The idea of medical miracles is an illusion.
    C. There is a great chance that TB could develop into a more difficult disease to treat.
    D. As the *bugs* get stronger, the disease becomes more prevalent.
    E. One day the miracle drugs which have been discovered will cause more harm than good.

2. *The bugs have been fighting back,* states the passage. 2.____
   This means:

    A. Higher doses of a particular drug become required.
    B. Patients develop an immunity to the disease.
    C. The *bugs* increase in number as a result of the drug.
    D. Some people have no reaction to the antibiotics.
    E. As the drugs become stronger, so do the *bugs*.

3. *Wonder drugs* are not the ultimate weapon because

   A. it remains for a drug to be discovered which the *bugs* cannot fight
   B. they only treat one disease, not all
   C. they are limited to certain people, i.e., many are allergic
   D. they sometimes carry their own diseases, with which they replace the ones they cure
   E. scientists deny the existence of a foreseeable day when the *ultimate weapon* against disease can be evolved

4. Wonder drugs were discovered

   A. by Jonas Salk
   B. 20 years ago
   C. less than five decades ago
   D. over a century ago
   E. as a by-product of research done in nuclear physics

5. *Animalcules* is another word for

   A. antibiotics   B. bacteria   C. drugs
   D. penicillin   E. oreomycin

6. Scientists realistically predict the day when

   A. there will be no more disease
   B. better drugs will be made
   C. the *bugs* may develop a resistance to all antibiotics
   D. antibiotics will not be needed to cure disease
   E. all bacteria will be conquered

KEY (CORRECT ANSWERS)

1. A   4. C
2. E   5. B
3. A   6. C

EXPLANATION OF ANSWERS

1. **CORRECT ANSWER: A**

   B is irrelevant; C is not stated; D is not stated or implied; E is pure conjecture and not inferred in the passage.

2. **CORRECT ANSWER: E**

   Items A and D are sometimes true but bear no relation to the question. C is false. Patients may develop an immunity to the antibiotics, but never to the disease. Therefore, B is false. The proper answer is E: *The battle today seesaws* (last sentence of the second paragraph).

3. **CORRECT ANSWER: A**

   While B and C are factually true, they do not satisfactorily complete the statement. D is scientifically unknown as yet. Item E is false. The correct answer is A (see the last sentence of the first paragraph).

4. **CORRECT ANSWER: C**

   The opening sentence is *Less than 50 years ago....a.... 'new era'....was ushered in by the 'wonder drugs'*. Therefore, C is the correct answer. The other answers are false.

5. **CORRECT ANSWER: B**

   Animalcules is a synonym for bacteria. Therefore, B is the proper answer. The other answers are completely incorrect as they are the substances which fight bacteria.

6. **CORRECT ANSWER: C**

   Though scientists are working constantly to perfect superior drugs, it has been their experience that the *bugs* are progressing in strength faster than the drugs can be improved. (See, particularly, the last paragraph.) Therefore, the correct answer is C.

TEST 2
PASSAGE

BILLINGS, Mont. — A 60-year-old Montanan traced on a map the other day the boundaries of the Bob Marshall Wilderness Area. As he lifted his finger, a smile creased his face. He said:

That's it. It has been pretty well explored for minerals, but you never can tell when somebody might want to try something again. Let's hope nobody can touch it now. It's something that should have been done long ago.

His reference was to the creation of the National Wilderness Preservation System, as set down in Public Law 88577, which went into effect September 3. The act is the compromise of a long and bitter fight to carve out of the national forests and other Federal lands a system that will, in the words of the legislation, *secure for the American people of present and future generations the benefits of an enduring resource of wilderness.*

The compromise was between conservationists and those who would put forest resources to commercial and other-than-wilderness uses.

It pins this down by its definition that a wilderness, *in contrast with those areas where man and his own works dominate the landscape, is hereby recognized as an area where the earth and the community of life are untrammeled by man, where man himself is a visitor who does not remain.*

1. The National Wilderness Preservation System was of great interest because it

    A. went into effect September 3
    B. was a compromise
    C. preserved an important resource
    D. worked hand-in-hand with commerce
    E. allowed for other-than-wilderness uses

2. What is meant by the statement ... *somebody might want to try something again*?

    A. It might be tapped for minerals
    B. Some party might damage the property.
    C. The property's resources might be tapped for commercial purposes.
    D. Building might take place.
    E. The general public might cause forest fires or sanitation problems.

3. *Untrammeled* means

    A. not trampled on
    B. not traveled
    C. something uninvestigated by man
    D. something abused by man
    E. something left in its original condition

4. After reading the passage, one gets the impression that the author

    A. appreciates the beauty of nature
    B. understands the needs of commerce in relation to natural resources
    C. is engaged in a bitter fight

2 (#2)

    D. will secure for the American people an enduring wilderness
    E. is on the side of the conservationists

5. A good title for this passage would be   5.____

    A. THE BOUNDARIES OF THE WILDERNESS
    B. EXPLORING FOR MINERALS
    C. SAVING THE WILDS
    D. HOW COMMERCE MAKES USE OF NATURAL RESOURCES
    E. THE WILDERNESS

6. The TVA, a conservation act, was enacted during the Presidency of   6.____

    A. Theodore Roosevelt   B. Woodrow Wilson
    C. Dwight D. Eisenhower   D. Franklin D. Roosevelt
    E. Harry Truman

KEY (CORRECT ANSWERS)

1.	C	4.	E
2.	C	5.	C
3.	E	6.	D

EXPLANATION OF ANSWERS

1. **CORRECT ANSWER: C**

   Item C is the correct answer, and it is clearly delineated in the quotation contained in paragraph 3, viz., ... *secure for the American people ... an enduring resource of wilderness.*

2. **CORRECT ANSWER: C**

   When the speaker says, *It has been pretty well explored for minerals, but you never can tell when somebody might want to try something again,* he is referring to a similar possibility of an exploitation by industry. This would designate C as the proper answer. Though B, D, and E are possible occurrences, he is not, in this statement, referring to these.

3. **CORRECT ANSWER: E**

   The last clause of the passage indicates that A, B, and C are incorrect because man can visit a wilderness area and leave it *untrammeled*. D is incorrect because it infers the opposite of the word's correct meaning.

4. **CORRECT ANSWER: E**

   The passage is not about the author's love of nature or the needs of commerce, nor does his work match the events or aims suggested in C and D. E would be most suited to his position on natural resources, and is the correct answer.

5. **CORRECT ANSWER: C**

   The best answer presented here would be C. The theme of the passage is in no way related to items B and D. A and E could be considered, but C is much more directly related to the passage.

6. **CORRECT ANSWER: D**

   The correct answer is D, Franklin Roosevelt (1933).

TEST 3
PASSAGE

Where others saw unrelated, individually created flowers or birds or people, he saw a mass of altering, dissolving, and interrelated forms flowing onward through earth's history. Living creatures were like cloud shapes contorted by the winds of time. As it happens, the years have proved him right.

What made Darwin a scientist? Let us ask again in particular because by modern school standards and measurements he was not a very good pupil, let alone a candidate for genius. His career was undecided; he dawdled and misspelled words, enraged his father and, giving up a career in medicine, was packed off to Cambridge with the notion that he might at least learn enough to become a country parson.

We cannot analyze Darwin's entire life, but we can say that his quoted letter to Joseph Hooker is enormously important and revelatory. Charles Darwin was a millionaire of facts but they happened not to be the facts in which the schools of his day were interested. Indeed, he spoke of his Cambridge studies as *next thing to intolerable*. As a result, his formal educational career was no measure of his real capacities. Later, as he remembered his experience in South America, he was to speak of lonely desert travels in which *the whole of my pleasure was derived from what passed in my mind*.

Yet the influences at work upon him were not all of a solitary character. His grandfather Erasmus had entertained evolutionary ideas about which Charles had learned as a youth; a kindly botanist, John Henslow, had obtained for him his post as naturalist on the Beagle. On the outward voyage to South America, Darwin had read Sir Charles Lyell's PRINCIPLES OF GEOLOGY and been convinced by Lyell's then-heretical views that the earth was extremely ancient—a necessary prelude to grasping the slow pace of plant and animal evolution.

1. As opposed to the individually created flowers or birds, Darwin saw

    A. living creatures
    B. masses of altering and dissolving cloud shapes
    C. interrelated forms
    D. people
    E. winds of time

2. The reader can assume from the passage that the author feels a formal education is

    A. necessary even for a candidate for genius
    B. what made Darwin a scientist
    C. not always a measure of real capacities
    D. necessary for a scientist
    E. not able to help a pupil beyond his potential

3. His first ideas about evolution may well have come from

    A. his grandfather
    B. Joseph Hooker
    C. John Henslow
    D. PRINCIPLES OF GEOLOGY
    E. his voyage to South America

4. Sir Charles Lyell's ideas were

   A. about animal evolution
   B. about plant life
   C. unaccepted by his period
   D. Darwin's primary inspiration
   E. extremely ancient

5. A work of Darwin's is

   A. ZOOLOGY OF THE VOYAGE OF THE BEAGLE
   B. ON THE TENDENCY OF VARIETIES TO DEPART INDEFINITELY FROM THE ORIGINAL TYPE
   C. TRAVELS ON THE AMAZON AND THE RIO NEGRO
   D. THE BOTANIC GARDEN
   E. ZOONOMIA

6. The famous Scopes trial brought him into conflict with

   A. William Jennings Bryan   B. Clarence Darrow
   C. the State of Tennessee   D. J.T. Scopes
   E. the State of Kentucky

KEY (CORRECT ANSWERS)

1. C   4. C
2. C   5. A
3. A   6. C

EXPLANATION OF ANSWERS

1. CORRECT ANSWER: C

   He saw, states the passage (sentence 1), *altering, dissolving, and interrelated forms flowing onward through earth's history.* And as he saw these things, he was envisioning the relationships of all living things. He seemed to see, implies the author, no one thing independent of another. C, then, is the proper answer.

2. CORRECT ANSWER: C

   Judging from Darwin's various failures and indecisions discussed in paragraph 2, the reader can only accept C as the correct completion of the statement. While A, D, and E are probably acceptable statements in themselves, they have nothing to do with the man about whom the author is writing. B, apparently, is not the opinion of the author.

3. CORRECT ANSWER: A

   The evolutionary ideas about which he learned as a youth came from his grandfather long before, presumably, his many other influences. Therefore, A must be the correct answer.

4. CORRECT ANSWER: C

   The last paragraph mentions *Lyell's then-heretical views* . . . . Therefore, C is the only possible answer. Item D is not indicated in the passage, and A, B, and E are false.

5. CORRECT ANSWER: A

   Items D and E were works of Erasmus Darwin, grandfather of Charles. Items B and C are the works of Alfred Russell Wallace. Item A is the work of Charles Darwin-his work on the Beagle mentioned in the passage and is the correct answer.

6. CORRECT ANSWER: C

   Scopes was charged with teaching Darwinian evolution in violation of a state law forbidding such instruction. The state was Tennessee, and the correct answer is C. Clarence Darrow was attorney for the defense and William Jennings Bryan, attorney for the prosecution.

TEST 4
PASSAGE

The most fascinating thing about a greenhouse is the opportunity provided for growing unusual plants. A greenhouse gardener need not limit himself to the plants he once grew in his home. He can branch out to plants from all over the world–depending on the temperature maintained in the greenhouse.

In a greenhouse where the temperature is kept just above freezing, alpine plants can be grown. Edelweiss, bottle gentian, creeping phlox, and columbines like Aquilegia akitensis and A. flabellata are just a few of the candidates. A book on rock gardening or a catalogue from a specialist nursery will suggest many other plants. A practical advantage to growing these cold-greenhouse plants is the saving on wintertime fuel bills.

Under warmer conditions, many kinds of dwarf shrubs will be fun to grow. Do not overlook some of the berried kinds like pyracantha Victory, which is hardy outdoors only about as far north as Zone 7. Tender shrubs and trees such as kumquat, calamondin orange, and dwarf lemon are satisfying to grow, for they will often have flowers and fruit at the same time.

The charming wax plant, Hoya oarnosa, develops beautifully in a warm greenhouse. Others are hibiscus, lantana, oleander, and osmanthus or sweet olive.

1. According to the passage, kumquat is a

    A. sturdy shrub
    B. dwarfed plant
    C. tender shrub
    D. fruit
    E. form of berry

2. An oleander develops

    A. in a warm greenhouse
    B. in a cold greenhouse
    C. outdoors in a southern climate
    D. well in the home
    E. in a northern climate

3. The advantage to growing plants like edelweiss in the wintertime is

    A. they are far more attractive plants than most
    B. they are too fragile for summer cultivation
    C. temperature
    D. the saving on fuel bills
    E. that they are an alpine plant

4. A good title for the passage might be

    A. HOW TO GROW NORTHERN PLANTS
    B. HOW TO GROW TROPICAL PLANTS
    C. THE FLORIDIAN PLANTS: HIBISCUS, OLEANDER, LANTANA
    D. HOW TO GROW CITRUS IN A GREENHOUSE
    E. CANDIDATES FOR A GREENHOUSE

2 (#4)

5. Broadly, the subject covered in the passage would come under the heading of   5._____

    A. botany
    B. nurseries
    C. gardens
    D. rock gardening
    E. pyracantha

6. A flowering plant, discovered by an American traveling in Mexico, and destined to become our most popular Christmas plant, thanks to the temperature control of the green house, is the   6._____

    A. mistletoe
    B. philodendron
    C. poinsettia
    D. rhododendron
    E. hibiscus

KEY (CORRECT ANSWERS)

1. C   4. E
2. A   5. A
3. D   6. C

EXPLANATION OF ANSWERS

1. CORRECT ANSWER: C

   Paragraph 3, sentence 3, contains the description of a kumquat as a *tender shrub,* indicating C as the correct answer.

2. CORRECT ANSWER: A

   Paragraph 4 contains the completion of the statement. It mentions Hoya carnosa as needing a warm greenhouse and goes on to state that, of other plants needing the same environment, one is oleander. Thus, the answer is A. Though an oleander will flourish outdoors in a southern climate, this is not indicated by the author in the passage.

3. CORRECT ANSWER: D

   The last sentence of paragraph 2 states that edelweiss is a cold-greenhouse plant and such plants are a *saving on wintertime fuel bills.* Therein lies its practical advantage. C and E could be considered adequate answers if the requirements only of the plant were the consideration, but D is the better answer because of the word *advantage* in the question (inferring that which is an advantage to the grower).

4. CORRECT ANSWER: E

   Though A, B, C, and D are all mentioned in the passage, the all inclusive title in item E presents the best possible choice and is the correct answer.

5. CORRECT ANSWER: A

   Botany being the science discussed in the passage is the most enveloping choice and, therefore, the best answer. Thus, the answer is A. B, C, D, and E, were they to be catagorized, would all come under the heading of A since they are all parts of the whole-botany.

6. CORRECT ANSWER: C

   Joel R. Poinsett, an American diplomat, discovered the flowering plant, poinsettia, in 1851, and it has since become our most popular Christmas plant. Thus, the answer is C.

TEST 5
PASSAGE

In a provocative series of experiments, a team of scientists at Western Reserve University in Cleveland has developed techniques to remove the brain of a monkey from its body and keep it alive for many hours. Bare except for two small bits of bone to help support it, the nerves and blood vessels that once connected it to the monkey's body severed, the brain is suspended above a laboratory table. Attached to it are the tubes of a mechanical heart to maintain its blood supply; from it run wires to recording instruments. Their measurements of its electrical activity not only show that it remains alive but even suggest that sometimes this isolated brain is conscious.

While the immediate goal of the team, headed by Dr. Robert J. White, is the development of methods for obtaining answers to basic questions related to the physiology of the brain, one cannot help being fascinated by less specifically scientific, but perhaps more profoundly philosophic, considerations. Can the truly *detached minds* of the Cleveland monkeys really be conscious? If so, conscious of what?

Sensation, for example, is an important ingredient of the conscious state. Does biological science give us any clues as to what sensations, if any, the conscious incorporeal brains of the Western Reserve monkeys could have felt? After all, the nerves that normally carry to the brain indications of touch, taste, odor, light, and sound were all cut, and the associated sensory organs were far removed. Does this mean that, during its conscious periods, the isolated monkey brain floated in a sensory void, with no flashes of touch, pain, sight, or sound to remind it of the kind of existence it once knew?

1. What is used by the scientists to support the brain?

    A. Nerves and blood vessels that once connected it to the monkey's body
    B. Two small bits of bone
    C. A mechanical heart
    D. A laboratory table
    E. The tubes of the mechanical heart

2. The suggestion that the brain is sometimes conscious comes from

    A. the measurements on the recording instruments
    B. associated sensory organs
    C. the memory of the kind of existence it once knew
    D. the maintenance of its blood supply
    E. the mechanical heart

3. By the term *incorporeal brains,* the author means

    A. brains without nerves
    B. brains with mechanical tubes
    C. brains in a sensory void
    D. that the brain, though isolated, has artificial support
    E. disembodied brains

4. The author states that the brain can be kept alive

   A. indefinitely
   B. until it normally expires corporeally
   C. until the mechanical heart fails
   D. a few minutes
   E. for many hours

5. Scientists, by such experiments as these, are PROBABLY trying to determine

   A. how certain parts of the brain can be mechanically replaced
   B. how the brain feels and thinks
   C. whether the brain of a monkey is superior to the human brain
   D. how they might duplicate this experiment with a human brain
   E. how long brains can be kept alive without their bodies

6. A part of the brain called the brainstem is

   A. the seat of mental activity
   B. the coordinator of muscular activity
   C. an extension of the spinal cord
   D. the mantle that fits the skull
   E. controller of voluntary action and the senses

7. The cerebral cortex is

   A. divided into two equal hemispheres
   B. that part of the brain through which all nerve impulses are channeled
   C. that part which controls breathing
   D. that part which controls heartbeat
   E. that part which generates feelings, i.e., hunger, anger, pleasure

---

KEY (CORRECT ANSWERS)

1. B   5. B
2. A   6. C
3. E   7. A
4. E

EXPLANATION OF ANSWERS

1. CORRECT ANSWER: B

   It is stated in paragraph 1 that the brain is *bare except for two small bits of bone to help support it*. The answer, then, is B. Items C and E refer to things connected to the brain but not supporting it.

2. CORRECT ANSWER: A

   Item C is stated as a question in the passage and goes unanswered. However, item A is stated in the last sentence of paragraph 1 and is the correct answer. Items D and E are artificial appendages on which the recording instruments depend, but cannot, themselves, estimate or measure consciousness.

3. CORRECT ANSWER: E

   Incorporeal means without a body, or a disembodied brain. Therefore, E is the correct answer. The other answers are characteristic of (or related to) the brain described in the passage but do not relate to the term *incorporeal*.

4. CORRECT ANSWER: E

   In sentence 1, paragraph 1, the author states there are techniques to *remove the brain. . . . and keep it alive for several hours*. Item E, then, is the correct answer. C is not correct because, should a mechanical heart fail, it would be replaced, and the brain would continue its *life course* for the prescribed length of time.

5. CORRECT ANSWER: B

   The correct answer is B (see paragraph two-*basic questions related to the physiology of the brain*). Item E, the scientists have obviously ascertained; items A, C, and D are neither mentioned nor implied in the passage.

6. CORRECT ANSWER: C

   Items A, D, and E relate to the cerebral cortex. Item B refers to the cerebellum.

7. CORRECT ANSWER: A

   Items B, C, D, and E refer to functions of the brainstem. Item A, which describes the make-up of the cerebral cortex, is the correct answer.

TEST 6
PASSAGE

The highest honors bestowed in the world of science were given last Thursday to an American, two Russians, and a British woman.

The Nobel Prize in physics was shared by Dr. Charles H. Townes, now provost of the Massachusetts Institute of Technology, and Drs. N.G. Basov and A.M. Prokhorov of the Soviet Union. The three men, during the early nineteen fifties, paved the way for a major invention: the maser. Dr. Townes also helped show how the maser principle could be applied to light, resulting in discovery of the laser.

The Nobel Prize in chemistry went to Mrs. Dorothy C. Hodgkin of Great Britain for her work in deciphering the structure of such complex molecules as those of penicillin and vitamin B-12. The latter is vital in treating a fatal form of pernicious anemia. Its structure was spelled out after eight years of work. *Never before,* the award announcement said, *has it been possible to determine the precise structure of so large a molecule.*

The analyses were performed by shining x-rays through crystals of the substance in question and recording the manner in which the rays were diffracted by the crystal structure.

Applied light was first achieved by Dr. Townes and his colleagues at Columbia University at a radar or *microwave* frequency. Hence, they called it *microwave amplification by stimulated emission of radiation,* or, more briefly, the maser, from the initials of these words.

When the same principle was applied to the production of intense light, it was called an optical maser or *laser*

One of the earliest applications of the maser was to increase many-fold the sensitivity of radar systems used to detect distant missiles.

1. The invention of the maser

    A. occurred in Great Britain
    B. made it possible to determine the precise structure of a molecule
    C. was related to the work of Drs. Basov, Townes, and Prokhorov
    D. was the work of Mrs. Dorothy C. Hodgkin
    E. was the work of Dr. Charles H. Townes

2. Vital in treating a form of pernicious anemia is

    A. deciphering the structure of complex molecules
    B. vitamin B-12
    C. the analysis performed by shining x-rays through crystals
    D. recording the manner in which the rays are defracted
    E. penicillin

3. The *laser* got its name from the

    A. microwave amplification by stimulated emission of radiation
    B. initials of its earliest application
    C. initials of the principle of the laser applied to light

D. application of the maser to increase the sensitivity of radar systems
E. optical laser

4. The Nobel Prize in physics was

   A. given for the work of deciphering the structure of molecules
   B. given for the invention of the laser
   C. given to Mrs. D.C. Hodgkin
   D. shared
   E. given to Drs. Basov and Prokhorov

5. The above passage might be found in a(n)

   A. scientific journal dealing with nuclear physics
   B. article on the detection of missiles
   C. brochure from the Massachusetts Institute of Technology
   D. article in a medical journal on the treatment of pernicious anemia
   E. article on Nobel Prize winners

6. A word MOST CLOSELY related to amplification is

   A. stimulation   B. enlargement
   C. emission   D. light
   E. radiation

KEY (CORRECT ANSWERS)

1. C   4. D
2. B   5. E
3. C   6. B

EXPLANATION OF ANSWERS

1. **CORRECT ANSWER: C**

   Paragraph 2 states, *The three men...paved the way for a major invention: the maser.* The correct answer, therefore, is item C. Item B relates to the work of Mrs. Hodgkin (item D), who lives in Great Britain (item A). Item E is incomplete and, therefore, false.

2. **CORRECT ANSWER: B**

   The answer is contained in paragraph 3, where it is stated, *...such complex molecules as those of penicillin and B-12. The latter is vital in treating...pernicious anemia.* The correct answer, then, is B. Item A relates to the work of Mrs. Hodgkin, as do items C and Item E is incorrect.

3. **CORRECT ANSWER: C**

   The laser is an optical maser (item E), but it got its precise name from the initials of the principle of the maser (item A) applied to light; that is, item C, which is the correct answer. The earliest application of the laser (item B) was item D and has nothing to do with the laser.

4. **CORRECT ANSWER: D**

   The prize was given to Drs. Basov, Prokhorov, and Townes. It was shared by these three men; therefore, the correct answer is D. E is incorrect because it is incomplete. The prize in Chemistry was given to Mrs. Hodgkin, item C. As for items A and B, if the reader were to check for the reason that the prize was given, he would find that it was the invention of the maser, discounting both A and B.

5. **CORRECT ANSWER: E**

   The correct answer, and the most inclusive one, regarding the source of the passage is item E. Item A is obviously false, as is C. B and D refer to things mentioned in the passage but not the substance or the main theme of it.

6. **CORRECT ANSWER: B**

   Item B is the correct meaning of amplification and, thus, the correct answer for the question. Items A, B, C, and E are incorrect.

TEST 7
PASSAGE

Thus for most of the earth's history, life, in the form of primitive algae, fungi, and bacteria, had little more than a toehold in these pools. The oldest fossil evidence of such algae dates back two or three billion years, yet diverse, large scale life forms did not appear in the fossil record until some 600 million years ago.

It is this sudden appearance of diverse life that has puzzled scientists. The assumption has been that the earlier record was destroyed or that previous life forms did not have shells or skeletons hard enough to leave a record. Yet soft plants and animals also leave their prints in the sands of time and they, too, were absent.

What really happened, according to the new hypothesis, was that when volcanic growth produced continents, and hence shallow pools of considerable extent, the pond-bottom plants slowly raised the oxygen content of the air until, at one percent of the present level, it was sufficient to filter out almost all the lethal ultraviolet. The latter, henceforth, could poison only the top few inches of the oceans and life, which had been hardly more than microscopic, erupted in all evolutionary directions.

The eruption of oceanic life increased photosynthesis and the oxygen level rose high enough to make the dry land habitable. This led to great forests and photosynthesis became so extensive that there was perhaps ten times as much oxygen in the air as today. The carbon dioxide of the air, that acts like the glass of a green-house in keeping the earth warm, was depleted, and the Permian ice ages of 250 million years ago resulted.

1. An example of algae is

    A. a form of mushroom plant
    B. fossiliferous
    C. seaweed
    D. a form of bacteria
    E. cryptogamous plants

2. The scientists were puzzled because

    A. of the production of shallow pools
    B. of the evidences of fossiliferous life prior to 600 million years ago
    C. they did not feel that the oldest forms of life did not have hard shells or skeletons
    D. they did not think volcanic growth produced continents
    E. they did not understand how plants could lower the oxygen content of the air

3. Continents were produced by

    A. fermentation
    B. a high level of oxygen
    C. photosynthesis
    D. volcanic growth
    E. the Permian ice ages

4. How could the ultraviolet poison only the top few inches of the oceans and life? Because

    A. salt water reflects the rays
    B. ultraviolet rays are poisonous to certain ocean plants
    C. the pond-bottom plants raised the oxygen content of the air
    D. the pond-bottom plants acted as a filter
    E. ultraviolet cannot penetrate below the ocean's surface

5. Ultraviolet rays are 5.____

   A. the strongest rays of the sun
   B. rays within the violet of the visible spectrum
   C. the rays of the sun which promote growth
   D. rays beyond the violet of the visible spectrum
   E. those rays which are attracted by salt or fresh water

6. Photosynthesis is the 6.____

   A. growth from within plant or animal life
   B. process by which plants manufacture food for their growth with the aid of light
   C. impulse of fluids to mix and become diffused through each other
   D. tendency of elements to pass through one another with unequal rapidity
   E. pressures produced by osmosis

KEY (CORRECT ANSWERS)

1. C   4. D
2. B   5. D
3. D   6. B

EXPLANATION OF ANSWERS

1. CORRECT ANSWER: C

   Algae is a subaqueous plant, that is a plant growing beneath the water. Therefore, the answer would be C. Items A and E are fungi. Item B, fossiliferous, means *containing or bearing fossils*. Item D is incorrect because algae is a form of plant life.

2. CORRECT ANSWER: B

   The answer to this question is to be found in paragraph 1, towards the end, and the beginning of paragraph 2. Items A and D are accepted concepts. Item E is a false statement, as is C. Item B is the correct answer.

3. CORRECT ANSWER: D

   At the beginning of paragraph 3, it is mentioned that *volcanic growth produced continents*. Therefore, item D is the correct answer, aside from being the only direct statement made about the production of continents. Items A, C, and E are not mentioned in relation to the production of continents.

4. CORRECT ANSWER: D

   The pond-bottom plants slowly raised the oxygen content of the air...until it was sufficient to filter out almost all the lethal ultraviolet states the passage in paragraph 3. Therefore, item D is the correct answer. A and E are false statements. Item C is true but not pertinent. Item B is misleading.

5. CORRECT ANSWER: D

   Ultraviolet rays are those short rays beyond the violet of the visible spectrum. A, B, C, and E are not applicable to ultra-violet rays.

6. CORRECT ANSWER: B

   Items C and D relate to the process of osmosis. Items A and E are incorrect.

TEST 8
PASSAGE

The discovery and use of metals was one of the crucial steps that put mankind on the long road to modern civilization.

New clues to the discovery were reported last week. They suggest that men were taking the first steps toward use of metal a millennium earlier than the dawn of real metallurgy. The clues are little bits of copper that appear to have been cold-hammered into shape as pins, a drill, and a sharply bent hook nearly 9,000 years ago by an artisan in one of man's earliest villages.

The copper specimens were discovered last summer by a team excavating an ancient village site at Cayonu, in southeastern Turkey.

Co-directors of the expedition that made the discoveries were Prof. Hale Cambel, from the University of Istanbul, and Prof. Robert J. Braidwood of the Oriental Institute and Department of Anthropology, University of Chicago.

In a telephone interview last week, Professor Braidwood said all the evidence indicates that the stone dwelling in which the tools were found was nearly 9,000 years old.

In the Shanidar Valley of northern Iraq, scientists from Columbia University independently have found a specimen that also seems to be cold-hammered copper and suggests the same conclusion as that reached by Professor Braidwood and his colleagues.

1. The discovery of the cold-hammered copper specimens was made

    A. in southwestern Turkey
    B. 9,000 years ago
    C. in Istanbul
    D. in the Shanidar Valley
    E. on the African continent

2. Why does the author suggest that metal was used before the dawn of real metallurgy? Because

    A. The scientists found evidences of copper
    B. The scientists found evidences of cold-hammers
    C. There was evidence of life in the site at Cayonu
    D. They assumed that people must have lived in Cayonu 9,000 years ago
    E. The scientists found copper worked into certain forms

3. Metallurgy is the

    A. discovery of metals
    B. discovery of minerals that could be worked into metals
    C. discovery of ore
    D. art of working metals
    E. application of metals to the body

4. A millennium is _____ years.

    A. thousands of
    B. a few thousand
    C. several thousand
    D. a thousand
    E. an incalculable number of

5. The dominant religion of Turkey today is

    A. Hinduism   B. Hebrew
    C. Islam   D. Buddhist
    E. Greek Orthodox

5. ____

6. The capital of Turkey today is

    A. Istanbul   B. Ankara
    C. Constantinople   D. Smyrna
    E. Izmir

6. ____

KEY (CORRECT ANSWERS)

1. D   4. D
2. E   5. C
3. D   6. B

3 (#8)

EXPLANATION OF ANSWERS

1. CORRECT ANSWER: D

   A place, apart from Cayonu, where scientists found cold-hammered copper specimens is the Shanidar Valley, item D, which is the correct answer. Istanbul is the location of the university of one of the scientists (item C). And Cayonu is in southeastern Turkey, thus discounting item A. Item B refers to the age of the specimens. Item E is false.

2. CORRECT ANSWER: E

   The evidences that the scientists found were copper that had been cold-hammered into different shapes, indicating E as the correct answer. A and B are insufficient or incomplete answers. C does not represent enough evidence, nor does D.

3. CORRECT ANSWER: D

   Metallurgy is *the art of working metals*. It has nothing to do with the discovery of or the existence of metal substances, discounting items A, B, and C, but rather with such activities as smelting, refining, parting, etc. Thus, the correct answer is D. Item E is incorrect.

4. CORRECT ANSWER: D

   A millennium is a thousand years. Thus, the answer is D. Items A, B, C, and E are incorrect.

5. CORRECT ANSWER: C

   The dominant religion of Turkey is Islam. The other choices are practiced in Turkey, but have very small followings throughout the country.

6. CORRECT ANSWER: B

   Turkey's capital is Ankara, item B, which is the correct answer. Constantinople, item C, was the former name and the former capital; it was replaced by the name, Istanbul, in the 20's. Izmir is the present-day name for Smyrna, a change which was made coincidentally with that for Constantinople.

TEST 9
PASSAGE

A radically new concept of evolution is being discussed in scientific circles. As presented by two Texans, it would explain the chief puzzle in the record of life's history on earth: the sudden appearance, some 600 million years ago, of most basic divisions of the plant and animal kingdoms.

There is virtually no record of how these divisions came about. Thus, the entire first part of evolutionary history is missing.

The theory says that evolution of a large proportion of the diverse species that have inhabited the earth–plants, fish, trees, and so forth–took place in two gigantic *revolutions* of comparatively short duration.

There is now general agreement that the earth was born as barren of an atmosphere as is the moon today, but volcanoes poured out gases, including an abundance of water vapor - enough to fill the oceans and produce an envelope of *air.*

It is agreed that the early air was radically different from that of today. Volcanoes do not produce oxygen gas, and the early air was dominated by hydrogen compounds. Hence, it was transparent to ultraviolet sunlight that no longer reaches the earth. Recent observations in space have documented the nature of sunlight before filtering by the atmosphere. It is clearly rich in wavelengths of ultraviolet that are lethal to all known forms of life.

This light not only penetrated the original air, but even pierced the top 15 to 30 feet of the oceans.

Since oceanic water circulates, any drifting life would have been carried into the layer bathed in ultraviolet. Hence, it seems unlikely to Drs. Berkner and Marshall that life could have originated in the oceans. Instead, they believe it probably sprang forth independently on the bottoms of numerous deep pools, possibly warmed by the volcanic activity widespread at that time.

1. The earth, at its beginning,

    A. contained craters like the moon
    B. was barren
    C. was fertile
    D. had animal and plant life only in its oceans
    E. had only plants, fish, and trees

2. The doctors mentioned in the passage seem to believe that

    A. life could have originated in the oceans
    B. life came about as the volcanoes poured out gases
    C. a gigantic revolution took place before a large proportion of the diverse species could inhabit the earth
    D. life sprang forth from numerous deep pools
    E. oceanic water, at the beginning, did not circulate

3. How was the volcanic air different from that of today?

   A. It did not come from volcanoes.
   B. The gases did not contain water vapor.
   C. It was dominated by oxygen.
   D. Ultraviolet light could easily penetrate it.
   E. It was not dominated by hydrogen compounds.

4. The air of today can filter ultraviolet rays because

   A. there are no more volcanoes
   B. they are absorbed by the earth
   C. of its oxygen content
   D. of its hydrogen content
   E. the ocean absorbs them

5. The BEST definition of an hypothesis is a(n)

   A. theory or formula derived by inference
   B. tentative assumption made in order to draw out and test its logical or empirical consequences
   C. assumption made in the form of a concession
   D. interpretation of a practical situation or condition taken as the ground for action
   E. statement of order and relation in nature that has been found to be invariable under the same conditions

6. In relation to the content of the passage, the BEST definition of air is the(a)

   A. mixture of invisible gases which surround the earth
   B. surrounding or pervading influence
   C. medium of transmission
   D. compound of 2 parts hydrogen and 1 part oxygen
   E. volcanic gas

KEY (CORRECT ANSWERS)

1. B   4. C
2. D   5. B
3. D   6. A

EXPLANATION OF ANSWERS

1. CORRECT ANSWER: B

   The earth was born as barren of an atmosphere as is the moon today, states the passage in paragraph 4. The only difference was that it had volcanoes which poured out gases, which in turn produced oceans and air. But since the correct answer must refer to the earth at its beginning (refer back to the question stem), B is the only possible answer. Item A is not mentioned. Item C does not refer to the earth at its beginning. Item E took place much later, during the *revolutions* mentioned in paragraph 3. Item D is not stated in the passage.

2. CORRECT ANSWER: D

   At the end of the passage, the two doctors are mentioned as believing that life *probably sprang forth independently on the bottoms of numerous deep pools.* Therefore, D is the correct answer. E is a false statement. The doctors did not believe A or B. C is false because two *gigantic revolutions* took place, according to paragraph 3.

3. CORRECT ANSWER: D

   Volcanic air was transparent to ultraviolet sunlight because it did not produce oxygen gas and was dominated by hydrogen compounds (paragraph 5). Item E is false. It did contain hydrogen compounds. C is false because the reverse is true.
   Items A and B are incorrect because the opposites are true.

4. CORRECT ANSWER: C

   It is the oxygen content in the air which filters out the ultra-violet rays before they reach the earth or the oceans. Therefore, the correct answer is C, and can be found in paragraph 5. Items A, B, and E have nothing to do with the ability of the air to filter the rays. Hydrogen, mentioned in item D, is transparent to ultraviolet rays.

5. CORRECT ANSWER: B

   Item E refers to a law. A and C are insufficient as definitions. D is a broad definition but not so precise as item B, which is the most accurate definition presented, and the correct answer.

6. CORRECT ANSWER: A

   Since the passage is concerned with natural science, item A is far superior to items B and C. Items D and E are incorrect. The correct answer, then, is A.

TEST 10
PASSAGE

Some 25,000 infants suffocate each year in the United States alone. The infants, most of them premature, turn blue and choke and die.

They die from something that is not to this day in most current medical directories, dictionaries, or guides. It is a mysterious condition called hyaline membrane disease. Many years ago this disease killed Patrick Bouvier, the younger son of John F. Kennedy, and it usually kills about half of the infants it strikes.

About 2,000 of the nation's pathologists met in Miami this week for the joint annual session of the College of American Pathologists and the American Society of Clinical Pathologists. They heard a report suggesting that a cure for hyaline membrane has been found.

It was through a series of autopsies of 150 infants who died of hyaline membrane disease that the new treatment for this disease evolved.

The study was done by a Louisville pathologist, Dr. Daniel Stowens, Director of Laboratories at Children's Hospital.

From his autopsies, Dr. Stowens determined that babies who are victims of hyaline membrane disease had too much water in their bodies. The baby's major organ systems may be all right. But they attempt to get rid of the water through the lungs. This clogs these organs and prevents the normal absorption of oxygen into the blood. So the babies die.

There are many complicated theories about how hyaline membrane disease blocks the lungs. The new simple theory had led to a simple therapy.

It is the use of two epsom salts enemas. The first enema clears away the mucus; the second, which relies on epsom salts' affinity for water, draws fluid away from the lungs.

Dr. Stowens reported that gasping and choking babies have been dramatically relieved of their symptoms in a matter of a few minutes after the treatment. In the last eight months, 28 babies suffering from hyaline membrane disease have been treated by epsom salts enemas in five Louisville hospitals, and all are reported to be alive today.

1. The babies who are victims of hyaline membrane disease die because they

    A. are organically defective
    B. absorb oxygen into the blood
    C. lack sufficient water in their system
    D. get rid of excess water through their lungs
    E. do not attempt to get rid of the excess water in their system

2. Before the new method of treating the disease was dis covered, it

    A. was always fatal
    B. killed half the infants it struck
    C. killed 25,000 infants a year all over the world
    D. killed 2,000 infants in the United States every year
    E. killed 150 infants a year

3. The success of the new method seems to

   A. be unpredictable
   B. be perfected
   C. involve some risk
   D. be disapproved of in some medical circles
   E. depend on the baby treated

4. The cause of death from hyaline membrane is

   A. the bloodstream
   B. the lungs
   C. the membrane
   D. suffocation
   E. the heart

5. Dr. Stowens might rightfully be compared to

   A. Dr. Spock
   B. the polio vaccine
   C. Dr. Teller
   D. Dr. Salk
   E. the hyaline membrane disease

6. Prior to the discovery of the therapy,

   A. there existed a simple theory about it
   B. hyaline membrane disease was not treated
   C. there was no theory on how to treat it
   D. the theories about causes were many and recondite
   E. there was a simple therapy

7. The new theory

   A. does not use epsom salts
   B. does not use water
   C. delivers fluid to the lungs
   D. relies on the affinity between epsom salts and water
   E. use various epsom salts enemas

8. With the new therapy, babies

   A. gasp and choke
   B. have been treated over the last 12 months
   C. are relieved of their symptoms in a matter of minutes
   D. are relieved of their symptoms in a few hours
   E. have now been treated in 28 hospitals

9. A pathologist is

   A. a doctor
   B. a specialist in children's diseases
   C. usually a pediatrician
   D. one versed in the nature of respiratory ailments
   E. one versed in the nature of diseases

KEY (CORRECT ANSWERS)

1. D
2. B
3. B
4. D
5. D
6. D
7. D
8. C
9. E

EXPLANATION OF ANSWERS

1. **CORRECT ANSWER: D**

   In the next to last sentence of paragraph 6, the reason is explained. The correct answer is D. Item B is incorrect because it is the prevention of the normal oxygen flow that leads to fatalities. C is incorrect because they have too much water in their system. Whether the baby is organically defective or not has nothing to do with the disease, discounting A. Item E is incorrect because the babies do make this attempt.

2. **CORRECT ANSWER: B**

   In the last sentence of paragraph 2, it is stated that the disease killed about half the infants it struck. Thus, the correct answer is B. 150 infants had autopsies performed (item E). 25,000 yearly in the United States died from it, discounting item C. Item A is false. The figure 2,000 in item D refers to the nation's pathologists.

3. **CORRECT ANSWER: B**

   It would seem, since all the babies treated are alive today, that Dr. Stowens' approach to the disease has been perfected and that the cure has been found. Therefore, the correct answer is B. Item D is not mentioned in the passage. And items A, C, and E are false.

4. **CORRECT ANSWER: D**

   The cause of death is suffocation. This is mentioned in the first sentence of the passage. The correct answer is D. Items A, B, C, and E are organs and parts of the body affected but not the cause of death. Item C refers to a part of the name of the disease.

5. **CORRECT ANSWER: D**

   Dr. Spock, a specialist in child growth and development, does not pioneer in the treatment of diseases, discounting A. Item C refers to a nuclear physicist. Item E refers to the disease Dr. Stowens sought to treat. But Dr. Salk, item D, found a way to treat polio successfully and, therefore, is the correct answer. Item B refers to the method he used.

6. **CORRECT ANSWER: D**

   The answer may be reached through paragraph 7, which ends in *The new simple therapy had led to a simple theory*. Before this, there were *many complicated theories about how ... disease blocks the lungs*. Therefore, item D is correct. (*Recondite* means complex, profound.) Item A is false; it occurred after the discovery of the therapy. Item B is false because it was treated. Item C is false; there were many theories. Item E is false although it contains a repetition of part of the statement appearing in the paragraph.

7. **CORRECT ANSWER: D**

   Item A is false because the opposite is stated in the passage. Item B is false for the same reason. Item C is false because fluid is drawn away from the lungs. Item D is correct because it is part of the second stage of the treatment (or therapy) indicated in paragraph 8. Item E is false because the two that are used do not justify the adjective *various*.

8. **CORRECT ANSWER: C**

   Item A is false because that is what occurs before they are treated. Item B is false because they have been treated over the last 8 months. Item C is correct, as indicated in para-graph 9. Item D is false because a different length of time *(a few minutes)* is mentioned in the passage. Item E is false because the passage actually states that 28 babies have been treated in 5 hospitals.

9. **CORRECT ANSWER: E**

   A pathologist is one versed in the nature of diseases. Therefore, E is the only possible answer and the correct one. Item A is insufficient. Items B, C, and D are false.

EXAMINATION SECTION
TEST 1

DIRECTIONS: Each question or incomplete statement is followed by several suggested answers or completions. Select the one that BEST answers the question or completes the statement. *PRINT THE LETTER OF THE CORRECT ANSWER IN THE SPACE AT THE RIGHT.*

Questions 1-5.

DIRECTIONS: Questions 1 through 5 are to be answered on the basis of the following passage.

The Grand Canyon carves through 279 miles of northern Arizona. No one expects what he finds here, and no one forgets what he sees and hears.

For more than ten years, Paul Winter has come to the Grand Canyon with his soprano saxophone. He has stood on the rim at Shoshone Point and played to cliffs that send back a triple echo. He has played with his fellow musicians in the side canyons, and together they have floated down the Colorado River. *I felt put back together on the river,* Winter says, *and I wanted to make music from that place. I wanted to make music of the canyon rather than just about it.*

Even when non-musicians come to these great spaces, they want to fill the stillness with sound. John Wesley Powell, first to describe the experience of a river trip through the canyon, wrote in 1895: *The wonders of the Grand Canyon cannot be adequately represented in symbols of speech, nor by speech itself.... It is the land of music.*

Winter and his group of musicians would certainly agree. On a fall evening, they play Japanese wood flutes, improvisations in answer to the local chorus of canyon tree frogs. Upstream the next morning the saxophone calls, sounding like a great bird, first raven, then great blue heron. The sounds of the wind mix with the rhythms of a frame drum. Much of this is recorded, and a small part will become part of a record the musicians are making.

The Grand Canyon is like a journey through time, life, Earth, underworld: It is any reality we care to invent. Paul Winter tries to recapture this in his music.

Adapted from PAUL WINTER'S CANYON CONSORT
by Stephen Trimble, SIERRA, March/April 1986

1. Paul Winter visits the Grand Canyon to

   A. trap ravens
   B. take photographs
   C. record frogs and animals
   D. play his saxophone

   1._____

2. In 1895, John Wesley Powell suggested that

   A. only words could describe the Grand Canyon
   B. symbols are needed for nature
   C. music can best express the canyon's beauty
   D. stillness is required in nature

   2._____

203

3. The word <u>improvisations</u> in this passage means

   A. producing high pitched sounds
   B. performing without preparation
   C. echoing the exact sound
   D. playing melodies

4. The musicians in this passage enjoy

   A. hiking in the wilderness
   B. playing old fashioned music
   C. responding in music to nature
   D. playing their music indoors

5. The author suggests that the Grand Canyon

   A. has many meanings
   B. stands for lack of freedom
   C. will be destroyed
   D. is a poor setting for art

Questions 6-10.

DIRECTIONS: Questions 6 through 10 are to be answered on the basis of the following passage.

Write about beauty and truth. Write about life, Miss Lowy had said.

Jeanie tore a page out of her notebook and opened her pen. Pulling over a chair she rested her book on the sooty window sill. She stared out at the dusk falling sadly, sadly, thickening into darkness over the coal yards.

A crash of the kitchen door caused a reverberation in the window sill. The notebook slipped out of her hands.

Where you get that soda? She heard her mother's voice, hard and more Southern-sounding than usual.

A lady give me a nickel. She come down the street and ask me—

You lyin'! I know where you got it. Gamblin? — that's what you was doin'!

I was pitchin' pennies, Ma. It's just a game.

Gamblin' an' stealin'! Takin' up with bad friends! I told you to stay away from them boys. Didn't I? Didn't I?

Her mother's voice rose. *I'm goin' to give you a beating you ain't goin' to forget for a good long time.*

Billy wailed on a long descending note.

Later, after the supper dishes were washed, Jeanie brought her books into the kitchen and spread them out under the glaring overhead light. Billy had been asleep, huddled in his clothes. Tears had left dusty streaks on his face.

Her mother sat in an armchair, ripping out the sides of a black dress. Her spectacles made her look strange. *Beauty is truth,* Jeanie read in her notebook. Hastily, carelessly, <u>defiantly</u> disregarding margins and doubtful spellings, letting her pen dig into the paper, she began to write: *Last night my brother Billy got a terrible beating....*

                    Adapted from BEAUTY IS TRUTH
                    by Anna Guest

6. The author suggests that Jeanie

   A. hated her mother
   B. was jealous of her brother
   C. had trouble writing at first
   D. enjoyed gambling

7. An overheard conversation serves to

   A. distract the writer
   B. inspire the writer
   C. involve the writer in a fight
   D. discourage the writer

8. The word <u>defiantly</u> as used in the passage means

   A. sadly   B. falsely
   C. fearlessly   D. carefully

9. Jeanie decides to write about

   A. life around her   B. her school experiences
   C. her secret dreams   D. an ideal family

10. The author suggests that a writer

    A. depends upon imagination
    B. finds inspiration in reality
    C. must ignore life experience
    D. needs a quiet place to work

Questions 11-15.

DIRECTIONS: Questions 11 through 15 are to be answered on the basis of the following passage.

LIFE

A crust of bread and a corner to sleep in,
A minute to smile and an hour to weep in,
A pint of joy to a peck of trouble,
And never a laugh but the moans come double:
    And that is life!

A crust and a corner that love makes precious,
With the smile to warm and the tears to refresh us;
And joy seems sweeter when cares come after,
And a moan is the finest of foils for laughter:
    And that is life!

by Paul Lawrence Dunbar

11. This poem is built on

    A. an abstract definition   B. comparisons and contrasts
    C. a view of loneliness   D. impressions of poverty

12. Lines 5 and 10 express

    A. the same meaning   B. different meanings
    C. a unique message   D. a poet's doubts

13. The rhyme schemes in stanzas 1 and 2 are

    A. totally different   B. somewhat different
    C. the same   D. difficult to identify

14. In line 4, sorrow is contrasted to

    A. suspicion   B. happiness   C. fear   D. insecurity

15. *And a moan is the finest of foils for laughter* means

    A. a moan is a prerequisite for happiness
    B. laughter follows tragedy
    C. sadness helps us appreciate joy
    D. unhappiness and happiness are equal

Questions 16-20.

DIRECTIONS: Read the following passage. In each question, select the word that BEST completes the passage.

Immigration, which played an important part in America's rapid progress, increased greatly in the 1830's and 1840's. Europe suffered from a number of revolutions and crop failures during this period. Most of the revolutions failed, and many people with advanced ideas had to flee for their (16) . This was especially true in Germany, where absolute monarchy was still strong. The worst crop (17) occurred in Ireland. There, several million people faced starvation during the *potato famines* of 1845 and 1846.

Large numbers of Germans, Irish, and other Europeans were attracted to the United States by its cheap land, economic prosperity, and democratic government. But they met with an unexpected problem, a growing feeling among Americans of dislike for (18). Most of the Irish were very poor. Since they could not afford to buy farms, they (19) in the cities. There they performed the most difficult and unpleasant types of work for very low wages. Native American (20) resented the Irish for keeping wages down and for taking away jobs. The newcomers were also disliked because they were generally uneducated and had very low living standards.

16. A. wealth B. safety
    C. country D. importance

17. A. success B. likelihood
    C. failures D. knowledge

18. A. foreigners B. democracy
    C. farms D. dreams

19. A. farmed B. met C. bought D. settled

20. A. standards B. immigrants
    C. workers D. bosses

Questions 21-35.

DIRECTIONS: Each of the following sentences may have a mistake in it. The error may be in sentence structure, usage, capitalization, or punctuation. If there is an error, choose the CORRECT response, and write the letter of your answer in the space at the right. If the sentence is correct as it is written, choose the letter of the answer for *correct as is*.

SAMPLE: I have always <u>chose</u> to follow my <u>mother's</u> advice.
  A. Correct as as
  B. chosen; mother's
  C. choosed; mothers
  D. chose; mothers'

CORRECT ANSWER: B

21. We <u>should of stayed</u> home.

    A. correct as is
    C. should of stay
    B. should have stayed
    D. should have stay

22. John and <u>I</u> are going to my <u>uncle's</u> house.

    A. correct as is
    C. me; uncle's
    B. me; uncles
    D. I; uncles

23. <u>"How are you," she asked.</u>

    A. correct as is
    C. "How are you? she asked."
    B. "How are you," she asked?
    D. "How are you?" she asked.

24. If you had brought your homework, you wouldn't needed to do it over.

    A. correct as is
    B. have brought; wouldn't needed
    C. had brought; wouldn't need
    D. had brung; wouldn't need

25. She sung that song worse than anyone I ever heard before.

    A. correct as is
    B. sung; worst
    C. sung; worser
    D. sang; worse

26. More people than we expected.

    A. correct as is
    B. Many more people than we expected.
    C. More people than expected to the party.
    D. More people than we expected came to the party.

27. You can do that problem many ways, the teacher will explain them.

    A. correct as is
    B. You can do that problem many ways; The teacher will explain them.
    C. You can do that problem many ways. The teacher will explain them.
    D. You can do that problem many ways the teacher will explain them.

28. We was born in New York, but we are living in New Jersey for the last two years.

    A. correct as is
    B. we was born; we was living
    C. we were born; we are living
    D. we were born; we have been living

29. After the thief had robbed his wallet, he told the police of its contents.

    A. correct as is
    B. robbed; it's
    C. stolen; it's
    D. stolen; its

30. If you think he don't do nothing carefully, you're right.

    A. correct as is
    B. he don't do nothing careful
    C. he doesn't do nothing carefully
    D. he doesn't do anything carefully

31. I learned in English class that London was the home of the Globe theater.

    A. correct as is
    B. English class; London; Globe Theater
    C. english class; London; Globe Theater
    D. English Class; London; Globe Theater

32. He asked each of the men for their dollar contribution to the charity, like he had promised. 32._____

 A. correct as is B. their; as
 C. his; like D. his; as

33. John, as well as Mary, deserves credit for having past advanced math. 33._____

 A. correct as is B. deserves; having passed
 C. deserve; having passed D. deserve; having past

34. The dance was lovely all the students dressed in formals. 34._____

 A. correct as is
 B. The dance was lovely, all the
 C. "The dance was lovely," all the
 D. The dance was lovely. All

35. I do good on this kind of test. 35._____

 A. correct as is B. good; these kinds
 C. well; this kind D. well; these kinds

Questions 36-40.

DIRECTIONS: A dictionary page has been reprinted on the next page. Use the information on this dictionary page to answer Questions 36 through 40.

mer·ci·less \\'mər-sē-ləs, 'mərs-l-əs\\ *adj.* Without mercy; pitiless. — **mer·ci·less·ly**, *adv.*

mer·cu·ri·al \\mər-'kyùr-ē-əl\\ *adj.* 1 Having qualities associated with being born under the planet Mercury or attributed to the god Mercury; swift; clever; fickle; changeable. 2 Of, relating to, containing, or caused by the element mercury; as, *mercurial* medical preparations; a *mercurial* thermometer. — *n.* A drug containing mercury.

mer·cu·ric \\mər-'kyùr-ik\\ *adj.* Of, relating to, or containing mercury.

mer·cu·ry \\'mərk-yər-ē, 'mərk-r(-)ē\\ *n.; pl.* **mer·cu·ries.** 1 A messenger; a guide. 2 A heavy, silver-white metallic element, the only metal that is liquid at ordinary temperatures; quicksilver. 3 The column of mercury in a thermometer or barometer.

mer·cy \\'mər-sē\\ *n.; pl.* **mer·cies.** 1 Kind and gentle treatment of an offender, an opponent, or some unfortunate person. 2 A kind, sympathetic manner or disposition; a willingness to forgive, to spare, or to help. 3 The power to be merciful; as, to throw oneself on an enemy's *mercy*. 4 An act of kindness; a blessing.

— The words *clemency* and *leniency* are synonyms of *mercy*: *mercy* usually refers to a compassionate and forgiving attitude on the part of a person who has the power or right to impose severe punishment on another; *clemency* may indicate a habit or policy of moderation and mildness in one whose duty it is to impose punishment for offences; *leniency* often indicates a deliberate overlooking of mistakes or an overindulgent acceptance of another's faults.

mere \\'mir\\ *n.* *Archaic* or *Dial.* A sheet of standing water; a lake or pool.

mere \\'mir\\ *adj.; superlative* **mer·est** \\'mir-əst\\. Only this, and nothing else; nothing more than; simple; as, a *mere* whisper; a *mere* child.

mere·ly \\'mir-lē\\ *adv.* Not otherwise than; simply; only.

mer·e·tri·cious \\,mer-ə-'trish-əs\\ *adj.* Attracting by a display of showy but superficial and tawdry charms; falsely attractive. — **mer·e·tri·cious·ly**, *adv.*

mer·gan·ser \\(,)mər-'gan(t)s-r\\ *n.; pl.* **mer·gan·sers** or **mer·gan·ser.** A fish-eating wild duck with a slender, hooked beak and, usually, a crested head.

merge \\'mərj\\ *v.; * **merged; merg·ing.** 1 To be or cause to be swallowed up, combined, or absorbed in or within something else; to mingle; to blend; as, *merging* traffic. 2 To combine or unite, as two business firms into one.

merg·er \\'mərj-r\\ *n.* 1 The combining of business concerns or interests into one. 2 The resulting business unit.

me·rid·i·an \\mə-'rid-ē-ən\\ *adj.* 1 At or relating to midday. 2 Of or relating to a meridian. — *n.* 1 The highest apparent point reached by the sun or a star. 2 The highest point, as of success or importance; culmination. 3 An imaginary great circle on the earth's surface, passing through the North and South Poles and any given place between. 4 The half of such a circle included between the poles. 5 A representation of such a circle or half circle on a globe or map; any of a series of lines drawn at intervals due north and south or in the direction of the poles and numbered according to the degrees of longitude.

me·ringue \\mə-'rang\\ *n.* A mixture of beaten white of egg and sugar, put on pies or cakes and browned, or shaped into small cakes or shells and baked.

me·ri·no \\mə-'rē-,nō\\ *n.; pl.* **me·ri·nos.** 1 A fine-wooled white sheep of a breed marked by the heavy twisted horns of the male. 2 A fine soft fabric resembling cashmere and originally made of the wool from this sheep. 3 A fine wool yarn.

merino

mer·it \\'mer-ət\\ *n.* 1 Due reward or punishment; especially, deserved reward; a mark or token of excellence or approval. 2 The condition or fact of deserving well or ill; desert; as, each according to his *merit*. 3 Worth; excellence; as, a suggestion having considerable *merit*. 4 A quality or act worthy of praise; as, an answer that at least had the *merit* of honesty. — *v.* To earn by service or performance; to deserve; as, a man who *merited* respect.

mer·i·to·ri·ous \\,mer-ə-'tōr-ē-əs, -'tòr-\\ *adj.* Deserving reward or honor; praiseworthy. — **mer·i·to·ri·ous·ly**, *adv.*

mer·maid \\'mər-,mād\\ *n.* [From medieval English *mermaide*, a compound formed from *mere* meaning "sea" and *maide* meaning "girl", "maid".] An imaginary sea creature usually represented with a woman's body and a fish's tail.

mer·man \\'mər-,man, -mən\\ *n.;* **mer·men** \\-,men, -mən\\. An imaginary sea creature usually represented with a man's body and a fish's tail.

mer·ri·ment \\'mer-ē-mənt, -ə-mənt\\ *n.* Gaiety; mirth; fun.

mer·ry \\'mer-ē\\ *adj.;* **mer·ri·er; mer·ri·est.** 1 Full of good humor and good spirits; laughingly gay. 2 Marked by gaiety or festivity; as, a *merry* Christmas. — **mer·ri·ly** \\'mer-ə-lē\\ *adv.*

mer·ry-an·drew \\'mer-ē-'an-,drü\\ *n.* A clown; a buffoon.

mer·ry-go-round \\'mer-ē-gō-,raùnd\\ *n.* 1 A circular revolving platform fitted with seats and figures of animals on which people sit for a ride. 2 Any rapid round of activities; a whirl; as, a *merry-go-round* of parties.

merry-go-round

mer·ry·mak·ing \\'mer-ē-,māk-ing\\ *adj.* Festive; jolly. — *n.* 1 The act of making merry; merriment. 2 A frolic; a festivity. — **mer·ry·mak·er** \\-,māk-r\\ *n.*

me·sa \\'mā-sə\\ *n.* A flat-topped hill or small plateau with steep sides.

mes·cal \\mes-'kal\\ *n.* 1 A small, spineless cactus

36. Which of the following groups contains ONLY adjectives? 36.____
    A. merciless, meritorious, merriment
    B. merciless, meridian, merry
    C. merit, meritorious, merry
    D. merciless, meritorious, merry

37. The word clemency is a synonym for 37.____

    A. mercurial   B. mercy   C. merit   D. merger

38. According to the pronunciation key for each word, the mark showing where the stress 38.____
    comes in the word occurs

    A. after the stressed syllable
    B. before the stressed syllable
    C. between stressed syllables
    D. at random

39. A word which means a sweet dessert is 39.____

    A. merge   B. meringue
    C. merit   D. merry-andrew

40. His invention was of such merit that the world honored him. 40.____
    Which is the CORRECT definition for the word merit, as used in the above sentence?
    Definition

    A. 1   B. 2   C. 3   D. 4

Questions 41-45.

DIRECTIONS: Select the BEST answer for each of the following media questions.

41. To find information on tonight's TV schedule, you should NOT look at 41.____

    A. this week's TV GUIDE
    B. this week's NEWSWEEK
    C. today's newspaper
    D. the weekend newspaper's TV section

42. An index 42.____

    A. gives an alphabetical list of topics and persons described in a book, with the pages listed
    B. gives the geographic location of all places in a book
    C. only lists the famous people mentioned in a book, with the appropriate page references
    D. gives the chapter headings found in the book

43. Magazines may concentrate on one particular subject such as 43.____

    A. sports   B. hobbies
    C. fashion   D. all of the above

44. People listen to the radio and watch television 44._____
   A. for information only
   B. for entertainment only
   C. lacking anything better to do
   D. for all of the above reasons

45. TV advertising frequently appeals to everything EXCEPT our desire 45._____
   A. to hear the whole truth about products
   B. to impress people
   C. to be up-to-date
   D. for the best in life

Questions 46-55.

DIRECTIONS: In each of Questions 46 through 55, only one of the words is misspelled. In each case, write the misspelled word CORRECTLY in the space at the right.

46. banana 46._____
    regional
    apolagize
    anticipate
    grievance

47. medicine 47._____
    interruption
    weird
    benifit
    fatigue

48. clothe 48._____
    religious
    aquarium
    brillianse
    vacuum

49. adjourn 49._____
    gorgeus
    precious
    category
    possess

50. diogram 50._____
    absence
    maturity
    pitiful
    intrusion

51. reccommend 51.____
    comparative
    assurance
    prisoner
    hilarious

52. attempt 52.____
    feminine
    independant
    orchestra
    hopeful

53. parallel 53.____
    transparent
    fantacy
    arguing
    hysterical

54. accidentally 54.____
    minimum
    cathedral
    responsable
    nuclear

55. approximatly 55.____
    committing
    fascinate
    minority
    privilege

KEY (CORRECT ANSWERS)

1.	D	16.	B	31.	B	46.	apologize
2.	C	17.	C	32.	D	47.	benefit
3.	B	18.	A	33.	B	48.	brilliance
4.	C	19.	D	34.	D	49.	gorgeous
5.	A	20.	C	35.	C	50.	diagram
6.	C	21.	B	36.	D	51.	recommend
7.	B	22.	A	37.	B	52.	independent
8.	C	23.	D	38.	B	53.	fantasy
9.	A	24.	C	39.	B	54.	responsible
10.	B	25.	D	40.	C	55.	approximately
11.	B	26.	D	41.	B		
12.	B	27.	C	42.	A		
13.	C	28.	D	43.	D		
14.	B	29.	D	44.	D		
15.	C	30.	D	45.	A		

EXAMINATION SECTION
TEST 1

DIRECTIONS: Each question or incomplete statement is followed by several suggested answers or completions. Select the one that BEST answers the question or completes the statement. *PRINT THE LETTER OF THE CORRECT ANSWER IN THE SPACE AT THE RIGHT.*

Questions 1-5.

DIRECTIONS: Questions 1 through 5 are to be answered on the basis of the selection below.

The school term ended. I was selected as valedictorian of my class and assigned to write a paper to be delivered at graduation. One morning the principal summoned me to his office.

"Well, Richard Wright, here's your speech," he said with smooth bluntness and shoved a stack of stapled sheets across his desk.

"What speech?" I asked as I picked up the papers.

"The speech you're to say the night of graduation," he said.

"But, professor, I've written my speech already," I said.

He laughed confidently, indulgently.

"Listen, boy, you're going to speak to both white and colored people that night. What can you alone think of saying to them?
You have no experience..."

I burned.

"I know that I'm not educated, professor," I said. "But the people are coming to hear the students, and I won't make a speech that you've written."

He leaned back in his chair and looked at me in surprise.

"You know, we've never had a boy in this school like you before," he said. "You've had your way around here. Just how you managed to do it, I don't know. But, listen, take this speech and say it. I know what's best for you. You can't afford to just say anything before those white people that night." He paused and added meaningfully: "The superintendent of schools will be there; you're in a position to make a good impression on him. I've been a principal for more years than you are old, boy. I've seen many a boy and girl graduate from this school, and none of them was too proud to recite a speech I wrote for them.

I had to make up my mind quickly; I was faced with a matter of principle. I wanted to graduate, but I did not want to make a public speech that was not my own.

"Professor, I'm going to say my own speech that night," I said.

He grew angry.

"You're just a young, hotheaded fool," he said. He toyed with a pencil and looked up at me. "Suppose you don't graduate?"

"But I passed my examinations," I said.

"Look, mister," he shot at me, "I'm the man who says who passes at this school."

I was so astonished that my body jerked. I had gone to thisschool for two years and I had never suspected what kind of man the principal was; it simply had never occurred to me to wonder about him.

"Then I don't graduate," I said flatly.

I turned to leave.

"Say, you. Come here," he called.

I turned and faced him; he was smiling at me in a remote superior sort of way.

"You know, I'm glad I talked to you," he said. "I was seriously thinking of placing you in the school system, teaching. But, now, I don't think that you'll fit."

He was tempting me, baiting me; this was the technique that snared black young minds into supporting the southern way of life.

"Look, professor, I may never get a chance to go to school again," I said.

"But I like to do things right. You're just a young, hot fool," he said. "Wake up, boy. Learn the world you're living in. You're smart and I know what you're after. I've kept closer track of you than you think. I know your relatives. Now, if you play safe," he smiled and winked, "I'll help you to go to school, to college."

"I want to learn, professor," I told him. "But there are some things I don't want to know."

Adapted from <u>Black Boy</u>, the
Autobiography of Richard Wright

1. The conflict between Richard and the principal of the school concerns

    A. whose speech is better—Richard's or the principal's
    B. whether there should be a prepared speech at graduation or informal remark
    C. whether the speech that is given should be written by Richard or the principal
    D. whether the superintendent of schools should be allowed to hear the speech

2. As used in the next to the last paragraph of the selection, the word *track* means a(n)

   A. watching or an observing
   B. athletic competition
   C. footprint
   D. route or course

3. Richard's words and actions in this incident can be BEST explained by Richard's

   A. fear of what the principal could do to him
   B. always wanting to get his own way in everything
   C. realizing that the principal knew what was best for him
   D. belief that, as a matter of principle, he had to be true to what he considered to be right

4. The principal was surprised at Richard's reaction when he handed him the speech because

   A. Richard had always been a cooperative student
   B. no other student had ever acted this way with the principal before
   C. Richard had promised to do whatever the principal told him to do
   D. Richard could barely read and write

5. The frequent use of quotation marks in this passage indicates that

   A. a conversation is going on
   B. the titles of short stories, poems, and other short works being mentioned
   C. the characters do not always mean exactly what their words are saying
   D. that writer does not understand the proper uses of quotation marks

Questions 6-10.

DIRECTIONS: Questions 6 through 10 are to be answered on the basis of the selection below.

We call it Sunrise Dance. But it lasts for four days. It's the biggest ceremony of the White Mountain Apache – when a girl passes from childhood to womanhood. When my time came at 14, I didn't want to have one. I felt embarrassed. All my friends would be watching me. But my parents really wanted it. My mother – she never had one – explained it was important, "Then you will live strong to an old age." So I didn't say no.

My parents prepared for a year. They asked relatives, "Help us so our daughter's dance will be a good one." Older relatives helped choose my sponsors; I call them Godparents. One morning my mother and father took an eagle feather to Godmother Foster and placed it at her foot saying, "Would you prepare a dance for my daughter?" Mrs. Foster picked up the feather. "Yes."

We held the dance at the fairgrounds at Whiteriver. There was room for everyone to camp. One Friday evening Godmother dressed me and pinned an eagle feather on my head. It will help me live until my hair turns gray. The abalone shell pendant on my forehead is the symbol of Changing Woman, mother of all Apache people.

The most important thing Godmother does in the whole ceremony is to massage my body. She is giving me all her knowledge. That night for hours around the fire, I follow a crown dancer who <u>impersonates</u> a protective spirit. We all believe the spirit is present.

Saturday is like an endurance test. Men begin the chants at dawn. They are really praying. Grandmother tells me to dance while kneeling on a buckskin pad facing the sun — the Creator. In that position, Apache women grind corn. When the times comes for running, I go fast around a sacred cave, so nobody evil will ever catch up with me. Rain begins, and my costume, which weighs ten pounds, gets heavier and heavier. But I don't fall. I don't even get tired.

I'm really glad I had a sunrise dance. It made me realize how much my parents care for me and want me to grow up right. They know my small age is past and treat me like a woman. If I have a daughter, I want her to have a sunrise dance, too.

Adapted from the February 1980 issue
of <u>National Geographic Magazine</u>

6. A young Apache girl participates in the ceremony described above when she

   A. is born
   B. is about to enter womanhood
   C. is about to be married
   D. needs godparents

7. The speaker of this selection changed her feelings toward her sunrise dance from

   A. anger to resignation
   B. embarrassment to humiliation
   C. refusal to resignation
   D. embarrassment to pride

8. In paragraph four, the word *impersonates* means

   A. acts the part of   B. dances with
   C. obeys   D. challenges

9. We can conclude that the sunrise dance

   A. is performed each week
   B. brings rain for the crops
   C. will make the speaker live a long time
   D. is a traditional Apache ritual

10. The MOST important part of the ceremony, according to the speaker, is the

    A. eagle feather   B. massage
    C. chanting men   D. sacred cave

Questions 11-15.

DIRECTIONS: Questions 11 through 15 are to be answered on the basis of the following passage.

I really knew I would like New York, but I thought I'd like it immediately, as I had liked the red brick of Venice and London's massive, somber houses. I didn't know that, for a newly arrived European visitor, there was a "New York sickness," like seasickness, air sickness, and mountain sickness.

In Europe, you stop along the streets, meet people, drink, eat, and linger. On Sundays, you get dressed and take a stroll for the sole pleasure of greeting friends. These streets are filled with a community spirit that changes from hour to hour. You do not go for walks in New York; you fly through it. It is a city in motion. Each street looks the same as any other. I feel like anybody, anywhere. I know nobody, nowhere.

In Europe, we become attached to a neighborhood, to a cluster of houses or a street corner, and we are no longer free. But hardly have you entered New York than your life is cut to New York size. You can gaze down in the evening from the top of the Queensborough Bridge, in the morning from New Jersey, at noon from the Empire State Building. Your world is much larger when you live in New York.

I have learned to love New York, especially its sky. In European cities where roofs are low, the sky crawls close to the earth and seems tamed. The New York sky is beautiful because the skyscrapers push it back, very far over our heads. Pure and lovely as a wild beast, it guards and watches over the city. This sky stretches into the distance over all America. It is the whole world's sky.

That thought alone is enough to lend softness to the world's harshest city.

Adapted from "New York"
by Jean-Paul Sartre

11. The author's purpose in writing this passage is to

    A. criticize New York
    B. praise Europe
    C. compare New York with Europe
    D. praise New York

12. The word *stroll* in paragraph two means a

    A. nap   B. walk   C. look   D. ride

13. The author's feelings about New York change from

    A. uneasiness to love   B. love to hatred
    C. fear to shock   D. uneasiness to hatred

14. The word *it* in paragraph four refers to

    A. skyscrapers   B. the beast
    C. New York   D. the sky

15. We can conclude from this passage that the author

    A. dislikes Europe now that he has discovered New York
    B. has travelled widely
    C. left Europe permanently
    D. was seasick on his journey to New York

Questions 16-20.

DIRECTIONS: Read the passages below and select from the words in each question the one that BEST completes the passages. Study the sample below and then proceed on your own.

Sample: Jim Hawkins in TREASURE ISLAND boarded a huge ship and 1 off that day to go in search of a hidden treasure.

1. A. drove   B. called   C. sailed   D. nodded

The CORRECT answer is C.

The Burgos' house was a poor one with a thatched roof of palm leaves, but there was the warmth of a loving home within. Paula, the mother, kept a small 16 nearby. She grew vegetables and grain to help feed the family, selling the produce to buy food and clothing. Since she had no one with whom to leave her small daughter, Paula would take Julia on her trips to the market. Down by the river, while the washing was done in the stream, Julia and her sisters played in the grass, smelled the flowers, climbed the trees, and bathed in a pond they called the Deep Well. It was then that the child began to recognize and love 17 .

Life was simple for the Burgos family. Their world was limited to the countryside surrounding their house. But it seemed 18 and wondrous to Julia. Her eyes would discover the beauty of every wild flower, the living miracle of a bird's nest tucked away in a bush. Years later 19 about her childhood, she confided, "I would cry disconsolately over the leaves of a MORIVINI because it would not awaken." The MORIVINI is a plant so sensitive that its leaves shrivel and die if someone touches it.

If Julia's childhood was poor in material wealth, it was rich in vital experiences and in emotions. Unfortunately, it also abounded in 20 . One by one she saw six of her brothers die. The first time she saw her mother cry over the loss of one of her sons, Julia was devastated. She would not accept that the dead child had to be buried. "Why don't they place him on a raft and cast him off to sea?" she asked.

16. A. factory   B. garden   C. warehouse   D. dairy
17. A. families   B. bathing   C. exercise   D. nature
18. A. enormous   B. poor   C. boring   D. small
19. A. forgetting   B. singing   C. reminiscing   D. complaining
20. A. love   B. sorrow   C. fear   D. anger

Questions 21-35.

DIRECTIONS: The sentences numbered 21 through 35 make up the paragraph that follows. There is one error either in sentence structure, spelling, punctuation, or incorrect usage in each sentence. Find the error in each sentence and write the CORRECTION in the space at the right.

Sample: A. On the last day of our vacation, we saw men skiing down a mountain that was the best part of the vacation for me.
B. If we go back next year I plan to take skiing lessons.
C. They shouldnt be expensive.

Answers: A. mountain. That
B. year,
C. shouldn't or should not

21. You are now at the mid-point in this examination in english.   21.____

22. Have you notice anything about the test so far?   22.____

23. You should of noticed it; it is about beginnings and endings.   23.____

24. In a week, you are probably gonna experience an ending and a beginning of your own.   24.____

25. We are referring to the commencement exercises that represent your graduation from High School.   25.____

26. Commencement ceremonies can be a beginning or an ending it depends on how you look at it.   26.____

27. Some students see there graduation as the completion of their formal education.   27.____

28. Others sees it as the first step to higher education or employment.   28.____

29. Are you looking at it as a beginning or an ending.   29.____

30. Both views are probably true. Because every ending begins something else.   30.____

31. As someone once said Every exit is an entrance somewhere else."   31.____

32. It is also true that each beginning contain's its own ending.   32.____

33. For example the beginning of life also contains the beginning of the end.   33.____

34. The moment we are born we begin both living and dieing.   34.____

35. "That's life," you may be thinking, and your right.   35.____

Questions 36-40.

DIRECTIONS: A dictionary page has been reprinted below. Use the information on this dictionary page to answer Questions 36 through 40.

panegyrist — pants

pan·e·gyr·ist \,pan-ə-'jir-əst\ *n.* A person who formally praises a person or event.

pan·el \'pan-l\ *n.* **1** A section or part of a wall, ceiling, or door, often sunk below the level of the frame; especially, a thin and usually rectangular board set in a frame, as in a door. **2** A thin, flat piece of wood on which a picture is painted. **3** A painting on such a surface. **4** A lengthwise strip or band sewn in a dress; as, an embroidered *panel* on a skirt. **5** A list or group of persons appointed for some service; especially, a group of persons called to serve on a jury. **6** A group of no less than three persons, often experts in various fields, conducting before an audience an unrehearsed discussion on a topic of interest, either to a special audience or to the general public; a similar group, usually of persons well-known to the public, acting as players in a quiz game or guessing game conducted by a master of ceremonies on a radio or television program. — *v.;* **pan·eled** or **pan·elled; pan·el·ing** or **pan·el·ling** \-l(-)ing\. To furnish, fit, trim, or decorate with panels; as, to *panel* a wall.

pan·el·ing or **pan·el·ling** \'pan-l(-)ing\ *n.* **1** Wood or other material made into panels. **2** Panels considered collectively.

pan·el·ist \'pan-l-əst\ *n.* A member of a panel for discussion or entertainment.

pang \'pang\ *n.* **1** A sudden sharp attack of pain; a throe. **2** A sudden sharp feeling of any emotion; as, a *pang* of regret.

pan·han·dle \'pan-,hand-l\ *n.* **1** The handle of a pan. **2** An arm or projection of land shaped like the handle of a pan.

pan·han·dle \'pan-,hand-l\ *v.;* **pan·han·dled; pan·han·dling** \-l(-)ing\. To approach people on the street and beg for money. — **pan·han·dler** \-lər\ *n.*

pan·ic \'pan-ik\ *n.* **1** A sudden, terrifying fright, especially without reasonable cause. **2** A sudden, widespread fear in financial circles, causing hurried selling of securities and a rapid fall in prices. — *v.;* **pan·icked** \-ikt\; **pan·ick·ing** \-ik-ing\. **1** To affect with panic; to be affected with panic; as, one who *panics* easily. **2** *Slang.* To call forth a show of appreciation on the part of someone. The comedian's performance *panicked* the audience. — **pan·icky** \'pan-ik-ē\ *adj.* — **pan·ic-strick·en** \'pan-ik-,strik-n\ *adj.*

pan·i·cle \'pan-ik-l\ *n.* A flower cluster, loosely branched and often in the shape of a pyramid, in which the branches of the flowerless main stem are elongated clusters in the form of a raceme, blooming from the bottom toward the top and outward, as in the oat.

pan·nier \'pan-yər, 'pan-ē-ər\ *n.* **1** A large basket, especially one of wicker, carried on the back of an animal or the shoulder of a person. **2** A framework worn by women to expand their skirts at the hips. **3** An overskirt puffed out at the sides and back.

pan·o·ply \'pan-ə-plē\ *n.; pl.* **pan·o·plies. 1** A full suit of armor. **2** Anything defending or protecting completely by covering; anything forming a magnificent covering or environment. The automobiles in the parade were covered with *panoplies* of flowers and bunting. — **pan·o·plied** \-plēd\ *adj.*

pan·o·ra·ma \,pan-r-'am-ə, -'äm-, -'am-\ *n.* **1** A picture that is unrolled little by little as a person looks at it. **2** A clear, complete view in every direction. **3** A complete view or treatment of any subject; as, a *panorama* of history. — **pan·o·ram·ic** \-'am-ik\ *adj.*

pan·pipe \'pan-,pīp\ *n.* A wind instrument consisting of a series of hollow reeds or pipes of different lengths, closed at one end and bound together with the mouth pieces in an even row.

panpipe

pan·sy \'pan-zē\ *n.; pl.* **pan·sies.** [From medieval English *pensee*, there borrowed from medieval French *pensée*, meaning literally "thought".] A low-growing, commonly annual plant belonging to the violet group and derived from the wild pansy or Johnny-jump-up, with small purple and violet flowers and, in its various garden forms, with showy five-petaled flowers that are usually of cream, violet, or yellow.

pant \'pant\ *v.* **1** To breathe hard or quickly; to gasp; as, to *pant* from running. **2** To want intensely; to long. **3** To breathe or say quickly and with difficulty. — *n.* **1** One of a series of short, quick breaths, as after exercise; a gasp. **2** A puff, as of a steam engine.

pan·ta·lets or **pan·ta·lettes** \,pant-l-'ets\ *n. pl.* Long, loose drawers with ruffles around each ankle, worn by women and girls.

pan·ta·loon \,pant-l-'ün\ *n.* **1** A clown. **2** [in the plural] Trousers.

pan·the·ism \'pan(t)th-ē-,iz-m\ *n.* **1** Any doctrine or belief that the universe taken as a whole is God. **2** The worship of gods of various creeds or religions at one time, as at one period in ancient Rome.

pantalets

pan·ther \'pan(t)th-r\ *n.* **1** The leopard. **2** In America, the cougar.

pant·ies \'pant-ēz\ *n. pl.; sing.* **pant·ie** or **panty** \'pant-ē\. A child's or woman's undergarment covering the lower trunk, with a closed crotch and very short legs.

pan·to·mime \'pant-m-,īm\ *n.* **1** A performer skilled in the art of conveying emotions and ideas without the use of words. **2** A play in which the actors use few or no words. **3** Silent movements or facial expressions that show how a person feels about something. — *v.;* **pan·to·mimed; pan·to·mim·ing.** To represent by pantomime. — **pan·to·mim·ist** \-,ī-məst, -,im-əst\ *n.*

pan·to·then·ic ac·id \'pant-ə-,then-ik\. A substance in the vitamin-B complex that promotes growth, found especially in liver and yeast.

pan·try \'pan-trē\ *n.; pl.* **pan·tries.** A small room where food and dishes are kept.

pants \'pan(t)s\ *n. pl.* **1** Trousers. **2** Drawers; especially, panties.

---

j joke; ng sing; ō flow; ȯ flaw; ȯi coin; th thin; t͟h this; ü loot; u̇ foot; y yet; yü few; yu̇ furious; zh vision

36. A word that originally comes from French meaning *thought* is 36.____
    A. panoply B. panicle
    C. pansy D. pantheism

37. If I had a *panoramic* view of the countryside, I would see 37.____
    A. only those things that are moving
    B. in all directions
    C. part of the scene
    D. only the grass

38. In an illustration on the page, an example of a musical instrument is a 38.____
    A. pantalet B. pantaloon
    C. pannier D. panpipe

39. A word that has at least six different meanings as a noun is 39.____
    A. pant B. pantomine C. panel D. panic

40. The play was performed as a _____ , so that the audience had to watch the actors' 40.____
    faces and movements very carefully.
    Select the word that BEST completes the above sentence.
    A. panelist B. pantomine
    C. panegyrist D. panic

Questions 41-43.

DIRECTIONS: Questions 41 through 43 are to be answered on the basis of the library card reproduced below.

```
                    Working for yourself
      658.1         Hewitt, Geof
      H               Working for yourself; how to be successfully
                    self-employed. Photos by T. L. Gettinsts. Rodale
                    [ c 1977 ] 304p illus

                      Features the stories and advice of nearly one
                    hundred self-employed people as well as guide-
                    lines for selecting, promoting, financing, and
                    managing a business or trade.

                    1 Professions 2 Small business
              ISBN  0-87857-162-0

                                        © THE BAKER & TAYLOR CO
```

41. The Dewey Decimal number you would use to locate this book on a library shelf is 41.____
    A. 1977 B. 658.1H
    C. ISBN 0-87857-162-0 D. 304

42. All of the following questions would be answered by reading this book EXCEPT:

   A. How have other people started their own businesses?
   B. How do I go about financing my business?
   C. What do I need to know to become a good manager?
   D. How should my boss treat me?

43. If you wanted additional books on the same topic, you would look in the card catalogue under the cross-reference

   A. Hewitt
   B. professions
   C. government service
   D. Rodale

Questions 44-45.

DIRECTIONS: Questions 44 and 45 are to be answered on the basis of the newspaper advertisement for a Broadway play shown below.

BOX OFFICE OPENS TOM'W at 10 AM
LIMITED ENGAGEMENT! 10 WEEKS ONLY!
PREVIEWS BEGIN WED. EVG., APRIL 29th
OPENS THURS. EVG., MAY 7th at 6:15
CHARGIT: (212) 944-9300
TICKETRON: (212) 977-9020 Group Sales: (212) 398-8383

MAIL ORDERS NOW!

Monday thru Saturday Evenings at 8 and Saturday Matinees at 2: Orchestra $30.00; Mezzanine $30.00, 27.50, 25.00. Wednesday Matinees at 2: Orchestra $28.50; Mezzanine $28.50, 25.00, 22.50. Please enclose a self-addressed, stamped envelope along with your check or money order made payable to: Martin Beck Theatre. List several alternate dates.

MARTIN BECK THEATRE 302 West 45th Street, New York, N.Y.

---

44. Missing from the ad is

   A. the times of the performance
   B. information on how to purchase tickets
   C. the name of the play
   D. the opening night of the play

45. For a Wednesday matinee performance, the LEAST expensive ticket is

   A. $30.00   B. $28.50   C. $22.50   D. $20.00

Questions 46-50.

DIRECTIONS: Questions 46 through 50 are to be answered on the basis of the following poem.

Summons

Keep me from going to sleep too soon
Or if I go to sleep too soon
Come wake me up. Come any hour
Of night. Come whistling up the road.
Stomp on the porch. Bang on the door.　　　5
Make me get out of bed and come
and let you in and light a light.
Tell me the northern lights are on -
And make me look. Or tell me clouds
Are doing something to the moon　　　10
they never did before, and show me
See that I see. Talk to me till
I'm half as wide awake as you
and start to dress wondering why
I ever went to bed at all.　　　15
Tell me the walking is superb.
Not only tell me but persuade me.
You know I'm not too hard persuaded.

Robert Francis

46. When the speaker says he is afraid he will "go to sleep too soon," he is really saying that he is afraid he will

    A. die suddenly
    B. lose his interest in life
    C. miss his friend's visit
    D. forget to get undressed

47. We can conclude that the speaker's friend is

    A. a woman
    B. more alive and curious about life than the speaker
    C. less alive and curious about life than the speaker
    D. disillusioned with life

48. The last line of the poem expresses

    A. difficulty   B. hope
    C. fear   D. disappointment

49. The title of the poem refers to a

    A. written notice to appear in court
    B. refusal to cooperate
    C. call for help to another person not present in the poem
    D. traffic violation ticket

50. Lines 3-5 in the poem are effective because they
    A. rhyme
    B. are part of a pattern of requests for action
    C. start a new stanza
    D. make use of similes

50. _____

KEY (CORRECT ANSWERS)

1.	C	16.	B	31.	said: "Every	46.	B
2.	A	17.	D	32.	contains	47.	B
3.	D	18.	A	33.	example, the	48.	B
4.	B	19.	C	34.	dying	49.	C
5.	A	20.	B	35.	you are/you're	50.	B
6.	B	21.	English	36.	C		
7.	D	22.	noticed	37.	B		
8.	A	23.	should have	38.	D		
9.	D	24.	going to	39.	C		
10.	B	25.	high school	40.	B		
11.	D	26.	ending. It	41.	B		
12.	B	27.	their	42.	D		
13.	A	28.	see	43.	B		
14.	D	29.	ending?	44.	C		
15.	B	30.	true, because	45.	C		

ARITHMETICAL REASONING
EXAMINATION SECTION
TEST 1

DIRECTIONS: Each question or incomplete statement is followed by several suggested answers or completions. Select the one that BEST answers the question or completes the statement. *PRINT THE LETTER OF THE CORRECT ANSWER IN THE SPACE AT THE RIGHT.*

1. A class decided to cultivate a garden. The principal gave them a piece of ground 40 feet long and 30 feet wide. There were 18 boys and 12 girls in the class. The class voted that each pupil should be allowed an equal amount of the space in the garden.
The number of square feet which was set aside for the *exclusive* use of the boys was
   A. 30 B. 40 C. 480 D. 720

2. The chef allowed 20 minutes cooking time per pound for a roast weighing 6 lbs. 12 ozs.
If the roast was placed in the oven at 4:20 P.M., it *should be done* by
   A. 6:00 P.M. B. 6:32 P.M. C. 6:35 P.M. D. 7:12 P.M.

3. To check the correctness of the answer to a multiplication example, divide the
   A. product by the multiplier
   B. multiplier by the product
   C. multiplicand by the multiplier
   D. multiplier by the multiplicand

4. Of the following correct ways to solve .125 × .32, the MOST efficient is to
   A. write .125 under .32, multiply, point off 5 places
   B. write .32 under .125, multiply, point off 5 places
   C. multiply 125 by 32 and divide by 1000 × 100
   D. divide .32 by 6

5. If you were to eat each meal in a different restaurant in the city's eating places, assuming that you eat 3 meals a day, it would take you more than 19 years to cover all of the city's eating places.
On the basis of this information, the BEST of the following choices is that the number of restaurants in the city
   A. exceeds 20,500
   B. is closer to 21,000 than 22,000
   C. exceeds 21,000
   D. does not exceed 21,500

6. The cost of electricity for operating an 875-watt toaster, an 1100-watt steam iron, and four 75-watt lamps, each for one hour, at 7.5 cents per kilowatt hour (1 kilowatt equals 1000 watts) is
   A. 15 cents B. 17 cents C. $1.54 D. $1.71

2 (#1)

7. Of the following, the pair that is NOT a set of equivalents is: 7.____
   A. .021%, .00021
   B. ¼%, .0025
   C. 1.5%, 3/200
   D. 225%, .225

8. Assuming that the series will continue in the same pattern, the NEXT number in the series 3, 5, 11, 29......is 8.____
   A. 41
   B. 47
   C. 65
   D. 83

9. If the total area of a picture measuring 10 inches by 12 inches plus a matting of uniform width surrounding the picture is 224 square inches, the WIDTH of the matting is 9.____
   A. 2 inches
   B. 2 4/11 inches
   C. 3 inches
   D. 4 inches

10. The *net price* of a $25 item after SUCCESSIVE discounts of 20% and 30% is 10.____
    A. 11
    B. $12.50
    C. $14
    D. $19

KEY (CORRECT ANSWERS)

1.	D	6.	B
2.	C	7.	D
3.	A	8.	D
4.	D	9.	A
5.	A	10.	C

SOLUTIONS TO ARITHMETICAL REASONING

1. Answer: (D) 720

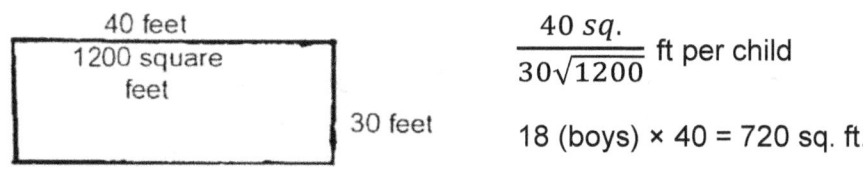

   18 (boys) × 40 = 720 sq. ft.

2. Answer: (C) 6:35 P.M.

   20 minutes per 1 lb.

   ```
   120
   +15
   135 minutes
   -120 minutes (2 hours
    15 minutes
   ```

   $\therefore \dfrac{12 \text{ oz.}}{16 \text{ oz}} = \dfrac{3}{4}$ lb.

   3/4 × 20 = 15 minutes
   20 × 6 = 120 minutes

   ```
    4:20 P.M.
   +2:15 (2 hours, 15 minutes)
    6:35 P.M.
   ```

3. Answer: (A) product by the multiplier

   12 (multiplicand
   ×2 (multiplier
   24 (product)

4. Answer: (D) divide .32 by 8

   The most efficient way is to divide .32 by 8.
   .125 = .12 ½ = 12 ½% = 1/8

   $1/8 \times .32 = \dfrac{.32}{8}$ $\quad\quad \dfrac{.04}{8\overline{).32}}$
   $\quad\quad\quad\quad\quad\quad\quad\quad\quad\quad\quad .32$

4 (#1)

5. Answer: (A) exceeds 20,500

    365 (days in 1 year)
  × 3 (meals)
  1095 (meals in 1 year)
  × 19 (number of years)
20,805 (number of meals eaten in 19 years)   4 (leap-year days)
+   12 (number of meals eaten in leap years)   × 3 (meals
20,817 (total)   12 (leap-year meals)

6. Answer: (B) 17 cents
875 + 1100 + 300 = 2275 watts
2275/1000 = 11/40 kilowatt hours
2 11/40 × 7.5 cents = $.17 approximately

7. Answer: (D) 225%, .225

A. .021% = .00021   B. $1/4\% = \dfrac{1}{400} = .0025$

C. $1.5\% = .015 + \dfrac{15}{1000} = \dfrac{3}{200}$ D. 225% = 2.25 (not .225)

8. Answer: (D) 83

Suggestions For Series Problems
1. Find the difference between the numbers (or squares of differences).
2. In this series, each difference is multiplied by 3 and added to the succeeding number.
    3,5:   the difference is 2; thus difference was multiplied by 3 giving 6, which was then added to 5, to make the next number in the series 11.
    5,11: the difference is 6; this difference was multiplied by 3, giving 18, which was then added to 11, to make the next number in the series 29.
   11,29: the difference is 18; this difference should be multiplied by 3, giving 54, which, when added to 29, will give the next number in the series, 83.

9. Answer: (A) 2 inches

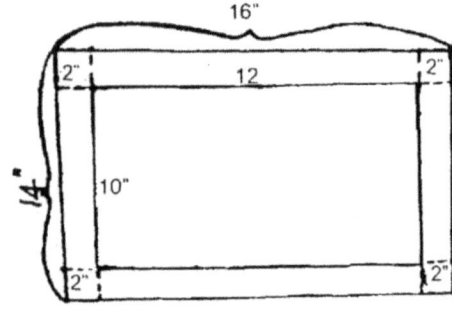

5 (#1)

The total area = 224 square inches (16 × 14).
If 2 inches are added to either side of the picture's width and to either side of the picture's length, we get a new width of 14 inches (10 + 4) and a new length of 16 inches (12 + 4).
Therefore, 14 × 16 = 224 square inches,
Or, a uniform matting width of 2 inches.

10. Answer: (C) $14

SOLUTION
Successful discounts
    20%   30%
1. Convert to decimals .2, .3
2. Subtract from 1.0, .8, .7
3. Multiply .8 × .7 = .56
4. 1.00 - .56 = .44
   25.00
   × .44
    100
    100
  $11.00
5. $25.00 - $11.00 = $14.00

ALTERNATE SOLUTION
 $ 25
 × .20
 $5.00
$25 - $5 = $20
 $ 20
 × .30
 $6.00
$20 - $6 = $14

TEST 2

DIRECTIONS: Each question or incomplete statement is followed by several suggested answers or completions. Select the one that BEST answers the question or completes the statement. *PRINT THE LETTER OF THE CORRECT ANSWER IN THE SPACE AT THE RIGHT.*

1. The cost of 63 inches of ribbon at 12 cent per yard is
   A. $.20   B. $.21   C. $.22   D. $.23

   1.____

2. If 1½ cups of cereal are used with 4½ cups of water, the amount of water needed with ¾ of a cup of cereal is
   A. 2 cups   B. $2^{1}/_{8}$ cups   C. 2¼ cups   D. 2½ cups

   2.____

3. Under certain conditions, sound travels at about 1100 ft. per second. If 88 ft. per second is approximately equivalent to 60 miles per hour, the above condition is, of the following, CLOSEST to _____ miles per hour.
   A. 730   B. 740   C. 750   D. 760

   3.____

4. Of the following, the MOST NEARLY accurate set of equivalents is
   A. 1 ft. equals 30.48 centimeters
   B. 1 centimeter equals 2.54 inches
   C. 1 rod equals 3.28 meters
   D. 1 meter equals 1.09 feet

   4.____

5. If one angle of a triangle is three times a second angle and the third angle is 20 degrees more than the second angle, the SECOND ANGLE is
   A. 32°   B. 34°   C. 40°   D. 50°

   5.____

6. Assuming that on a blueprint ¼ inch equals 12 inches, the ACTUAL length in feet of a steel bar represented on the blueprint by a line $3^{3}/_{8}$ inches long is
   A. $3^{3}/_{8}$ B. 6¾   C. 12½   D. 13½

   6.____

7. A plane leaves Denver, Colorado, on June 1st at 1 P.M. Mountain Standard Time and arrives at New York City on June 2nd A.M. Eastern Daylight Saving Time.
   The ACTUAL time of flight was _____ hours.
   A. 10   B. 11   C. 12   D. 13

   7.____

8. Of the following, the value CLOSEST to that of $\frac{42.10 \times .0003}{.002}$ is:
   A. .063   B. .63   C. 6.3   D. 63

   8.____

9. If Mrs. Jones bought 3¾ yards of dacron at $1.16 per yard and $4^{2}/_{3}$ yards of velvet at $3.87 per yard, the amount of change she receives from $25 is
   A. $2.12   B. $2.28   C. $2.59   D. $2.63

   9.____

2 (#2)

10. The water level of a swimming pool, 75 feet by 42 feet, is to be raised 4 inches. 10.____
The number of gallons of water needed for this purpose is (1 cubic foot equals
7½ gallons)
   A. 140   B. 7,875   C. 31,500   D. 94,500

KEY (CORRECT ANSWERS)

1.	B	6.	D
2.	C	7.	A
3.	C	8.	C
4.	A	9.	C
5.	A	10.	B

SOLUTIONS TO ARITHMETICAL REASONING

1. Answer: (B) $.21

   SOLUTION

   $63" = \frac{63}{36}$ yds; $\frac{6.3}{3.6} \times \frac{.01}{.12} = 21$¢

   ALTERNATE SOLUTION

   12¢ per yard

   $\frac{12}{36} = \frac{1}{3}$ ¢per inch; $\frac{63"}{1} \times \frac{1}{3}$ ¢ $= \frac{63}{3} = 21$¢

2. Answer: (C) 2¼ cups

   SOLUTION

   From the data given, we form the proportion,

Proportion	Cereal	Water
1st mixture	1½ cups	4½ cups
2nd mixture	¾ cups	x cups

   ¾ is half of 1½; therefore, half of 4½ is ¼

   ALTERNATE SOLUTION
   From the data given, we form the proportion,
   1½ (cups of cereal): 4½ (cups of water) = ¾ (cup of cereal): x ∴ 3/2 : 9/2 = ¾ : x
   3/2x = 27/4
   x = 9/4 – 2¼ (cups of water)

3. Answer: (C) 750 miles per hour
   Speed of sound = 1100 ft. per second
   88 ft. per second = 60 miles an hour
   $\frac{1100}{88}$ = 12½ (the number of times the speed of sound is greater than 60 miles an hour)
   ∴ 60 × 12½ = 750 miles per hour (the speed of sound)

4. Answer: (A) 1 ft. equals 30.48 centimeters
   Taking each alternative in turn:
   1. A meter = 100 centimeters
      A meter = 39 in. (approx.) = 3¼ ft. (39/12 = 3¼)
      3 ¼ ft. = 1 meter = 100 centimeters
      ∴ 1 ft. = $\frac{100}{3\ 1/4}$ = 30.48 centimeters (approx.)
   2. 1 meter = 39 in. = 3 ¼ ft. (approx.)
   3. 1 centimeter = .39 in.
   4. 1 rod = 5½ yds. = 16½ ft.
      ∴ 1 rod = 5 meters (approx.) (see item 2 above)

4 (#2)

5. Answer: (A) 32°
Let x = second angle
Let 3x = first angle
Let x + 20° = third angle
5x + 20 = 180°
x = 32°

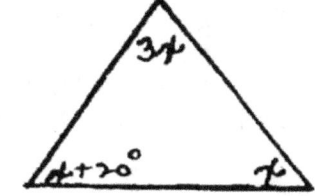

6. Answer (D) 13 ½

$$\frac{1/4"}{12} = \frac{3\,3/8"}{x}$$

¼ ÷ 12/1 = 27/8 ÷ x/1
¼ × 1/12 = 27/8 × 1/x

$$\frac{1}{4} = \frac{27}{8x}$$

8x = 48 × 27 = 1296
x = 162 inches
  = 13½ ft.

7. Answer: (A) 10 hours
TIME BELTS

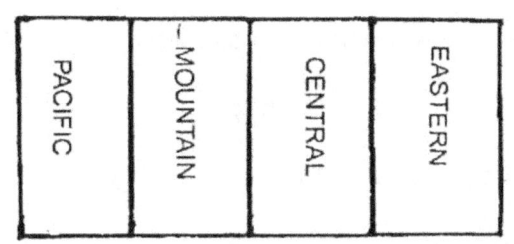

4 A. M. 5 A. M. 6 A. M. 7 A. M. E. S. T.
8 A.M. D.S.T.

In traveling eastward, we set our clocks forward for each time zone.

Plane left at 1 P.M.
Traveled around clock 12 hours or 13 hours at 2 A.M.

Subtract 2 hours' difference between Mountain Time and Eastern Standard Time. Subtract another hour for Daylight Saving Time. That is, 13 − 3 = 10 hours.

8. Answer: (C) 6.3

In 42.10, discard for practical purposes the .10 and perform as follows;

$$\frac{42 \times .003}{.002} = \frac{.0125}{.002} = \frac{12.6}{2}\ 63$$

9. $1.16 $ 3.86 $18.06 $25.00
   × 3 3/4   ×   4 2/3   + 4.35   - 22.41
   $4.35 $18.06 $22.42 $ 2.59

10. Answer: (B) 7,875
42 × 75 × 1/3 ft. (4") = 1050 cu. ft.
×   7 ½
7,875 gallons

TEST 3

DIRECTIONS: Each question or incomplete statement is followed by several suggested answers or completions. Select the one that BEST answers the question or completes the statement. *PRINT THE LETTER OF THE CORRECT ANSWER IN THE SPACE AT THE RIGHT.*

1. The part of the total quantity represented by a 24-degree sector of a circle graph is
   A. $6^2/_3$%   B. 12%   C. $13^1/_3$%   D. 24%

2. If the shipping charges to a certain point are 62 cents for the first 5 oz. and 8 cents for each additional ounce, the weight of a package for which the charges are $1.66 is
   A. 13 ounces   B. $1^1/_8$ lbs.   C. 1¼ lbs.   D. 1½ lbs.

3. If 15 cans of food are needed for 7 men for 2 days, the number of cans needed for 4 men for 7 days is
   A. 15   B. 20   C. 25   D. 30

4. The total saving in purchasing thirty 13-cent ice cream pops for a class party at a reduced rate of $1.38 per dozen is
   A. 35¢   B. 40¢   C. 45¢   D. 50¢

5. The quotient for the division of 36 apples among 4 children may be correctly found by thinking
   A. 36 ÷ ¼   B. $4\overline{)36.0}$ C. ¼ of 36   D. 4/36

6. The missing term in the equation 1/3 of ? = ½ of 90 is
   A. 45   B. 30   C. 15   D. 135

7. The fraction CLOSEST to 4/5 is
   A. 2/3   B. 7/9   C. 8/11   D. 5/8

8. Of the following, the one which may be used CORRECTLY to compute the value of 4 × 22½ is
   A. (4×45) + (4×1/2)
   B. (4×1/2) + (4×2)+(4×2)
   C. (1/2 if 4(+ (2×4)+(2×4)
   D. (4×20) + (4×2)+((4×1/2)

9. 16 ½ ÷ ¼ may CORRECTLY be expressed as
   A. (1/4×16) + (1/4×1/2)
   B. (4×16) + 4×1/2)
   C. $4\overline{)16.5}$
   D. ¼ times 33/2

10. In computation, ¾ may be CORRECTLY transformed into 6/8 for the same reason that
    A. 7(3+4) = 21 + 28
    B. 3 apples + 5 apples = 8
    C. $.2\overline{)3.4} = 2\overline{)34}$
    D. 3 + 4 = 4 + 3

KEY (CORRECT ANSWERS)

1. A   6. D
2. B   7. B
3. D   8. D
4. C   9. B
5. C   10. C

SOLUTIONS TO ARITHMETICAL REASONING

1. Answer: (A) 6 2/3%

   $$\frac{24}{360} = \frac{2}{30} = \frac{1}{15} = .06\ 2/3 = 6\ 2/3\%$$

2. Answer: (B) 1 1/8 lbs.
   Total charges = $1.66
   Charge for 1st 5 oz. =   .62
                         $1.04 (remaining charges at rate of .08/oz.)

   5 oz. + 13 oz. = 18 oz. (Total no. of oz. in weight of pkge.)
   OR $\frac{18}{16}$ 1 1/8 lb.

3. Answer: (D) 30
   If 15 cans of food are needed for 7 men for 2 days, therefore, 7½ cans are needed for these same 7 men for 1 day.
   7 ½ ÷ 7 = 15/14 the no. of cans needed by 1 man for 1 day.
   4 × 7 × 15/14 = 30, the number of cans needed by 4 men for 7 days.

4. Answer (C) 45¢
   $.13 × 30 = $3.90 (regular rate)
   30 = 2½ doz.; $1.38 × 2½ = $3.45 (reduced rate)
   Total saving = $.45 ($3.90 - $$3..45)

5. Answer: (C) ¼ of 36   36/4 = 9

6. Answer: (D) 135   1/3 of ? = ½ of 90
                    1/3x = 45
                    x = 3 × 45
                      = 135

7. Answer: (B) 7/9
   4/5 = .80   8/11 = .73
   2/3 = .66   5/8 = .63
   7/9 = .78

8. Answer: (D) (4 × 20) + (4× 2) + (4 × ½)

    $$\begin{array}{r} 22\ \tfrac{1}{2} \\ \times 4 \\ \hline 80 \\ 8 \\ 2 \\ \hline 10 \end{array}$$

    Choice (D) (4×20) + (4×2) + (4×1/2) = 80 + 8 + 2 = 90
    (This is an example of the Distribution Law which links the operations of addition and multiplication.)

9. Answer: (B) (4×16) + (4×1/2)

    $$16\ \tfrac{1}{2} \div 4 = \frac{16\ 1/2}{4} = 16\ \tfrac{1}{2} \times 4/1 = (4 \times 16) + (4 \times 1/2)$$

10. Answer: (C) $2\overline{)3.4} = 2\overline{)34}$

    $$\frac{3}{4} = \frac{6}{8}\ ;\ \frac{3.4}{.2} = \frac{34}{2} = 17$$

TEST 4

DIRECTIONS: Each question or incomplete statement is followed by several suggested answers or completions. Select the one that BEST answers the question or completes the statement. *PRINT THE LETTER OF THE CORRECT ANSWER IN THE SPACE AT THE RIGHT.*

1. The mathematical law of distribution is illustrated by all of the following EXCEPT:

    A. 15
        ×12

        150
        30

        180

    B. 15
        ×12

        30
        150

        180

    C. 15
        ×12

        180

    D. 15
        ×12

        30
        15

        180

    1._____

2. Of the following series of partial sums which might arise in the addition of 36 and 25, the one that is INCORRECT IS:
    A. 11, 31, 61   B. 11, 4, 6, 61   C. 11, 41, 61   D. 36, 56, 61

    2._____

3. Of the following, the one which equals one million is:
    A. ten hundred thousand
    B. 10^7
    C. 10×10×10×10×10×10×10
    D. 1 plus 6 zeros

    3._____

4. Of the following groups, the one containing four terms all associated with one algorismic process is:
    A. Added, quotient, dividend, divisor
    B. Dividend, quotient, divisor, minuend
    C. Dividend, quotient, addend; minuend
    D. Multiplicand, product, minuend, addend

    4._____

5. Depreciation of a certain machine is estimated, for any year, at 20% of its value at the beginning of the year.
    If the machine is purchased for $600, its estimated net value at the end of two years is CLOSEST to
    A. $325   B. $350   C. $375   D. $400

    5._____

6. Hats are purchased at the rate of $33 per dozen.
    If they are sold at a close-out sale for $2.50 each, the *percent loss* on the cost price is
    A. 3   B. 3 1/3   C. 9 1/11   D. 10

    6._____

7. The time, 3 hours, 58 minutes after 10:56 A.M. is
    A. 4:54 P.M.   B. 2:54 P.M.   C. 4:15 P.M.   D. 2:15 P.M.

    7._____

8. Mr. Brown had $20.00 when he took his three children on a bus trip. He spent $7.33 for the four tickets and bought each of the children a magazine costing 15¢, a candy bar costing 11¢, and a 5¢ package of chewing gum. His change from the $20.00 was
    A. $12.74   B. $11.43   C. $11.74   D. $12.84

    8._____

9. The loan value on a life insurance policy at the end of 5 years is $30.19 per $1,000 of insurance.
The LARGEST amount to the nearest dollar that can be borrowed n a $5,500 policy at the end of five years is
   A. $17 B. $151 C. $166 D. $1,660

10. Using cups that hold six ounces of milk, the number of cupfuls a person can obtain from 1 ½ gallons of milk is
    A. 16 B. 24 C. 32 D. 64

KEY (CORRECT ANSWERS)

1. C   6. C
2. B   7. B
3. A   8. C
4. B   9. C
5. C   10. C

SOLUTIONS TO ARITHMETICAL REASONING

1. Answer: (C)
   15
   ×12
   ───
   180

   The Distributive Law links the operations of addition and arithmetic.

2. Answer: (B) 11, 4, 6, 61

   Partial Sums

v36	(A) 11	(C) 11	(D) 36
+25	+20	+30	+20
61	31	41	56
	+30	+20	+5
	61	61	61

3. Answer: (A) ten hundred thousand 100,000 × 1,000,000

4. Answer: (B) dividend, quotient, divisor, minuend
   Division is repeated subtraction
   divisor   21   quotient
           12)256   dividend
             24
             16   minuend – partial dividend
             12
              4   partial dividend

     36   multiplicand
   ×45   multiplier
   ─────
   180   partial product   5 addend
   144   partial produce   +6 addend
   ─────
   1620   product   11 sum

   7,485   minuend
   2,648   subtrahend
   4,837   remainder (difference)

5. Answer: (C) $375

$600	$480	$600	$480
× .20	× .20	-120	96
120.00	96.00	$480	$384 (approximately

4 (#4)

6. Answer: (C) 9 1/11
Cost of one dozen
Selling price of one dozen $33.00 $2.50
                             30.00   ×   12
                            $ 3.00 $30.00 sold at close-out sale

$$\frac{L}{C} = \frac{\$3}{\$33} = \frac{1}{11} = 9\ 1/11\%$$

7. Answer: (B) 2:54 P.M.
A simple way to do this is to add 4 minutes to 10:56 A.M., making 11:00 A.M. Adding 3 hours = 2:00 P.M.
Adding 54 minutes (instead of 58 minutes, to compensate for the 4 minutes added to 10:56 A.M.) = 2:54 P.M.

8. Answer: (C) $11.74

15¢	31¢	$7.33	$20.00
11¢	×3	+.93	-8.26
5¢	93¢	$8.26	$11.74
31¢			

9. Answer: (C) $166
$30.19 × 5 = $150.95 (loan value on $5,000 policy at end of 5 years))
$150.95 ÷ 10 = $15.10 (approx.) (loan value on additional $500 at end of 5 years)
∴ $150.95 + $15.10 = $166 (approx.)

10. Answer: (C) 32
We must know that 1 cup = 8 oz. and that 1 qt. = 4 cups or 32 oz.
Since 1 gallon = 4 qts., 1 gallon = 128 oz. (4×32 oz.)
∴ ½ gallon = 64 oz. and 1 ½ gallon = 192 oz. (128 +64)
Finally, 192 ÷ 6 = 32 (cups)

TEST 5

DIRECTIONS: Each question or incomplete statement is followed by several suggested answers or completions. Select the one that BEST answers the question or completes the statement. *PRINT THE LETTER OF THE CORRECT ANSWER IN THE SPACE AT THE RIGHT.*

1. A storekeeper purchased an article for $36. In order to include 10% of cost for overhead and to provide $9 of net profit, the MARKUP should be
   A. 25%   B. 35%   C. 37 ½ %   D. 40%

   1.____

2. A rectangular carton has twice the height, one-third the length, and four times the width of a second carton. The ratio of the volume of the first carton to that of the second is
   A. 16 : 3   B. 3 : 1   C. 8 : 3   D. 3 : 8

   2.____

3. If a boy has a number of dimes and quarters in his pocket adding up to $3.10, the LARGEST possible number of dimes he can have is
   A. 16   B. 28   C. 26   D. 21

   3.____

4. In a number system using the base 10, the value represented by the first digit 3 reading from the left, in the number 82,364,371, is _____ times the value represented by the second digit 3.
   A. 30   B. 100   C. 1,000   D. 10,000

   4.____

5. The number of revolutions made by a bicycle wheel of 28-inch diameter in traveling ½ mile is CLOSEST to
   A. 720   B. 180   C. 360   D. 120

   5.____

6. Of the following, the property which is TRUE of all parallelograms is that the
   A. diagonals are equal   B. diagonals meet at right angles
   C. sum of the interior angles is 180°   D. diagonals bisect each other

   6.____

7.
```
      218
  32)6985
     64
     58
     32
     265
     256
       9
```

   7.____

244

Of the following explanations about steps in the above computation, the one which is LEAST meaningful or accurate is that the
- A. 64 represents 200 × 32
- B. 265 is the result of subtracting 320 from 585
- C. 9 is part of the quotient
- D. 256 symbolizes the subtraction of 32 eight times

8. Assuming that a system of meridians and parallels of latitude like that used on maps of the earth's surface, were designed for the moon's surface, the distance covered by a man traveling 1° on the moon, as compared to that covered in traveling 1° on the earth, would be
   - A. equal
   - B. less
   - C. greater
   - D. sometimes greater and sometimes less

9. 1958 may MOST correctly be expressed in Roman numerals as
   - A. MDCDLVIII
   - B. CMMLVIII
   - C. MCMLVIII
   - D. MCMLIIX

10. If the same positive quantity is added to both the numerator and the denominator of a proper fraction, the VALUE of the new fraction as compared to that of the original fraction will be
    - A. greater
    - B. less
    - C. equal
    - D. either greater or less

KEY (CORRECT ANSWERS)

1.	B	6.	D
2.	C	7.	C
3.	C	8.	B
4.	C	9.	C
5.	C	10.	A

SOLUTIONS TO ARITHMETICAL REASONING

1. Answer: (B) 35%
   Cost = $36
   Overhead = 10% of cost, OR $3.60
   Profit = $9.00 (Given)
   Selling Price = $48.60 (36 + 3.60 + 9)
   Markup = $12.60 (48.60 (S.P.) − 36 (Cost))

   Finally, $\dfrac{12.60 \text{ (markup)}}{36.00 \text{ (cost)}} = 35\%$

2. Answer: (C) 8 : 3

   First Carton

   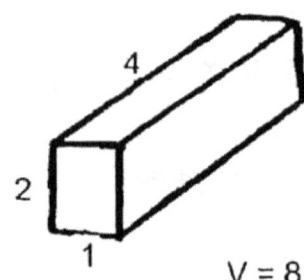

   V = 8

   Second Carton

   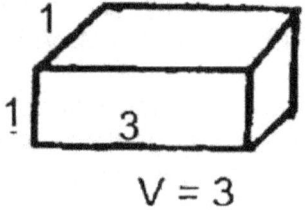

   V = 3

   $\dfrac{V1}{V2} = \dfrac{8}{3}$

3. Answer: (C) 26   26 × 10 = $2.60 + .50 = $3.10.

4. Answer: (C) 1,000 times the value represented by the second digit 3 (approximately)
   300 × 1,000 = 300,000

5. Answer: (C) 360

   C = πD
   C = 22/7 × 28 = 88"

   1 revolution of wheel covers 88"
   ½ × 5280 × 12/1 = traveling distance in inches

   6 × 5280 − 32680 inches

   ```
         360 revolutions
   88)31680
      264
      528
      528
   ```

6. Answer: (D) diagonals bisect each other

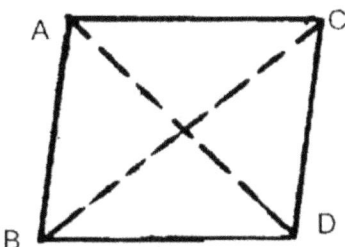

triangle = 180°

parallelogram = 360°

7. Answer: Answer (C) 9 is part of the quotient
Division is repeated subtraction
Below is a division "pyramid," which shows what actually happens when we divide.

```
         8
        10
       200
32)6985    dividend            32 × 100 = 3200
   6400                        32 × 200 = 6400
    585   partial dividend     32 × 10 = 320
    320
    265   partial dividend
    256
      9   partial dividend
```

8. Answer: (B) less
Diameter of moon = 2000 mile; diameter of earth = 8000 miles

Moon

Earth

The larger the circle, the larger the arc.
1° of arc = 1/360 of circle

Circumference of earth = 25,000 miles
Circumference of moon = 6,200 miles (1/4 of earth)

```
       69+
360)25,000            1° = 69+ miles on the equator (Earth)
    21 6              1° = 17+ miles (Moon)
     3 40
     3 24
       16
```

247

9. Answer: (C) MCMLVIII

   M   = 1000
   CM = 900
   L   = 50
   VIII = 8
         1958

10. Answer: (A) greater

    $\dfrac{2+2}{3+2} = \dfrac{4}{5} = \dfrac{12}{15}$ $\qquad\qquad \dfrac{2}{3} = \dfrac{10}{15}$

EXAMINATION SECTION
TEST 1

DIRECTIONS: Each question or incomplete statement is followed by several suggested answers or completions. Select the one that BEST answers the question or completes the statement. *PRINT THE LETTER OF THE CORRECT ANSWER IN THE SPACE AT THE RIGHT.*

1. 2/3 × 12 equals
   A. 4
   B. 6
   C. 8
   D. 18
   E. None of the above

   1.____

2. 83.97
   1.78
   14.36
   9.03
   The sum of the above column is
   A. 99.13   B. 99.24   C. 109.14   D. 109.23   E. 109.24

   2.____

3. The value of x in the equation 5x = 75 is
   A. 13
   B. 15
   C. 70
   D. 80
   E. None of the above

   3.____

4. 65 ÷ .13 equals
   A. .501
   B. 5.01
   C. 50.1
   D. 501
   E. None of the above

   4.____

5. The sum of 6 feet 8 inches and 3 feet 4 inches is
   A. 2 ft. 2 in.
   B. 9 ft.
   C. 10 ft.
   D. 10 ft. 12 in.
   E. None of the above

   5.____

6. 3/4 − 1/2 + 1/8 equals
   A. 3/10
   B. 3/8
   C. 5/8
   D. 1 3/8
   E. None of the above

   6.____

7. 4 5/16 − 2 3/8 equals
   A. 1 15/16
   B. 2 1/16
   C. 2 ¼
   D. 2 15/16
   E. None of the above

   7.____

8. (-12)+(-3) equals
   A. -9
   B. +15
   C. +9
   D. -15
   E. None of the above

   8.____

9. The ratio of the lengths of two lines is 5 to 3. The length of the shorter line is 30 inches. The length of the longer line is _____ inches.
   A. 18
   B. 48
   C. 50
   D. 140
   E. None of the above

   9.____

249

10. .025 written as a common fraction is
    A. 25/10   B. 25/100   C. 25/1000
    D. 25/10,000   E. None of the above

11. In the proportion 5/2 = 9/x the value of x is
    A. 1.8   B. 3.6   C. 22.5
    D. 36   E. None of the above

12. 33 1/3 percent of 3 equals
    A. 1   B. 10   C. 100/3
    D. 100   E. None of the above

13. √233 equals
    A. 15   B. 20.5   C. 25
    D. 112.5   E. None of the above

14. On the portion of the scale shown at the right, the reading to which the arrow points is _____ units.
    A. 6 3/16
    B. 6 3/5
    C. 6 3/4
    D. 7 5/8
    E. None of the above

15. If 4x/5 − 6 = 10, then x equals
    A. 15 1/5   B. 5   C. 4
    D. 3 1/5   E. None of the above

16. The difference between 8 hours 0 minutes 6 seconds and 6 hours 4 minutes 15 seconds is _____ hr. _____ min. _____ seconds.
    A. 0; 54; 51   B. 1; 54; 51   C. 2; 4; 9
    D. 2; 54; 45   E. None of the above

17. The scores made by nine pupils on a science test are: 2, 4, 6, 6, 8, 10, 12, 14, 19.
    The MEAN score is
    A. 6   B. 8   C. 9
    D. 81   E. None of the above

18. A certain cost formula is represented graphically in the figure at the right. From the graph, when n = 7, the value of C is about
    A. 140
    B. 120
    C. 110
    D. 102
    E. None of the above

19. A simplified form of the expression A = 1/2 bh + 1/2 ah is 19._____
    A. A = ½ h(b+a)   B. bh + ah   C. A = abh
    D. $\dfrac{A}{1/2bh}$ = 1/2 ah   E. None of the above

20. The ratio of 6 inches to 3 feet is 20._____
    A. 6/1   B. 2/1   C. 1/2
    D. 1/18   E. None of the above

21. The value of s in the equation 3s = 12 – s is 21._____
    A. 6   B. 4   C. 3 2/3
    D. 3   E. None of the above

22. 16 2/3 percent of what number is 30? 22._____
    A. 5   B. 18   C. 160
    D. 180   E. None of the above

23. The line graph shown at the right represents the temperature readings in Albany, New York, at two-hour intervals from 4 A.M. to 10 P.M. on a certain day in February. The APPROXIMATE change in temperature between 7 A.M. and 9 A.M. is _____ degrees. 23._____
    A. 3.5
    B. 3.0
    C. 2.5
    D. 2.0
    E. None of the above

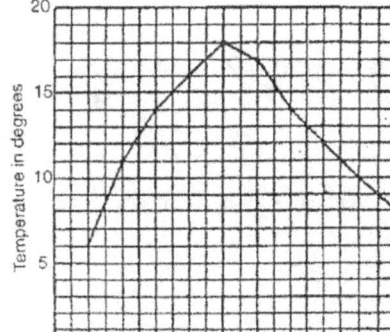

Questions 24-25.

DIRECTIONS: Questions 24 and 25 are to be answered on the basis of the following figure and information.

In the figure below, a square whose side is b is cut from a square whose side is a.

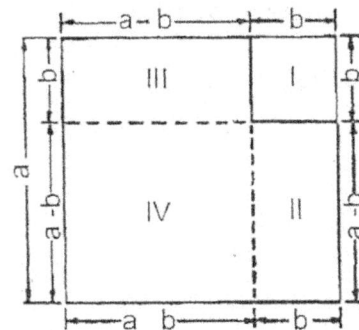

24. The sum of the perimeters of Section I and Section III can be represented by
    A. b^2 B. $4a - 2b$ C. $2a + 3b$
    D. $a(a-b)$ E. None of the above

24.____

25. The sum of the areas of Section II and Section IV can be represented by
    A. b^2 B. $4a - 2b$ C. $2a + 3b$
    D. $a(a-b)$ E. None of the above

25.____

26. The temperature reading (F) on the Fahrenheit scale equals 32 more than 9/5 of the Centigrade reading (C).
    This rule when translated into symbols is expressed by
    A. F = 9/5C + 32   B. F = 9/5(C+32)   C. F = 9/5 + 32C
    D. F + 32 = 9/5C   E. None of the above

26.____

27. In the equation 6x − 114 = .3x, the value of x is
    A. 38   B. 20   C. 12 2/3
    D. 2   E. None of the above

27.____

28. What percent of 42 is 84?
    A. 4%   B. 2%   C. 50%
    D. 200%   E. None of the above

28.____

29. The CORRECT name of the solid figure at the right is
    A. semicircle
    B. circle
    C. sphere
    D. cone
    E. cylinder

29.____

30. Which of these fractions has the LARGEST value?
    A. 1/2   B. 5/9   C. 7/12
    D. 2/3   E. 3/4

30.____

31. The formula for the area of a circle is A =
    A. π^2 B. $2/3\, \pi^2$ C. $2\pi r$
    D. bh   E. None of the above

31.____

32. The CORRECT name of the figure at the right is
    A. pentagon
    B. hexagon
    C. rectangle
    D. trapezoid
    E. square

32.____

33. The figure at the right is a
    A. rectangle
    B. square
    C. pentagon
    D. trapezoid
    E. parallelogram

33.____

34. If x = -18, y = 3, and z = -2, then x – y + z equals
    A. 3   B. -3   C. -23   D. -52   E. -56

34.____

35. The number 335,560 rounded off to the nearest thousand is
    A. 335,000   B. 335,500   C. 336,000
    D. 340,000   E. None of the above

35.____

36. In the triangle ABC at the right, the sum of the angles is _____ degrees.
    A. 360
    B. 180
    C. 90
    D. 35
    E. None of the above

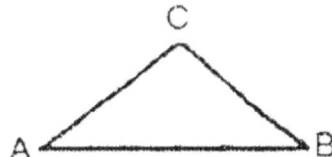

36.____

37. According to the map shown at the right, the APPROXIMATE distance between the southern point of New York City and Albany is _____ miles.
    A. 50
    B. 75
    C. 130
    D. 180
    E. 200

37.____

38. If 6 is added to a certain number n, the result is 1. An equation which expresses this relationship is
    A. n + 6 = 1   B. n – 1 = 6   C. 6 – n = 1
    D. n + 1 = 6   E. None of the above

38.____

39. In the expression $2n^3$, the 3 is called a(n)
    A. coefficient   B. factor   C. exponent
    D. multiplicand   E. None of the above

39.____

40. The number of inches in n feet is represented by
    A. 12n   B. 3n   C. n/3
    D. n/12   E. None of the above

40.____

41. The simple interest on $600 for 3 months at 4 percent per year is represented by 600 × .04x
    A. 1/4
    B. 1/3
    C. 3
    D. 4
    E. None of the above

    41.____

42. The circle graph shown at the right indicates how a family's annual budget of $3,000 was planned.
    Food   40 percent
    Shelter   25 percent
    Clothes   15 percent
    Operating Expenses 10 percent
    Insurance & Savings 10 percent
    The part of the circle representing Shelter is _____ degrees.
    A. 25
    B. 45
    C. 90
    D. 250
    E. None of the above

    42.____

43. In the parallelogram ABCD shown at the right, each small square represents 4 square inches. The area of the right triangle AED represents _____ square inches.
    A. 3
    B. 12
    C. 24
    D. 48
    E. None of the above

    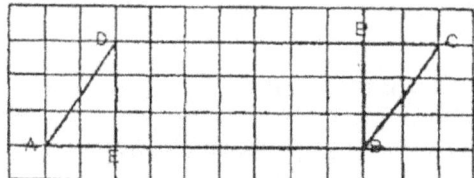

    45.____

44. A surveyor measured angle x with a transit. (See figure at the right.) Angle x is called
    A. the angle of depression B from A
    B. an obtuse angle
    C. the supplement of angle
    D. the angle of elevation of B from A
    E. none of the above

    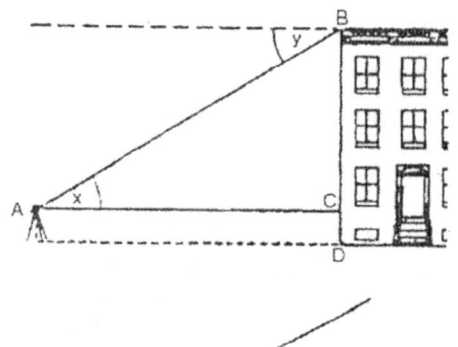

    44.____

45. In the figure at the right, AOB is a straight line. An equation showing the relationship between u and v is
    A. u = 1/2v
    B. u = 180 – v
    C. u + v = 90
    D. v = 3u
    E. None of the above

    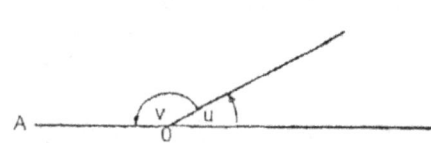

    45.____

46. If x = 4 when y = 6 and x varies directly as y, then when y = 15, x equals
   A. 20   B. 10   C. 1 3/5
   D. 1 1/3   E. None of the above

47. A discount of 15 percent from a marked price produces a net price which is _____ of the marked price.
   A. .15%   B. .85%   C. 15%   D. 85%   E. 115%

48. When the formula A = P + Prt is solved for t, t equals
   A. A − P − Pr   B. $\frac{A-Pr}{P}$ C. $\frac{A-P}{I+r}$
   D. $\frac{A-P}{Pr}$ E. None of the above

49. The Greek letter π
   A. was assigned the value 3.1416 by the International Court of Law
   B. was given an arbitrary value of 22/7 by a famous mathematician
   C. was discovered to be exactly 3.142
   D. when multiplied by the radius of a circle equals the area
   E. is used as a symbol for the ratio of the circumference of a circle to its diameter

50. If the base and altitude of a triangle are doubled, the area
   A. remains constant   B. is multiplied by 4   C. is doubled
   D. is divided by 4   E. is none of the above

51. Each side of the equilateral triangle in the figure at the right is s inches long. The length of an altitude of the triangle is represented as
   A. s in.
   B. $S\sqrt{2}$
   C. $S\sqrt{3}$
   D. $\frac{S\sqrt{3}}{2}$ in.
   E. None of the above

52. The length of a meter is about _____ inches.
   A. 1   B. 6   C. 12   D. 40   E. 100

53. A point which lies on the straight-line graph of the equation 2x − 3y = 12 is
   A. (3,-2)   B. (2,-3)   C. (-4,0)
   D. (0,6)   E. None of the above

8 (#1)

54. If the two parallel lines AB and CD in the figure at the right are cut by a third line, EF, then the FALSE statement is
 A. $\angle r + \angle s = \angle s + \angle y$
 B. $\angle y + \angle w = \angle t + \angle s$
 C. $\angle u + \angle w = \angle s + \angle x$
 D. $\angle r + \angle x = \angle t + \angle w$
 E. $\angle s + \angle u = \angle r + \angle t$

54.____

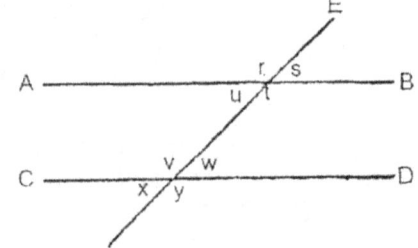

55. The product of n^4 and n^2 equals
 A. $2n^8$ B. $2n^6$ C. n^8
 D. n^2 E. None of the above

55.____

56. The volume of the rectangular solid shown at the right is
 A. 12 cu. in.
 B. 44 sq. in.
 C. 48 cu. in.
 D. 88 sq. in.
 E. None of the above

56.____

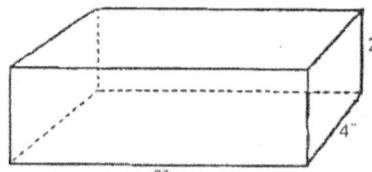

57. Baseball bats listed at twenty-one dollars per dozen are sold to schools at a discount of 20 percent.
 How much do they cost the schools per dozen?
 A. $4.20   B. $16.80   C. $20.80
 D. $25.20   E. None of the above

57.____

58. Last year a Chicago merchant's total business amounted to $30,000. For the goods sold, he paid $12,000, for rent he paid $2,500, for clerk services $4,742, and for other expenses $1,058.
 His average monthly net profit was
 A. $676.67   B. $891.67   C. $2,500.00
 D. $9,700.00 E. None of the above

58.____

59. If the marked price of an article is $100 and the first discount is 10 percent and the second discount 2 percent, the sale price is
 A. $78.20   B. $88.00   C. $88.20
 D. $88.80   E. None of the above

59.____

60. Mr. Smith agreed to pay an automobile agency a commission of 18 percent of the selling price of his car.
 If the selling price was $1,250, Mr. Smith would receive
 A. $225.00   B. $1,025.00   C. $1,227.50
 D. $1,475.00 E. None of the above

60.____

61. Mr. Browne receives $30.45 per year on an investment of $870.
 At this rate, if his total investment was $1,500, his annual interest would be
 A. $52.50   B. $62.50   C. $625.00
 D. $655.45   E. None of the above

61.____

62. The Ephrata National Bank discounted a 60-day note for $3,500 at 3½ percent per year.
    The proceeds of the note were
    A. $3,377.50 B. $3,479.58 C. $3,520.42
    D. $3,622.50 E. None of the above

    62._____

63. The normal weight of an adult can be found by using the formula w = 5.5(20+d), where w represents the weight in pounds and d the number of inches one's height exceeds 5 feet.
    By this formula, the normal weight of an adult who is 5'6" tall is _____ pounds.
    A. 134 B. 140.25 C. 140.8
    D. 143.0 E. None of the above

    63._____

64. In the figure at the right, triangles ACB and ADE are similar triangles. The length of side DE is _____ feet.
    A. 30
    B. 32
    C. 48
    D. 50
    E. None of the above

    64._____

65. A square piece of tin shown in the figure at the right is used to make an open box. One-inch squares are cut from each corner of the piece of tin and the sides then turned up, to form a box containing 49 cubic inches.
    The length of a side of the original square piece of tin required to make this box is _____ inches.
    A. 5
    B. 7
    C. 8
    D. 9
    E. None of the above

    65._____

KEY (CORRECT ANSWERS)

1. C	11. B	21. D	31. A	41. A	51. D	61. A
2. C	12. A	22. D	32. A	42. C	52. D	62. B
3. B	13. A	23. C	33. E	43. B	53. A	63. D
4. D	14. E	24. E	34. C	44. D	54. E	64. B
5. C	15. E	25. D	35. C	45. B	55. E	65. D
6. B	16. E	26. A	36. B	46. B	56. C	
7. A	17. C	27. B	37. C	47. D	57. B	
8. D	18. A	28. D	38. A	48. D	58. E	
9. C	19. A	29. E	39. C	49. E	59. C	
10. C	20. E	30. E	40. A	50. B	60. B	

SOLUTIONS TO PROBLEMS

1. $2/3 \times 12 = \frac{12}{1} = \frac{24}{3} = 8$

2. Adding, we get 109.14

3. If 5x = 75, x = 75/5 = 15

4. 65.13 ÷ 13 = 501

5. 6 ft. 8 in. + 3 ft. 4 in. = 9 ft. 12 in. = 10 ft.

6. 3/4 − 1/2 + 1/8 = 6/8 − 4/8 + 1/8 = 3/8

7. 4 15/16 − 2 3/8 = 3 21/16 − 2 6/16 = 1 15/16

8. (-12) + (-3) = -15

9. Let x = length of longer line. Then, 5:3 = x:30. Solving, x = 50

10. .025 = 25/1000 (Can also be reduced to 1/40)

11. Cross-multiplying, 5x = 18. Thus, 18/5 = 3.6

12. 33 1/3% of 3 = (1/3)(3) = 1

13. $\sqrt{225}$ = 15, since 15^2 = 225

14. The arrow points to 6 3/8

15. 4x/5 − 6 = 10. Adding 6, 4x/5 = 16. Then, x = 16 ÷ 4/5 = 20

16. 8 hrs. 0 min. 6 sec. − 6 hrs. 4 min. 15 sec. can be written as 7 hrs. 59 min. 66 sec. − 6 hrs. 4 min. 15 sec. to get 1 hr. 55 min. 51 sec.

17. Mean = (2+4+6+8+10+12+14+19) ÷ 9 = 9

18. When n = 0, c = 0. When n = 5, c = 100. Thus, c = 20n. Finally, for n = 7, c = (20)(7) = 140

19. A = 1/2 bh + 1/2 h(b+a)

20. 6 inches : 3 feet = 6 inches : 36 inches = 1/6

21. Add 5 to both sides to get 4s = 12, so s = 3

22. 16 2/3% of x is 30. Then, 1/6 x = 30. Then, 1/6 x = 180

23. At 7:00 A.M. the temperature was 12.5, while at 9:00 A.M. the temperature was 15. The change was 2.5 degrees.

24. Perimeter of Section I is 4b and the perimeter of Section III is 2b + 2a − 2b = 2a. The sum of the perimeters is 4b + 2a,

25. Area of Section II is b(a-b) = ab − b^2 and the area of Section IV is $(a-b)^2 = a^2 − 2ab + b^2$. The sum of the areas is a^2 − ab = a(a-b).

26. Direct translation of words to symbols yields F = 9/5C + 32

27. Subtract 6x to get -114 = 5.7x. Solving, x = 20

28. (84/42)(100)% = 200%

29. The figure is a cylinder.

30. Converting each choice to a decimal, we get .5, .$\bar{5}$, .58$\bar{3}$, .6, .75. The largest is .75 corresponding to 3/4.

31. For a circle, A = πr^2

32. A five-sided enclosed figure with straight sides is called a pentagon.

33. A quadrilateral with opposite sides parallel is called a parallelogram. Rectangles and squares are parallelograms with 90° angles.

34. x − y + z = 18 − 3 − 2 = 23

35. Since the digit in the hundreds place is 5 or greater, the answer is 336,000.

36. The sum of the angles of any triangle is 180°.

37. The scale difference is about 2 inches, and since 50 miles corresponds to 3/4 inch, the actual distance is about (50)(2÷3/4) = 133 1/3 mi. Closest answer given s 130 mi.

38. 6 added to n means 6 + n. Thus, 6 + n = 1 or n + 6 = 1.

39. 3 is an exponent for $2n^3$.

40. 12 inches in 1 foot means 12n inches in n feet.

41. 3 months = 1/4 year

42. 25% of 360 degrees = 90 degrees.

43. Area of △AED = (1/2)(2)(3) = 3 square units = 12 sq. inches.

44. Angle X is the angle of elevation to B from A.

13 (#1)

45. Since u + v = 180, we can also write u = 180 − v

46. 4/x = 6/15 Cross-multiplying, 6x = 60. Solving, x = 10

47. 100% - 15% = 85%

48. A = P + Prt becomes A − P = Prt. Dividing by Pr, we get: t = (A-P)/Pr

49. π = ratio of circumference to diameter of a circle.

50. Let B = base, H = altitude. Original area of triangle = 1/2BH. If new base and altitude are 2B and 2H, new area = ½(2B)(2H) = 2BH, which is 4 times the value of 1/2BH.

51. Let x = altitude. Then, $x^2 + (s/2)^2 = s^2$. This becomes $3/4 s^2 = x^2$. Solving, x = s $\sqrt{3}$ /2

52. 1 meter ≈ 39.37 inches ≈ 40 inches.

53. Substituting (3,-2), 2(3) − 3(-2) = 12. The other points do not lie on 2x − 3y = 12.

54. The false statement is ∠2 + ∠u = ∠r + ∠t. It is only true that ∠x = ∠u and ∠r = ∠t).

55. $n^4 \cdot n^2 = n^6$, since exponents are added in multiplication.

56. Volume = (6)(4)(2) = 48 cu. in.

57. ($21)(.80) = $16.80

58. $30,000 - $12,000 - $2,500 - $4,742 - $1,058 = $9,700. The monthly amount is $9,700 ÷ 12 = $808.33

59. ($100)(.90) = $90. Then, ($90)(.98) = $88.20

60. 1,250 − (1,250)(.18) = $1,025

61. $30.45/$870 = 3.5%. Then, 3.5% of $1,500 = $52.50

62. (.035)(60/360) = .005$\overline{83}$ = discount for 60 days.
The value of the note = (1 - .005$\overline{83}$)($3500) = $3,479.58.

63. W = 5.5(20+6) = (5.5)(26) = 143

64. x/80 = 40/100. Solving, x = 32. Note that AD:AC = DE:BC

65. When folded, each new side is $\sqrt{49}$ = 7

EXAMINATION SECTION
TEST 1

DIRECTIONS: Each question or incomplete statement is followed by several suggested answers or completions. Select the one that BEST answers the question or completes the statement. *PRINT THE LETTER OF THE CORRECT ANSWER IN THE SPACE AT THE RIGHT.*

1. Which of the following fractions is the SMALLEST?
   A. 2/3   B. 4/5   C. 5/7   D. 5/11

2. 40% is equivalent to which of the following?
   A. 4/5   B. 4/6   C. 2/5   D. 4/100

3. How many 100's are in 10,000?
   A. 10   B. 100   C. 10,000   D. 100,000

4. $\frac{6}{7} + \frac{11}{12}$ is approximately
   A. 1   B. 2   C. 17   D. 19

5. The time required to heat water to a certain temperature is directly proportional to the volume of water being heated.
   If it takes 12 minutes to heat 1 ½ gallons of water, how many minutes will it take to heat 2 gallons of water?
   A. 12   B. 16   C. 18   D. 24

6. The cost of an item increased by 25%.
   If the original cost was C dollars, identify the expression which gives the new cost of that item.
   A. C + 0.25   B. 1/4 C   C. 25C   D. 1.25C

7. Given the formula PV = nRT, all of the following are true EXCEPT
   A. T = PV/nR   B. P = nRTN   C. V = P/nRT   D. n = PV/RT

8. If a Fahrenheit (F) temperature reading is 104, find its Celsius (C) equivalent, given that C = i(F-32).
   A. 36   B. 40   C. 72   D. 76

9. If 40% of a graduating class plans to go directly to work after graduation, which of the following must be TRUE?
   A. Less than half of the class plans to go directly to work.
   B. Forty members of the class plan to enter the job market.
   C. Most of the class plans to go directly to work.
   D. Six in ten members of the class are expected not to graduate.

10. Given a multiple-choice test item which has 5 choices, what is the probability of guessing the correct answer if you know nothing about the item content?
   A. 5%   B. 10%   C. 20%   D. 25%

10.____

11.

S	T
0	80
5	75
10	65
15	50
20	30
25	5

Which graph BEST represents the data shown in the above table?

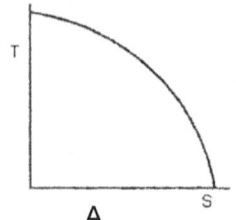 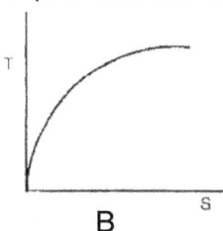 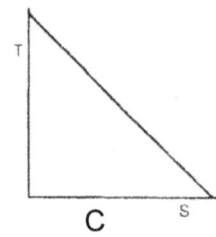 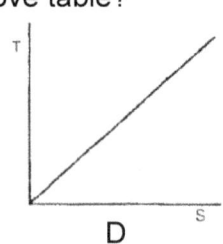

A   B   C   D

11.____

12. If 3(x+5y) = 24, find y when x = 3.
   A. 1   B. 3   C. 33/5   D. 7

12.____

13. The payroll of a grocery store for its 23 clerks is $395,421. Which expression below shows the average salary of a clerk?
   A. 395,421 × 23
   B. 23 ÷ 395,421
   C. (395,421 × 23
   D. 395,421 ÷ 23

13.____

14. If 12.8 pounds of coffee cost $50.80, what is the APPROXIMATE price per pound?
   A. $2.00   B. $3.00   C. $4.00   D. $5.00

14.____

15. A road map has a scale where 1 inch corresponds to 150 miles. A distance of 3 3/4 inches on the map corresponds to what actual distance? _____ miles.
   A. 153.75   B. 375   C. 525   D. 562.5

15.____

16. How many square feet of plywood are needed to construct the back and 4 adjacent sides of the box shown at the right?
   A. 63
   B. 90
   C. 96
   D. 126

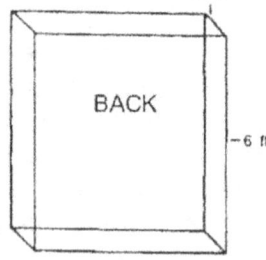

16.____

17. One thirty-pound bag of lawn fertilizer costs $20.00 and will cover 600 square feet of lawn. Terry's lawn is a 96 foot by 75 foot rectangle. How much will it cost Terry to buy enough bags of fertilizer for her lawn?
Which of the following do you NOT need in order to solve this problem? The
   A. product of 96 and 75
   B. fact that one bag weighs 30 pounds
   C. fact that one bag covers 600 square feet
   D. fact that one bag costs $20.00

17.____

18. On the graph shown at the right, between which hours was the drop in temperature GREATEST?
   A. 11:00 – Noon
   B. Noon – 1:00
   C. 1:00 – 2:00
   D. 2:00 – 3:00

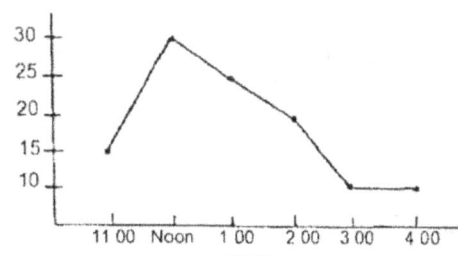

18.____

19. If on a typical railroad track the distance from the center of one railroad tie to the next is 30 inches, approximately how many ties would be needed for one mile of track?
   A. 180   B. 2,110   C. 6,340   D. 63,360

19.____

20. Which of the following is MOST likely to be the volume of a wine bottle?
   A. 750 milliliters   B. 7 kilograms
   C. 7 milligrams   D. 7 liters

20.____

21. What is the reading on the gauge shown at the right?
   A. -7
   B. -3
   C. 1
   D. 3

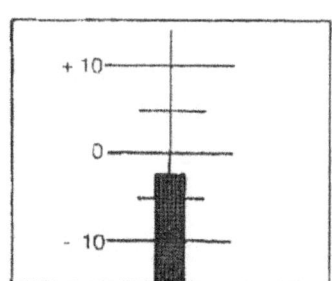

21.____

22. Which statement below disproves the assertion, *All students in Mrs. Marino's 10th grade geometry class are planning to go to college?*
   A. Albert is in Mrs. Marino's class, but he is not planning to take mathematics next year.
   B. Jorge is not in Mrs. Marino's class, but he is still planning to go to college.
   C. Pierre is in Mrs. Marino's class but says he will not be attending school anymore after this year.
   D. Crystal is in Mrs. Marino's class and plans to attend Yale University when she graduates.

22.____

23. A store advertisement reads, *Buy not while our prices are low. There will never be a better time to buy.*
    The customer reading this advertisement should assume that
    A. the prices at the store will probably never be lower
    B. right now, this store has the best prices in town
    C. prices are higher at other stores
    D. prices are always lowest at this store

24. *Given any positive integer, there is always a positive number B such that A × B is less than 1.*
    Which statement below supports this generalization?
    A. 8 × 1/16 = 1/2
    B. 8 × 1/2 = 4
    C. 5/2 × 1/10 = 1/4
    D. 1/2 × 1/2 = 1/2

25. Of the following expressions, which is equivalent to 4C + D = 12E?
    A. C = 4(12E-D)
    B. 4 + D = 12E − C
    C. 4C + 12E = -D
    D. $C = \frac{12E-D}{4}$

KEY (CORRECT ANSWERS)

1.	D		11.	A
2.	C		12.	A
3.	B		13.	D
4.	B		14.	C
5.	B		15.	D
6.	D		16.	C
7.	C		17.	B
8.	B		18.	D
9.	A		19.	B
10.	C		20.	A

21.	B
22.	C
23.	A
24.	A
25.	D

SOLUTIONS TO PROBLEMS

1. Converting to decimals, we get $.\overline{6}$, .8, .714 (approx..), $\overline{45}$. The smallest is $.\overline{45}$ corresponding to 5/11.

2. 40% = 40/100 = 2/5

3. 10,000 ÷ 100 = 100

4. $\frac{6}{7} + \frac{11}{12}$ = (72+77) ÷ 84 = $\frac{149}{84}$ ≈ 1.77 ≈ 2

5. Let x = required minutes. Then, 12/1 ½ = x². This reduces to 1 1/2x = 24. Solving, x = 16.

6. New cost is C + .25C = 1.25C

7. For PV = nRT, V = nRT/P

8. C = 5/9 (104-32) = 5/9(72) = 40

9. Since 40% is less than 50% (or half), we conclude that less than half of the class plans to go to work directly after graduation.

10. The probability of guessing right is 1/5 or 20%

11. Curve A is most accurate since as S increases, we see that T decreases. Note, however, that the relationship is NOT linear. Although S increases in equal amounts, the decrease in T is NOT in equal amounts.

12. 3(3+5y) = 24. This simplifies to 9 + 15y = 24. Solving, y = 1

13. The average salary is $395,421 ÷ 23

14. The price per pound is $50.80 ÷ 12.8 = $3,96875 or approximately $4.

15. Actual distance is (3 3/4)(150) = 562.5 miles.

16. The area of the back = (6)(5) = 30 sq. ft. The combined area of the two vertical sides is (2)(6)(3) = 36 sq. ft. The combined area of the horizontal sides is (2)(5)(3) = 30 sq. ft. Total area = 30 + 36 30 = 96 square feet.

17. Choice B is not relevant to solving the problem since the cost will be [(96)(75)/600][$20] = $240. So, the weight per bag is not needed.

18. For the graph, the largest temperature drop was from 2:00 P.M. to 3:00 P.M. The temperature dropped 20 – 10 = 10 degrees.

19. 1 mile = 5280 feet = 63,360 inches. Then, 63,360 ÷ 30 = 2112 or about 2110 ties are needed.

20. Since 1 liter = 1.06 quarts, 750 milliliters = (750/1000)(1.06) = .795 quarts. This is a reasonable volume for a wine bottle.

21. The reading is -3.

22. Statement C contradicts the given information, since Pierre is in Mrs. Marino's class. Then he should plan to go to college.

23. Since there will never be a better time to buy at this particular store, the customer can assume the current prices will probably never be lower.

24. Statement A illustrates this concept. Note that in general, if n is a positive integer. then $(n)(\frac{1}{n-1}) < 1$

25.

TEST 2

DIRECTIONS: Each question or incomplete statement is followed by several suggested answers or completions. Select the one that BEST answers the question or completes the statement. *PRINT THE LETTER OF THE CORRECT ANSWER IN THE SPACE AT THE RIGHT.*

1. Which of the following lists numbers in INCREASING order?
   A. 0.4, 0.04, 0.004
   B. 2.71, 3.15, 2.996
   C. 0.7, 0.77, 0.777
   D. 0.06, 0.5, 0.073

   1.____

2. $\frac{4}{10}+\frac{7}{100}+\frac{5}{1000} =$
   A. 4.75
   B. 0.475
   C. 0.0475
   D. 0.00475

   2.____

3. 700 times what number equals 7?
   A. 10
   B. 0.1
   C. 0.01
   D. 0.001

   3.____

4. 943-251 is approximately
   A. 600
   B. 650
   C. 700
   D. 1200

   4.____

5. The time needed to set up a complicated piece of machinery is inversely proportional to the number of years' experience of the worker.
   If a worker with 10 years' experience needs 6 hours to do the job, how long will it take a worker with 15 years' experience?
   A. 4
   B. 5
   C. 9
   D. 25

   5.____

6. Let W represent the number of waiters and D, the number of diners in a particular restaurant.
   Identify the expression which represents the statement: There are 10 times as many diners as waiters.
   A. 10W = D
   B. 10D = W
   C. 10D + 10W
   D. 10 = D + W

   6.____

7. Which of the following is equivalent to the formula F = XC + Y?
   A. F − C = X + Y
   B. Y = F + XC
   C. $C = \frac{FY}{X}$
   D. $C = \frac{FX}{Y}$

   7.____

8. Given the formula A = BC/D, if A = 12, B = 6, and D = 3, what is the value of C?
   A. 2/3
   B. 6
   C. 18
   D. 24

   8.____

9. 5 is to 7 as X is to 35. X =
   A. 7
   B. 12
   C. 24
   D. 49

   9.____

10. Kramer Middle School has 5 seventh grade mathematics teachers: two of the math teachers are women and three are men.
    If you are assigned a teacher at random, what is the probability of getting a female teacher?
    A. 0.2
    B. 0.4
    C. 0.6
    D. 0.8

    10.____

11. Which statement BEST describes the graph shown at the right?
    Temperature
    A. and time decrease at the same rate
    B. and time increase at the same rate
    C. increases over time
    D. decreases over time

12. If $3x + 4 = 22y$, find y when $x = 2$.
    A. 0   B. 3   C. 4 1/2   D. 5

13. A car goes 243 miles on 8.7 gallons of gas.
    Which numeric expression should be used to determine the car's miles per gallon?
    A. 243 × 87   B. 8.7 ÷ 243   C. 243 ÷ 8.7   D. 243 − 8.7

14. What is the average cost per book if you buy six books at $4.00 each and four books at $5.00 each?
    A. $4.40   B. $4.50   C. $4.60   D. $5.40

15. A publisher's sale offers a 15% discount to anyone buying more than 100 workbooks.
    What will be the discount on 200 workbooks selling at $2.25 each?
    A. $15.00   B. $30.00   C. $33.75   D. $67.50

16. A road crew erects 125 meters of fencing in one workday.
    How many workdays are required to erect a kilometer of fencing?
    A. 0.8   B. 8   C. 80   D. 800

17. Last month Kim made several telephone calls to New York City totaling 45 minutes in all.
    What does Kim need in order to calculate the average duration of her New York City calls?
    The
    A. total number of calls she made to New York City
    B. cost per minute of a call to New York City
    C. total cost of her telephone bill last month
    D. days of the week on which the calls are made

18.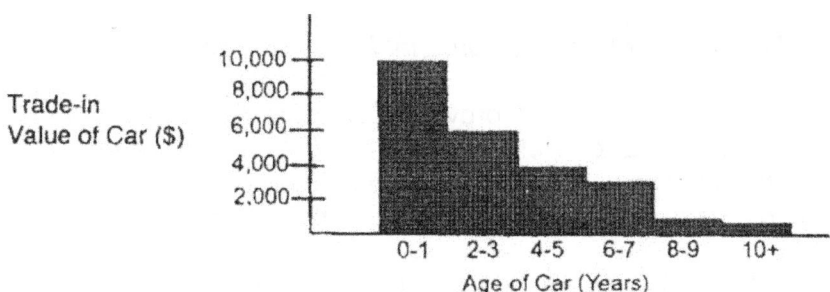

The above chart relates a car's age to its trade-in value.
Based on the chart, which of the following is TRUE?
   A. A 4- to 5-year old car has a trade-in value of about $2,000
   B. The trade-in vale of an 8- to 9-year old car is about 1/3 that of a 2- to 3-year old car.
   C. A 6- to 7-year old car has no trade-in value.
   D. A 4- to 5-year old car's trade-in value is about $2,000 less than that of a 2- to 3-year old car.

18.____

19. Which of the following expressions could be used to determine how many seconds are in a 24-hour day?
   A. 60 × 60 × 24
   B. 60 × 12 × 24
   C. 60 × 2 × 24
   D. 60 × 24

19.____

20. For measuring milk, we could use each of the following EXCEPT
   A. liters
   B. kilograms
   C. millimeters
   D. cubic centimeters

20.____

21. What is the reading on the gauge shown at the right?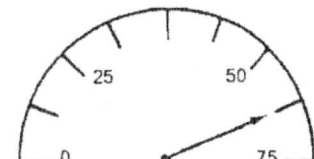
   A. 51
   B. 60
   C. 62.5
   D. 70

21.____

22. Bill is taller than Yvonne. Yvonne is shorter than Sue. Sue is 5' tall.
Which of the following conclusions must be TRUE?
   A. Bill is taller than Sue.
   B. Yvonne is taller than 5'4".
   C. Sue is taller than Bill.
   D. Yvonne is the shortest.

22.____

23. The Bass family traveled 268 miles during the first day of their vacation and another 300 miles on the next day. Maria Bass said they were 568 miles from home.
Which of the following facts did Maria assume?
   A. They traveled faster on the first day and slower on the second.
   B. If she plotted the vacation route on a map, it would be a straight line.
   C. Their car used more gasoline on the second day.
   D. They traveled faster on the second day than they did on the first day.

23.____

24. *The word LEFT in a mathematics problem indicate that it is a subtraction problem.*
   Which of the following mathematics problems prove this statement FALSE?
   A. I want to put 150 bottles into cartons which hold 8 bottles each. After I completely fill as many cartons as I can, how many bottles will be left?
   B. Sarah has 5 books but gave one to John. How many books did Sarah have left?
   C. Carlos had $4.25 but spent $3.75. How much did he have left?
   D. We had 38 models in stock but after yesterday's sale, only 12 are left. How many did we sell?

24._____

25. Let Q represent the number of miles Dave can jog in 15 minutes.
   Identify the expression which represents the number of miles Dave can jog between 3:00 P.M. and 4:45 P.M.
   A. 1 3/4 Q
   B. 7Q
   C. 15 × 1 3/4xQ
   D. Q/7

25._____

KEY (CORRECT ANSWERS)

1. C
2. B
3. C
4. C
5. A

6. A
7. C
8. B
9. C
10. B

11. D
12. D
13. C
14. A
15. D

16. B
17. A
18. D
19. A
20. C

21. C
22. D
23. B
24. A
25. B

SOLUTIONS TO PROBLEMS

1. Choice C is in ascending order since .y < .77 < .777

2. Rewrite in decimal form: .4 + .07 + .005 = .475

3. Let x = missing number. Then, 700x = 7. Solving, x = 7/700 = .01

4. 943 − 251 = 692 ≈ 700

5. Let x = hours needed. Then, 10/15 = x/6. Solving, x = 4

6. The number of diners (D) is 10 times as many waiters (10W). So, D = 10W, or 10W = D

7. Given F = XC + Y, subtract Y from each side to get F − Y = XC. Finally, dividing by X, we get (F−Y)/X = C

8. 12 = 6C/3. Then, 12 = 2C, so C = 6

9. 5/7 = x/35. Then, 7x = 175, so x = 25

10. Probability of a female teacher = 2/5 = .4

11. Statement D is best, since as time increases, the temperature decreases.

12. (3)(2) + 4 = 2y. Then, 10 = 2y, so y = 5.

13. Miles per gallon = 243/8.7

14. Total purchase is (6)($4) + (4)($5) = $44. The average cost per book is $44 ÷ 10 = $4.40

15. (220)($2.25) = $450. The discount is (.15))($450) = $67.50

16. The number of workdays is 1000 ÷ 125 = 8

17. Choice A is correct because the average duration of the phone calls = total time ÷ total number of calls.

18. Statement D is correct since a 4-5 year old car's value is $4,000, whereas a 2-3 year-old car's value is $6000.

19. 60 seconds = 1 minute and 60 minutes = 1 hour. Thus, 24 hours = (24)(60)(60) or (60)(60)(24) seconds.

20. We can't use millimeters in measuring milk since millimeters is a linear measurement.

21. The reading shows the average of 50 and 75 = 62.5

6 (#2)

22. Since Yvonne is shorter than both Bill and Sue, Yvonne is the shortest.

23. Statement B is assumed correct since 568 = 269 + 300 could only be true if the mileage traveled represents a straight line.

24. To find the number of bottles left, we look only for the remainder when 150 is divided b 8 (which happens to be 6).

25. 3:00 P.M. to 4:45 P.M. = 1 hour and 45 minutes = 105 minutes
Let Q = 15 minutes
105 / 15 = 7
7(15) = 105 = 7Q

MATHEMATICAL RELATIONSHIPS AND CONCEPTS

1. SOLVING LINEAR EQUATIONS

When solving simple linear equations, the goal is to rewrite the equation in the form *variable = constant* or *constant = variable*. To achieve the goal, you generally need to add the same quantity to both sides of the equation or to multiply both sides of the equation by the same quantity. Thus, to solve $3x - 6 = 14$, we would add 6, the opposite of -6, to both sides, obtaining $3x = 20$. We would then multiply both sides by 1/3, the *opposite* or *inverse* of 3, to obtain the final answer.

$$3x = 20$$
$$\frac{1}{3} \cdot 3x = \frac{1}{2} \cdot 20$$
$$x = \frac{20}{3} \text{ or } 6\frac{2}{3}$$

Notice that the equation has been reduced to the form *variable = constant*, that is $=6\frac{2}{3}$. Here is another example. Solve for x:

Add -7 (the opposite of 7) to both sides
This reduces to

Multiply both sides by $\frac{3}{2}$ because $\frac{3}{2}$ is the inverse of $\frac{2}{3}$

$$\frac{2}{3}x + 7 = 18$$
$$\phantom{\frac{2}{3}x} -7 \quad -7$$
$$\frac{2}{3}x = 11$$
$$\frac{3}{2} \cdot \frac{2}{3}x = \frac{3}{2} \cdot \frac{11}{1}$$
$$x = \frac{33}{2} \text{ or } 16\frac{1}{2}$$

Some equations have variables on both sides of the equality symbol.

Problem: Solve for x: $3x + 7 = 5x - 11$
Solution:

Add -3x to both sides
This reduces to:
Add 11 to both sides: This reduces to:
Multiply both sides by $\frac{1}{2}$:
The answer is:

$$3x + 7 = 5x - 11$$
$$-3x -3x$$
$$7 = 2x - 11$$
$$+11 +11$$
$$18 = 2x$$
$$\frac{1}{2} \cdot 18 = \frac{1}{2} \cdot 2x$$
$$9 = x$$

Problem: Solve for t: $4 + 3(t-2) = t + 1$

Solution: When equations contain parentheses, always remove the parentheses first and then proceed as usual. Here, $3(t-2)$ is equivalent to $3t - 6$. Thus,

	4	+ 3t	− 6	=	t	+	1
	3t	+ 4	− 6	=	t	+	1
Reordered: | | 3t | − 2 | = | t | + | 1 |
Reduced:
Add -t to both sides: | −t | | | = | −t | | |
The result is: | 2t | − 2 | | = | | | 1 |
Add 2 to both sides: | | + 2 | | | | | +2 |
The result is: | 2t | | | = | | | 3 |

Multiply both sides by 1/2:
$$\frac{1}{2} \cdot 2t = \frac{1}{2} \cdot 3$$
$$t = \frac{3}{2}$$

The answer is:

Problem: Solve for x: $0.17x + 1.2 = 6.3$

Solution: Sometimes you must multiply both sides by an appropriate power of ten in order to remove the decimals. Because the equation above has as many as two digits to the right of the decimal point, we multiply both sides by 10^2 or 100.

$$100(0.17x + 1.2) = 100(6.3)$$
$$17x + 120 = 630$$
$$17x = 510$$
$$x = 30$$

EXERCISES

1. Solve for x:
    A. $2x - 3 = 15$
    B. $5x + 8 = 20$
    C. $15 = 3x - 6$
    D. $\frac{2}{3}x - 7 = 4$
    E. $3/5x + 4 = 12$

2. Solve for x:
    A. $3x + 5 = 6x - 1$
    B. $4x - 5 = 12 - 9$
    C. $4 - 2x = 6x + 5$
    D. $12 - x = \frac{3}{2}x = 2$
    E. $300 - 140x = 3860x - 20$

3. Solve for the variable:
    A. $2x - 5 = 4(3x+1) - 2$
    B. $10t + 1 = 2(3t+5) - 1$
    C. $2(x+2) = 1 + 3(1-x)$
    D. $5 - (11 - 2x) = 7x + 7$

4. Solve for the variable:
   A. $0.42x - 1.2 = 7.2$
   B. $1.1a + 3 = 0.712$
   C. $-6.54 = 1.48t - 3.062$
   D. $\dfrac{1}{a} + 1 = 3$

2. EVALUATING ALGEBRAIC EXPRESSIONS

Evaluating algebraic expressions is mostly a matter of replacing variables with numbers. You may need to use your equation-solving knowledge to complete the process.

Problem: Find the value of y when x= 3 if $x = 3y - 6$.

Solution: $x = 3y - 6$
Replace x by 3 $3 = 3y - 6$
                                                   $+6 \quad\quad +6$
                                                   $9 = 3y$
                                                   $\dfrac{1}{3} \times 9 = \dfrac{1}{3} \times 3y$
The answer is: $3 = y$

EXERCISES

5. Evaluate the following when a=2, b=3, c=2:
   A. $-3a + 5b$
   B. $a(b+c)$
   C. $3a + 2b + 4c$

6. Find the value of y when x = 3 if
   A. $y = 3x - 9$
   B. $x + y = 11$
   C. $2x + 3y = 7$
   D. $5 - (x+y) = 11$
   E. $3y = 2x$

7. Solve for y if x = 20:
   A. $y = \dfrac{2}{3}x - 4$
   B. $y = \dfrac{9}{5}x + 32$
   C. $\dfrac{1}{3}y + \dfrac{1}{4}x = \dfrac{1}{5}$

8. Interest (I) equals principal (P) multiplied by the interest rate per unit of time (r) multiplied by the number of the time periods (t) of the loan: I = Prt. What is the rate per year if an invested principal of $2000 earns $320 interest over a 2-year period?

9. What is the value of a if b = 0.2 and 3.2 + a + 0.3b = 0.25?

3. SOLVING LITERAL EQUATIONS

A literal equation is one involving more than one variable; for example, 3x + 2y = 6 or d = rt. Often literal equations need to be solved for one or another of the variables in the equation. Thus, d = rt is in a form where d is the solution. To *solve for* r, we may divide both sides of the equation by t to obtain $\frac{d}{t} = \frac{rt}{t}$ or $\frac{d}{t} = r$. We might also divide both sides by r to obtain $\frac{d}{r} = t$.

Thus, we have three *equivalent* equations: $d = rt$; $\frac{d}{t} = r$; $\frac{d}{r} = t$.

Solving literal equations involves our usual equation-solving techniques: We add (or subtract) the same quantity to both sides of the equation, and we multiply (or divide) both sides by the same quantity.

Problem: Rewrite 2x + 9y - 18 = 0 in terms of y:

Solution:

$$2x + 9y - 18 = 0$$
$$\underline{\ +18\ \ +18}$$
$$2x + 9y\ \ \ = 18$$
$$\underline{-2x\ \ \ \ -2x}$$
$$9y\ \ \ = 18 - 2x$$

now divide both sides by 9:

$$\frac{9}{9}y = \frac{18 - 2x}{9}$$
$$y = \frac{18 - 2x}{9}$$

Problem: Solve the following for c: $F = \frac{9}{5}C + 32$

Solution:
$$F = \frac{9}{5}C + 32$$
$$\underline{-32 -32}$$
$$F - 32 = \frac{9}{5}C$$

$$\frac{5}{9}(F - 32) = \frac{5}{9} \times \frac{9}{5}C$$

$$\frac{5}{9}(F - 32) = C$$

Problem: Solve for x: $y = 14 - 8x$

Solution:

$$\begin{array}{rcl} y & = & 14 - 8x \\ -14 & & -14 \\ \hline y - 14 & = & -8x \end{array}$$

$$\frac{y-14}{-8} = \frac{-8x}{-8}$$

Multiply numerator and denominator by -1 to eliminate the negative denominator

$$\frac{y\ 14}{8} = x$$

$$\frac{14\ \ y}{8} = x$$

EXERCISES

10. Solve the equations in terms of y
    - A. $3x + y = 12$
    - B. $xy = 8$
    - C. $A = bry$
    - D. $4x + 3y = 12$
    - E. $4x - 13y = 17$
    - F. $3x = 6y$

11. Rewrite $I = Prt$ in terms of P

12. Solve $s = a + (n - 1)d$ for d

13. Rewrite $L = a(l + ct)$ in terms of c

14. Suppose $x\ y\ z = 10$. Solve for x and then for y

15. Give two equivalent forms of the equation $7x - 2y = 14$ by solving for x and for y

4. DIRECT AND INVERSE VARIATION

If the numbers involved are simple, direct and inverse variation problems can be done mentally.

Consider this problem: Suppose y varies directly as x. If y is 8 when x is 2, what is y when x is 3?

To say, *y varies directly as x* means y is a multiple of x. Now, if y is 8 when x is 2, what multiple of x must y be? Clearly, 8 is 4 times 2 so y must be 4 times x: $y = 4x$. At this point, you can answer the question, *What is y when x is 3?* Since $y = 4x$, it follows that when x is 3, y is 12.

Consider this problem: Suppose y varies directly as x. When $y = 5$, then $x = 10$. What is the value of y when $x = 6$? The variable y varies directly as x. This means that y is a multiple of x. What do you multiply the x-value of 10 by to get the y-value 5? The multiplier is 1/2 because 1/2 10 = 5. Thus, if $x = 6$, then $y = 1/2 \,.\, 6 = 3$.

EXERCISES

16. Solve these direct variation problems. In each case, y varies directly as x.
    A. If y is 3 when x is 1, then y = _____ when x = 6.
    B. If y is 10 when x is 2, then y = _____ when x = 4.
    C. If y is 2 when x is 4, then y = _____ when x = 9.
    D. If y is 5 when x is 15, then y = _____ when x = 9.
    E. If y is 3 when x is 2, then y = _____ when x = 10.
    F. If y is 12 when x is 4, then y = 15 when x = _____.
    G. If y is 3 when x is 9, then y = 4 when x = _____.
    H. If y is 3/2 when x is 1, then y = 6 when x = _____.
    I. If y is 5 when x is 2, then y = _____ when x = 6.

Although many variation problems can be solved or approximated mentally, there are mechanical, rote methods for solving such problems.

Consider problem 16I above: If y is 5 when x is 2, then y = _____ when x = 6. Some people might reason this way: *So y = 5 when x 2. That means that y equals two and a half times x. So if x = 6, then two and a half x's make 6 + 6 + 3 = 15, so when x = 6, then y = 15.*

Here is a mechanical way to do the same problem. Since y varies directly as x, y is a multiple of x: y = kx. By substituting the known values 5 and 2 for y and x respectively, you can solve for k. We know that y = kx, 5 = k.2. Therefore, 5/2 = k. If y = 5/2x and if x = 6, then y = 5/2.6 = 15. Thus, we have this procedure:

Use formula y = kx where $\frac{\text{Known y-value}}{\text{Known x-value}}$

EXERCISES

17. Solve these direct variation problems by using the formula y = kx. In each case, y varies directly as x. For each problem, identify the value of k you used and the value that goes in the blank.
    A. If y is 6 when x is 2, then y = _____ when x = 10.
    B. If y is 6 when x is 3, then y = _____ when x = 18.
    C. If y is 12 when x is 1/3, then y = _____ when x = 5.
    D. If y is 28 when x is -4, then y = _____ when x = 7.
    E. If y is 12 when x is 4, then y = 12.36 when x = _____.
    F. If y is 459 when x is 17, then y = 27 when x = _____.
    G. If y is 100 when x is -10, then y = -10 when x = _____.
    H. If y is 1.4 when x is 7, then y = 10 when x = _____.

18. The salary of an hourly worker varies directly with the number of hours she works per week. According to the records, she worked 24 hours last week and made $108. How many hours would she need to work this week to make $45?

19. The weight of a collection of machine screws varies directly as the number of screws in the collection. If 110 screws weigh 1.1 kg, how many screws are in a collection weighing 0.56 kg.?

By now you have noticed that y varies directly as x, when x increases so does y and when x decreases so does y. For instance, if x doubles then y also doubles. For inverse variations, however, if x doubles, then y decreases by half! Overall, for inverse variations one variable moves in the opposite direction from the other.

Direct Variation: If y = 8 when x = 4, then when x = 8, y = 16.
Inverse Variation: If y = 8 when x = 4, then when x = 8, y = 4.

Direct Variation: If y = 15 when x = 3, then when x = 9, y = 45.
Inverse Variation: If y = 15 when x = 3, then when x = 9, y = 5.

Suppose y is inversely related to x. Then if x doubles, y is 1/2 its former value. If the value of x is multiplied by 3, then the y-value is multiplied by 1/3, and so forth.

EXERCISES

20. Solve these inverse variation problems mentally. In each case, assume that y varies inversely as x.
    A. If y = 6 when x = 8, then y = _____ when x = 16.
    B. If y = 6 when x = 8, then y = _____ when x = 24.
    C. If y = 6 when x = 8, then y = _____ when x = 2.
    D. If y = 10 when x = 10, then y = _____ when x = 5.
    E. If y = 10 when x = 10, then y = _____ when x = 2.
    F. If y = 24 when x = 6, then y = 12 when x = _____.
    G. If y = 24 when x = 12, then y = 2 when x = _____.
    H. If y = 15 when x = 12, then y = 10 when x = _____.
    I. If y = 1 when x = 1, then y = 1/3 when x = _____.

As is the case with direct variation, there is also a formula (if you need it) for solving inverse variation problems:

$$y = \frac{k}{x} \text{ where } k = \text{(known x-value)} \cdot \text{(known y-value)}$$

Let us solve problem 20C by means of the formula. In this problem, k = 8·6 = 48. Thus, $y = \frac{48}{x}$. So, to find y when x = 2, we calculate y = 48/x = 48/2 = 24.

Let us use the formula to solve 20G. Here, k = 12·24 = 288. So the formula is $y = \frac{288}{x}$. If y = 2, then to find x we proceed as follows:

$$y = \frac{288}{x}.$$
$$2 = \frac{288}{x}$$
$$2x = 288$$
$$x = 144$$

21. Solve these inverse variation problems by using the formula $y = \frac{k}{x}$. In each case, y varies inversely as x. For each problem, identify the value of k you used and then the value that goes in the blank.
    A. If y is 12 when x = 2, then y = _____ when x = 1.
    B. If y is 6 when x = 2, then y = _____ when x = 3.
    C. If y is 2 when x = -3, then y = _____ when x = 1/2.
    D. If y is 6 when x = 4, then y = _____ when x = 3.
    E. If y is 3 when x = 2, then y = 1 when x = _____.
    F. If y is 10 when x = 9, then y = 45 when x = _____.

22. The pressure of a gas varies inversely as its volume. If the pressure is 21 pounds per square inch when the volume is 350 cubic inches, find the pressure when the volume is 70 cubic inches.

In place of phrases *varies directly as* or *varies inversely as,* you may encounter terms like *is directly proportional to* or *is inversely proportional to.* Problems 23-26 use this alternate wording.

23. The time required to heat water to a given temperature is directly proportional to the volume of water being heated. If 1 1/2 gallons of water take 12 minutes to heat, how many minutes will 2 gallons take to heat?

24. The scaled score on a particular test is directly proportional to the raw score. Lee had a scaled score of 500 and a raw score of 40. If Carlos had a scaled score of 375, what was his raw score?

25. The time required to travel one lap on a racetrack is inversely proportional to a car's average speed. A car averaging 90 mph takes 2 minutes to complete one lap. How long will it take to complete one lap at 120 mph?

26. A sociologist has developed a test for measuring *teaching anxiety* among junior high school teachers. She estimates that test scores are inversely related to years of teaching experience. If a teacher with 3 years experience scores 60, how many years experience has a teacher who scores 15?

5. RATIO AND PROPORTION

Ratio may be considered to be another word for *fraction*. The ratio of x to y is written x/y or x:y. Just as the fractions 2/4 and 1/2 are equal, we consider the ratio 2:4 to be the same as 1:2.

Thus, if an office employs 18 men and 15 women, we might report the ratio of men to women as 18:15, but more likely we would use 6:5 (dividing both terms by 3). On the other hand, the ratio of women to men would be 5:6. Watch out for the order of the numbers when writing ratios. The order of terms should match the order of groups or things to which they refer.

EXERCISES

27. Give the ratios required (using lowest terms).
    A. An office employs 10 female employees and 3 males. What is the ratio of males to females?
    B. A rectangle has length 20 and width 15. What is the ratio of length to width?
    C. John spends $200 a month for food and $300 a month for rent. What is the ratio of the amount he spends for food to the amount he spends for rent?
    D. A TV station airs 40 drama shows in a given week and 24 news/sports shows. What is the ratio of news/sports to drama for the TV station?

A proportion is a statement that two ratios are equal. Proportions are commonly used to solve ratio problems. Consider this problem: Bill needs to paint 3 identical bedrooms. He needs 5 gallons of paint for 2 of the rooms. How much paint will he need for all 3 rooms? We express the relationship this way

$$\frac{5}{2} = \frac{x}{3}$$ (Read 5 is to 2 as x is to 3) or this way

$$\frac{2}{5} = \frac{3}{x}$$ (Read 2 is to 5 as 3 is to x)

Note that both proportions will yield the same solution for x.

To solve a proportion, simply multiply as follows and solve the resulting equation:

Product: 15   Product: 2x

$$\frac{5}{2} = \frac{x}{3}$$

Thus,   15   =   2x
         7 1/2 = x

So, 7 1/2 gallons are needed for 3 rooms.

Here is a second problem: 3 is to 7 as 8 is to what?

$$\frac{3}{7} = \frac{8}{x}$$

$$3x = 7 \times 8$$
$$3x = 56$$
$$x = \frac{56}{3}$$

28. A park ranger counts 16 trout out of 30 fish sampled in a given lake. If the lake contains 2000 fish in all, how many would you predict should be trout?

29. The ratio of a person's weight on Mars to the person's weight on Earth is 2:5. How much would a 120-pound Earth person weigh on Mars?

30. A map of your hometown has a scale that reads, *1 inch equals 6 miles.* If two locations on the map are 4 12 inches apart, what is the distance between them in miles?

31. Gerry's car burns 1 1/2 quarts of oil on a 700-mile trip. How much oil will be needed for a 3000-mile trip?

32. If a 6-foot person casts a 4-foot shadow, how tall is a tree that casts a 25-foot shadow?

33. The ratio of male to female faculty members in the Delendo School system is 2:5. If there are 36 male faculty, how many female faculty are there?

34. A collection of miniature dinosaur replicas are all constructed on the same scale. One dinosaur, whose length is estimated at 12 feet, measures 4 inches. Another measures 6 inches. Estimate its length in feet.

35. It is estimated that student scores on two different physical skills tests are proportional. John got 20 on the first test and 32 on the second. If Maria got 6 on the first test, estimate her score on the second.

6. PERCENT PROBLEMS

What is 10% of 60? Many percent problems, such as this one, can be done mentally:

10% of 60 becomes 1/10 of 60 or 6
10% of 90 is 9
10% of 463 is 46.3, etc.

More complicated problems involve changing percents to decimals and manipulating the resulting numbers

23% of 187 becomes 0.23 x 187 or 43.01
102% of 16 becomes 1.02 x 16 or 16.32

Proportions can be used to solve many percent problems. Consider this question: *50 is 25% of what number?* Since 25% = 1/4, you could determine the answer in this way: 50 is 1/4 of 200. But you could also set up a proportion: 50 is to x as 25 is to 100.

$$\frac{50}{x} = \frac{25}{100}$$

or 50 . 100 = 25x

200 = x

Problem: 10 is 30% of what number?

Solution:
$$\frac{10}{x} = \frac{30}{100}$$
1000 = 30x

$$\frac{1000}{30} = x$$

33.3 = x (rounding the answer)

So, 10 is 30% of 33.3 (rounded).

Problem: 25 is what percent of 60?

Solution: $\frac{25}{60} = \frac{x}{100}$

41.67 = x (rounding the answer)

So, 25 is approximately 41.67% of 60.

EXERCISES

36. What is:
    A. 10% of 50
    B. 1% of 50
    C. 20% of 50
    D. 21% of 50
    E. 25% of 40
    F. 50% of 160
    G. 100% of 86
    H. 150% of 50

37. What is:
    A. 17% of 80
    B. 12% of 116
    C. 8% of 21
    D. 7.5% of $15.60

38. Solve the following:
    A. 16 is 25% of what number?
    B. 13 is 86% of what number?
    C. 10 is what percent of 18?
    D. 17 is what percent of 51?

39. Solve the following:
    Example: A shirt that regularly sells for $15 is on sale for $12. What is the percent of the discount?
    The discount is $3 out of $15. 3 is what percent of 15?

    $$3 = x \cdot 15$$

    $$\frac{3}{15} = x$$

    $$0.2 = x$$

So, x = 20%. The discount is 20%.

Example: The sign says that all merchandise is marked down 12%, What should one pay for a dress normally priced $28? 12% of $28 becomes 0.12 m . $28 or $3.36. Thus, the sale price of the dress is $28 - $3.36 or $24.64.
- A. The price of a $32 shirt has just increased by 16%. What does it cost now?
- B. A used car is marked $6200, but the salesman claims that he can deduct another 15%. What would the new price be?
- C. A movie ticket that usually sells for $4 now costs $5.
 What is the percent of the mark-up?
- D. A tire selling for $60 has just been reduced to $56.
 What is the percent of the discount?

40. Three grapefruits weighing 14 oz. each were combined with seven oranges weighing 8 oz. each. What percent of the total weight was provided by
 - A. the grapefruits?
 - B. the oranges?

7. EXPRESSING RELATIONSHIPS SYMBOLICALLY

Consider this problem: In Academy School there are twenty times as many students as there are teachers. Express this fact symbolically, letting S represent the number of students and T, the number of teachers. Which of the following answers is correct?
- A. $T = S + 20$
- B. $S = T + 20$
- C. $T = 20S$
- D. $S = 20T$

The Academy School problem illustrates what is meant by *expressing relationships symbolically.* When you have taken a relationship expressed in words and have expressed it by means of an equation or formula, it is a good idea to create an example to test your answer to see if it is correct.

Consider the Academy School problem. There are twenty times as many students as teachers at the school. If Academy School had, for example, one teacher, how many students would there be? There would be 20. So, if $T = 1$, $S = 20$. If you take the number of teachers (T) and multiply it by 20, you will identify the number of students (S): $20T = S$. Therefore, choice D above is the correct answer.

Notice how choices A, B, C fail when you substitute $T = 1$, $S = 20$ in the equations. By testing your answer, you can avoid incorrect responses. A person who thought $T = 20S$ was the correct equation should discover the error by responding in this way: *I know that for 20 students I should have one teacher. If I let $S = 20$ in the equation $T = 20S$, I would get $T = 20 . 20 = 400$. Four hundred teachers for 20 students? Something is wrong!*

Problem: An item regularly sells for R dollars but is on sale for S dollars. Which expression gives the percent discount?

A. $\dfrac{(R-S)(100)}{R}$

B. $\dfrac{100S}{R}$

C. $\dfrac{R-S}{100}$

D. $(R-S)100$

Solution: How do we find percent discounts? Suppose something that normally sells for $10 is on sale for $8. This discount is $2 out of $10 or 2/10, 0.20, or 20%. The strategy used was this: The sale price (S) was subtracted from the regular price (R), then the answer was divided by the regular price (R) to get 2/10 or 0.20. We then moved the decimal point two places to the right to get the answer, 20%. This is the same as multiplying by 100. Thus, the formula is identified this way: R-S/R . 100. The answer is A.

Only practice and some familiarity with frequently encountered situations can help improve formula and equation-writing skills. Remember, if you have any difficulty at all with these problems, begin by creating an example to test your answer. We did this with both problems above.

EXERCISES

41. If 100 pounds of scrap metal cost p dollars, how much is 2 tons worth at the same rate? (Note: 2000 pounds = 1 ton)

    A. 2p   B. $\dfrac{100-p}{2}$ C. 40p   D. $\dfrac{2-p}{100}$

42. An item regularly sells for p dollars but is marked 25% *off*. Which of the following is not a correct expression for the sale price?

    A. $\dfrac{3}{4}p$ B. (1-0.25)p   C. p - 1/4p   D. p - 25

43. Given a car's odometer reading S at the start of a trip, the reading F at the trip's finish, and the elapsed time t, write an expression for the trip's average speed V.

44. The regular price p of an item has been increased by 20%. Write an expression for the new price.

45. If x is positive and increasing in value, then y = 1/x is
    A. increasing and always positive
    B. increasing and always negative
    C. decreasing and always positive
    D. decreasing and always negative
    E. none of the above

46. If x is positive and increasing in value, then $y = \dfrac{1}{x}$ is

    A. increasing and always positive
    B. increasing and always negative
    C. decreasing and always positive
    D. decreasing and always negative
    E. none of the above

47. Write an expression that gives the total number of jars we need if each jar holds 0.5 liters and we need T liters in all. (Create an example to test your answer.)

48. Louise is trying to write an equation involving P, Q, and R. She has created an example showing that when P and Q are both 1, R must be 4. Which one or more of the following equations indicates this relationship?

    A. R = 5P - Q
    B. $1 = \dfrac{P+Q+R}{6}$
    C. R = 5(P-Q)
    D. 4Q = PR

49. Which of the following have the property that when x is positive and decreasing, y is positive and increasing?

    A. y = 4 - 1/x
    B. y = (4+x) 100
    C. xy = 1
    D. 1/x + 1/y = 3

50. Textbooks you plan to order cost $P. However, you receive a 20% discount on each book after the first 100 ordered. Which of the following will express your dollar cost if you order T textbooks, where T is larger than 100?

    A. 100P + 0.8(T-100)
    B. (100-0.20)PT
    C. 20P + 0.8PT
    D. 100P + 0.8PT

51. Suppose that personal income is taxed at a 15% rate for the first $20,000 and 28% for all income over that amount. Write an expression for the total tax paid on an income of D dollars, where D is larger than $20,000.

8. GRAPHS AND TABLES

For most people, reading graphs and tables is a matter of attention to detail and common sense. Carelessness is the most frequent cause of error. The exercises below will give you some idea of the most frequently encountered ways of displaying data and relationships pictorially.

52.

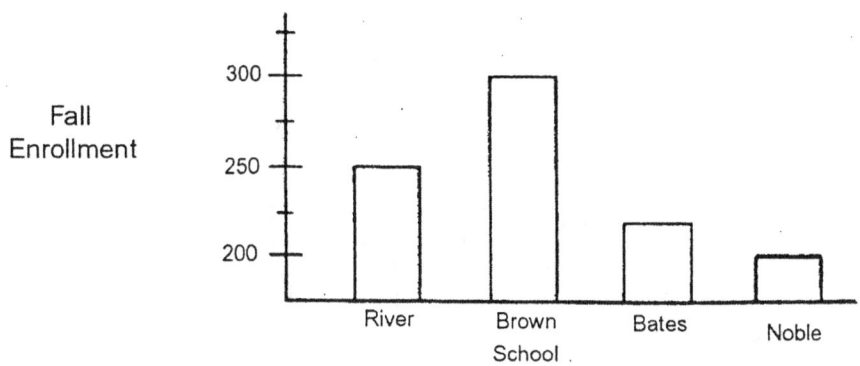

A. What is the total enrollment at the four schools?
B. What, approximately, is the ratio of the enrollment at Noble School to that at River School?
C. How many times greater is enrollment at Brown School than at Noble School?

53. This graph shows spending for the town of Amsden last year. What percentage went for police and fire protection?

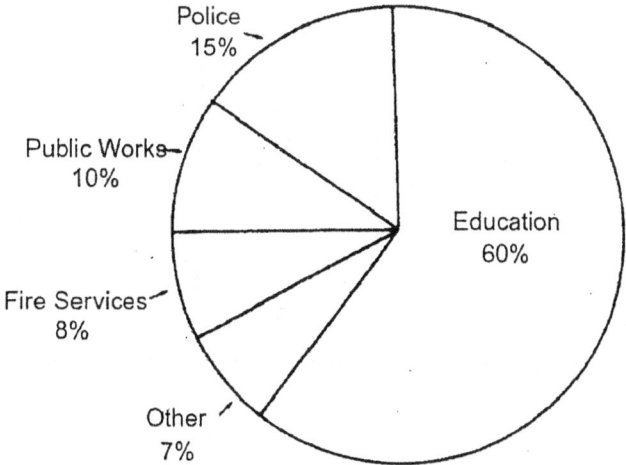

54. The graph below represents milk production for three counties last year. (Each symbol represents 10,000 gallons.) What was the approximate milk production in Balch County last year?

16

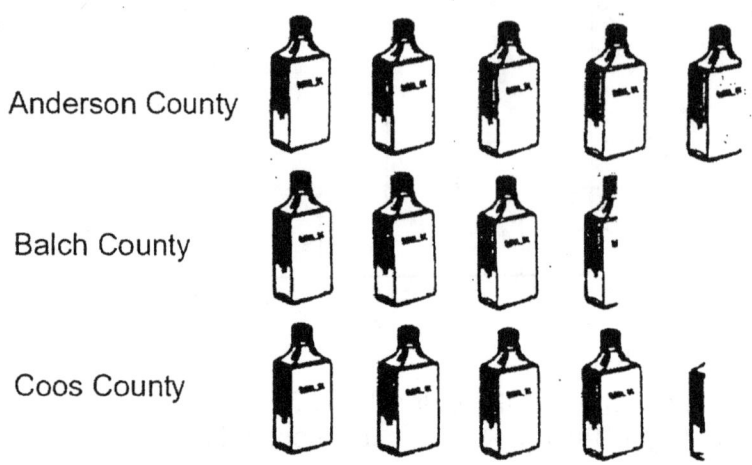

Anderson County

Balch County

Coos County

55. Mrs. Menon's mathematics group has been working independently on some lesson units. Mrs. Menon's record book is shown below. She enters S on the day a student starts Unit 1. On the day a student completes a unit, she enters that unit's number in her book.

DAY

	1	2	3	4	5	6	7	8	9	10	11	12	13
Andrew	S	1		2			3		4		5		6
Susan		S	1		2			3			4	5	
Louts				S		1	2		3		4		5
Tomas			S	1		2		3	4		5		6
Fran					S	1	2		4		5		6

UNITS COMPLETED

A. Susan took 11 days to complete units 1-5. How many days did Louis take to complete the same units?
B. At the end of the 11th day, which student had been working at the most rapid pace?

56. The distance (d) a person walks varies directly with time (t). Which graph best represents this situation?

A.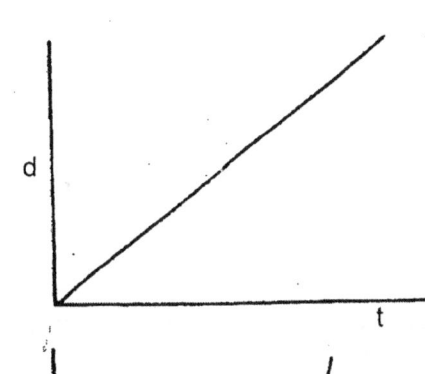
B.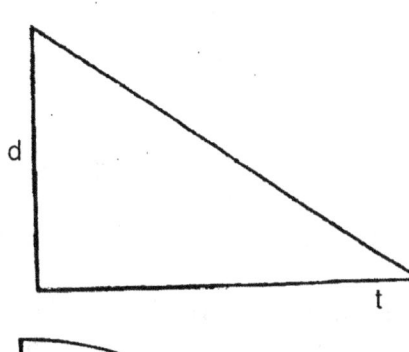
C.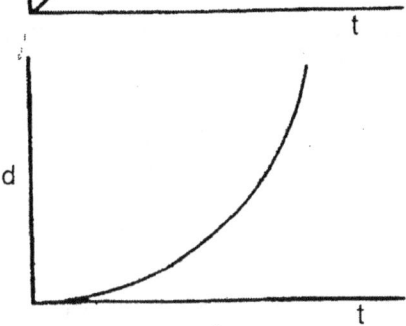
D.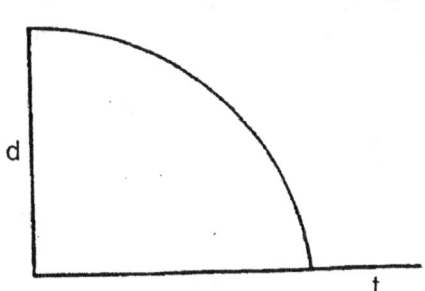

57. Which graph best represents the number of hours (T) from sunrise to sunset in Hartford, Connecticut, from January of one year to January of the next?

A.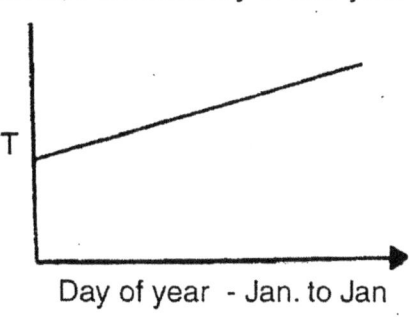
B.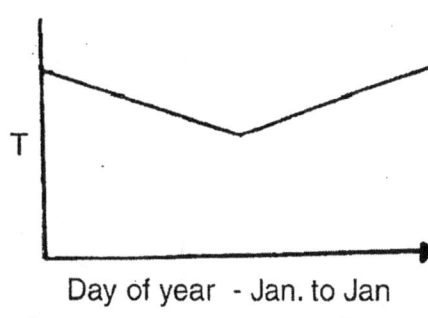
C.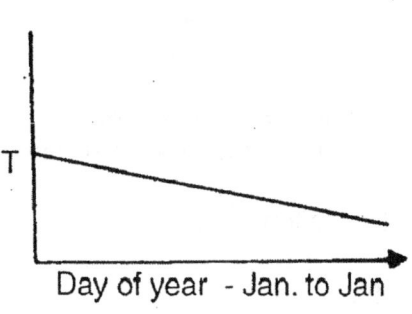
D.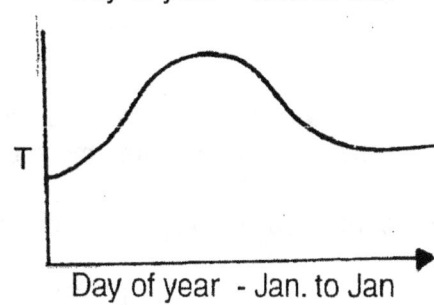

58.

City	TEMPERATURE Noon	6 PM
A	72°	54°
B	80°	70°
C	62°	50°
D	90°	66°

    A. In which city did the temperature drop the most rapidly between noon and 6 M.?
    B. Assuming an equivalent decrease in temperature per hour, what was the rate of temperature decrease in city A between noon and 6 P.M.?

59. Lee has been studying designs for picnic tables as shown below. Which design gives Lee the greatest surface area per dollar?

Design	Surface Area of Table	Cost of Materials
#1	20 square feet	$48.00
#2	18 square feet	$44.00
#3	24 square feet	$60.00

60. Ms. Haddad's 30 students took a standardized examination. The data below indicate the quartile in which each of her students' scores lie.

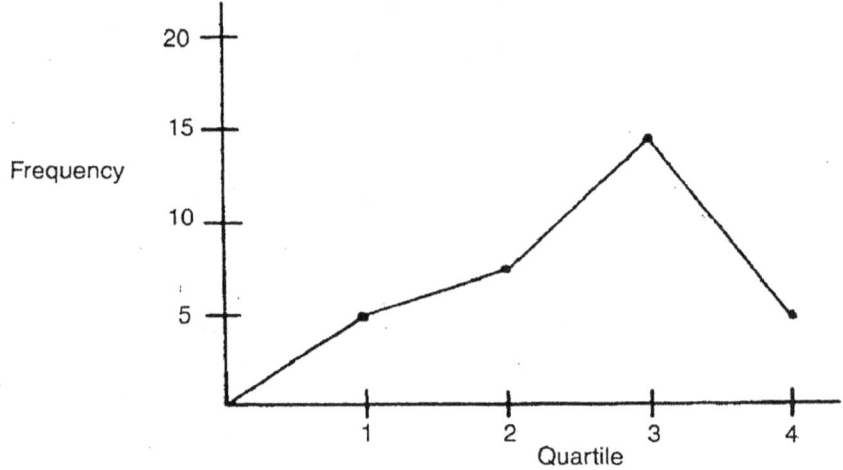

    A. Approximately how many students have scores in the 4th quartile?
    B. What quartile contains more of Ms. Haddad's students' scores than any other?

61. Use the table below to respond to the statements that follow.

SMOKERS BY FAMILY INCOME AND SEX

Family Income	Male	Female
Under $5,000	40%	32%
$5,000 - $14,999	36%	32%
$15,000 - $24,999	36%	30%
$25,000 or more	32%	26%

	Yes	No	Cannot Tell From Table Data
A. 60% of males with family incomes of under $5,000 are non-smokers	___		___
B. 58% of the people with family incomes of $25,000 or more are smokers	___	___	___
C. Among those with family incomes of $25,000 or more, more males than females smoke.	___	___	___
D. 36% of those with family incomes of under $5,000 smoke.	___	___	___
E. Among 600 females with family incomes in the $15,000-$24,999 range, there are about 180 smokers.	___	___	___

9. BASIC PROBABILITY CONCEPTS

When a student says, *The probability that I will pass the examination tomorrow is 2/3,* what does that student mean? She means that, were she to find herself in that situation many times, on about 2/3 of those occasions she would pass the exam. On about 1/3 of the occasions she would not pass.

Imagine a person playing a game which involves rolling a die. When he says, *The probability that I will roll a three is 1/6,* what does he mean? In this case, he means that of the six possible out-comes when rolling a die (1, 2, 3, 4, 5, 6), one possible outcome out of six is three. It is also true that, were he to roll that die a large number of times, about 1/6 of the times he would roll a three. (Thus, in 600 rolls, he would expect to get approximately 100 three's.)

Problem: The names of 5 students - Deborah, Andrew, Thomas, Jose, and Maria - are placed in a hat. One name is withdrawn at random. What is the probability that
    A. Deborah's name is chosen?
    B. The name chosen is either Deborah's or Andrew's?
    C. A boy's name is chosen?

Solution: A. Deborah's name is 1 of 5. Thus, the answer to A is 1/5.
    B. 2/5
    C. 3/5

Problem: Consider the data below on 100 different students.
If we choose one student at random from the 100 students shown on the chart, what is the probability of choosing
    A. a boy?
    B. a girl?
    C. a student with glasses?
    D. a girl with glasses?

	Glasses	No Glasses
Boys	15	45
Girls	10	30

Solution:
A. Of the 100 students, 15 + 45 = 60 are boys. Thus, the probability of choosing a boy is 60/100 = 6/10 = 3/5.
B. There are 10 + 30 = 40 girls. Thus, 40/100 = 2/5 is the probability of choosing a girl. You could also reason this way: The probability of choosing a boy is 3/5. The probability of not choosing a boy is, therefore, 1 - 3/5 = 2/5.
C. 15 + 10 = 25 out of 100 students. Thus, the answer is 25/100 = 1/4.
D. 10/100 or 1/10.

EXERCISES

62. A hat contains six tickets numbered 1, 1, 2, 2, 3, 3, respectively. One ticket is withdrawn at random. What is the probability that the ticket drawn
    A. is a 1?
    B. has an even number on it?
    C. is either a 2 or 3?
    D. has a 5 on it?
    E. has a number less than 3 on it?

63. Kim keeps records of his hens' daily egg production for 3 weeks and identifies the results listed in the table below. Based on these data, answer the questions that follow.

Eggs Laid Per Day	Number of Days
1	//
2	////
3	++++ //
4	/
5	///
6	//
7	//

    A. What is the probability of getting 5 or more eggs on a given day?
    B. What is the probability of not getting exactly 4 eggs on a given day?

64. Here are some data on student test performance at a particular school. Based on the data, answer the questions that follow.

	Above Mean	Below Mean
Boys	246	54
Girls	280	20

    A. What is the probability that a randomly chosen student scored above the mean?
    B. What is the probability that a randomly chosen female student scored below the mean?

65. The science students at our school have kept records indicating that the probability of rain at noon on a given day is 1/3 during the month of October.
    A. We have 21 school days this October. How many of rainy-days-at-noon do we anticipate?
    B. What is the probability of no rain at noon during October?
    C. Suppose that the probability of the sun shining at noon is 1/6 during October. What is the probability of neither rain nor sun at noon during October?

66. Here is a summary of student performance on a statewide test. Based on the data, answer the questions that follow.

Class	Number Passed	Number Failed
Ms. Adams	20	5
Ms. Blake	18	6
Ms. Gomez	22	2

    A. What is the probability that a randomly chosen student has passed the exam?
    B. What is the probability that a student who has failed belongs to Ms. Adams' class?

67. Based on statewide test data, here are probabilities of scoring in certain categories:

Score	Probability
0-50	0.16
51-60	0.24
61-70	0.30
71-80	0.20

    A. If 5,000 students took the test, how many would you predict had scores below 51?
    B. Eighty students at School A took the test. Fifteen students scored 50 or below. Is this better or worse than the state as a whole?
    C. Overall, what was the probability of scoring above 80 on the statewide test?

10. NEEDED AND EXTRANEOUS INFORMATION IN PROBLEM SOLVING

Problems with missing or with extra information are very common in real-life situations, but relatively rare in textbooks. These problems may not be necessarily difficult, but they often trap unwary readers whose schooling has led them to expect that all school problems and test problems contain precisely the information needed for a solution. But that is not always so. It is important to read problems carefully and use your common sense; imagine you are not faced with a *mathematics* problem on a test, but have encountered the problem in your daily life. Ask yourself, what information would you need to solve it?

EXERCISES

68. Pedro wants to tile a rectangular floor measuring 7.2 m by 5.4 m. Tiles cost 35¢ each at a store. What additional information will Pedro need before he can tell how much he needs to spend on tiles at a store?

69. Consider this situation: A manager bought 100 identical video cameras for $2,568. He sold them for $5,042. This situation includes three numerical pieces of information, not all of which may be needed to answer the questions below. What are the answers? What information is extraneous in each case?

	Answer	Extraneous Data
A. What was the total profit?	_____	_____
B. What was the selling price of each camera?	_____	_____
C. What did the manager pay for the cameras?	_____	_____
D. What was the manager's profit per camera?	_____	_____

70. Identify the additional information, if any, needed for each of the following problems.
    A. When mixing concrete for a patio, a contractor uses sand and gravel in a ratio of 3 to 4. How many cubic yards of gravel did the contractor use?
    B. The distance from Ampex to Bodwick is 38 miles. The distance from Bodwick to Cranmore is 20 miles. How far is it from Ampex to Cranmore?
    C. Ten percent of Ms. Mora's fourth graders failed the state's mastery test in reading. Four percent of Mr. Gomez's class failed. What was the total number of failing students in the two classes?
    D. All the rooms in Lauren's house are the same size. To paint two of those rooms she needs three gallons of paint. How many gallons does she need to paint all her rooms?
    E. A team wins 105 games. This is 70% of the games they played. How many games did they lose?

71. Identify any extraneous data.
    A. Of 180 class days last year, Lisa missed 9. If the probability of her missing school that year was 1/20, what was the probability of her being in school on a given day?
    B. The 30 students in Ms. Gate's class paid an average of $12.50 each during the year for special class materials, fees, etc. How much more, on the average, would each student need to pay for the class average to be $14 per student?
    C. A car averaged 20 miles per hour traveling from point A to point B. On the return trip, it averaged 40 miles per hour and took 2 1/2 hours. How far did the car travel for the entire trip?
    D. Tickets to the student production of OUR TOWN sell for $3 each. Yesterday, 30 students and 7 teachers bought tickets. Today $123 worth of tickets were sold, including another 30 student tickets. How many nonstudents bought tickets these two days?

KEY (CORRECT ANSWERS)

1. A. $x = 9$
   B. $x = \dfrac{12}{5}$
   C. $x = 7$
   D. $\dfrac{2}{3}x = 11$, so $x = \dfrac{3}{2} \cdot \dfrac{11}{1} = \dfrac{33}{2}$
   E. $\dfrac{3}{5}x = 8$, so $x = \dfrac{5}{3} \cdot \dfrac{8}{1} = \dfrac{40}{3}$

2. A. $x = 2$
   B. $x = 2$
   C. $x = x = -\dfrac{1}{8}$
   D. $x = 4$
   E. $x = \dfrac{320}{4000} = \dfrac{2}{25}$

3. A. $x = -\dfrac{7}{10}$
   B. $t = 2$
   C. $x = 0$
   D. $x = -\dfrac{13}{5}$

4. A. $x = 20$
   B. $a = -\dfrac{52}{25}$ or -2.08
   C. $t = -\dfrac{3478}{1480} = -\dfrac{47}{20}$
   D. $\dfrac{1}{a} = 2$, so $a = \dfrac{1}{2}$

5. A. 9
   B. 10
   C. 20

6. A. 0
   B. 8
   C. 1/3
   D. -9
   E. 2

7. A. $\dfrac{28}{3}$
    B. 68
    C. $-\dfrac{72}{5}$

8. $320 = \$2000 \times r \times 2$, so $r = \dfrac{320}{4000} = \dfrac{32}{400} = \dfrac{8}{100} = 8\%$

9. $a = -\dfrac{301}{100} = -3.01$

10. A. $Y = 12 - 3X$
    B. $y = \dfrac{8}{x}$
    C. $y = \dfrac{A}{br}$
    D. $y = \dfrac{12-4x}{3} = 4 - \dfrac{4}{3}x$
    E. $y = \dfrac{17-4x}{-13} = \dfrac{4x-17}{13}$
    F. $y = \dfrac{3x}{6} = \dfrac{1}{2}x$

11. $P = \dfrac{I}{rt}$

12. $\dfrac{s-a}{n-1} = d$

13. $L = a + act$; $L - a = act$; $\dfrac{L-a}{at} = C$

14. $x = \dfrac{10}{yz}$; $y = \dfrac{10}{xz}$

15. $x = \dfrac{14+2y}{7}$; $y = \dfrac{14-7x}{-2}$ or $y = \dfrac{7x-14}{2}$

16. A. 18   D. 3   G. 12
    B. 20   E. 15   H. 4
    C. 4 1/2   F. 5   I. 15

17. A. $k = \frac{6}{2} = 3$, so y = 3x and y = 30

B. $k = \frac{6}{3} = 2$, so y = 2x and y = 36

C. $k = 12 \div \frac{1}{3} = 12 \times \frac{3}{1} = 36$, so y = 36x and y = 180

D. $k = \frac{28}{4} = -7$, so y = -7x and y = -49

E. $k = \frac{12}{4} = 3$ so y = 3x and 12.36 = 3x. Therefore, x - 4.12

F. $k = \frac{459}{17} = 27$, so y = 27x and 27 = 27x. Therefore, x = 1

G. $k = \frac{100}{10} = -10$, so y = -10x and -10 = -10x. Therefore, x = 1

H. $k = \frac{14}{7} = 0.2$, so y = .2x and 10 = .2x. Thus, 100 = 2x and x = 50

18. $k = \frac{\text{known y-value}}{\text{known x-value}} = \frac{24}{108} = \frac{2}{9}$, so $y = \frac{2}{9}x$. If x = 45, then $y = \frac{2}{9} \cdot \frac{45}{1} = \frac{90}{9} = 10$.

She needs to work 10 hours this week. If you reversed the x's and y's, you should have obtained $k = \frac{108}{24} = \frac{9}{2}$, so, $y = \frac{9}{2}x$. When y = 45, we have $45 = \frac{9}{2}x$ and, multiplying both sides by $\frac{2}{9}$, we get $\frac{2}{9} \cdot \frac{45}{1} = x$, so x = 10.

19. If y = 110 when x = 1.1, then what is y when x = .56?

$K = \frac{110}{1.1} = \frac{1100}{11} = 100$ and y = 100x. So, when x = .56, then y = 100 x .56 = 56.

20. A. 3
B. 2
C. 24
D. 20
E. 50
F. 12
G. 144
H. The value of y has been multiplied by 2/3. The value of x will therefore be multiplied by 3/2 (or 1 1/2). Since x = 12 and 1 1/2 twelves are 18, the answer is x = 18.
I. 3

21. A. $k = 12 \times 2 = 24$, so $y = \frac{24}{x}$. Thus when $x = 1$, $y = 24$.

  B. $k = 6 \times 2 = 12$, so $y = \frac{12}{x}$. Thus when $x = 3$, $y = 4$.

  C. $k = 2(-3) = -6$, so $y = -\frac{6}{x}$. Thus when $x = \frac{1}{2}$, $y = -6 \div \frac{1}{2} = -\frac{6}{1} \times \frac{2}{1} = -12$

  D. $k = 6 \cdot 4 = 24$, so $y = \frac{24}{x}$. Thus when $x = 3$, $y = 8$.

  E. $k = 3 \cdot 2 = 6$, so $y = \frac{6}{x}$. Thus if $y = 1$, we have $1 = \frac{6}{x}$ and $x = 6$.

  F. $k = 10 \cdot 9 = 90$, so $y = \frac{90}{x}$. Thus if $y = 45$, we have $45 = \frac{90}{x}$ and $x = 2$.

22. If y is 21 when x = 350, then what is y when x = 70?
   $k = 21 \cdot 350$, so $y = \frac{21 \cdot 350}{x}$. If $x = 70$, then $y = \frac{21 \cdot 350}{70}$ $21 \cdot 5 = 105$ pounds per square inch.

23. If y = 1 1/2 when x = 12, then when y = 2, what is x?
   Here, $1\,1/2 \cdot 8 = 12$, so $2 \cdot 8 = 16$. Therefore, $x = 16$ when $y = 2$.

24. Let y represent the scaled score and x represent the raw score. Then,
   $k = \frac{500}{40} = \frac{25}{2}$, so $y = \frac{25}{2}x$. Thus, if $y = 375$, we have $375 = \frac{25}{2}x$. Therefore, $x = \frac{2}{25} \cdot 375 = 30$.

25. Let y represent the speed and x the number of minutes. Notice that 90 plus one-third of 90 is 120. So, since y has increased by $1\frac{1}{3}$ (or $\frac{4}{3}$), x will decrease by $\frac{3}{4} \cdot \frac{3}{4} \cdot 2 = \frac{6}{4} = \frac{3}{2}$ so the answer is 3/2 minutes, or 1 1/2 minutes.

26. Going from 60 to 15 represents a decrease by a factor of 1/4. Thus, the years of experience will increase by a factor of 4, and the answer is 12.

27. A. three to ten or $\frac{3}{10}$ or 3:10

    B. $\frac{20}{15} = \frac{4}{3}$ or 4:3 or four to three

    C. $\frac{200}{300} = \frac{2}{3}$ or 2:3 or two to three

    D. $\frac{24}{40} = \frac{3}{5}$ or 3:5 or three to five

28. 16 trout out of 30 fish. How many trout out of 2000 fish?
    $\frac{16}{30} = \frac{x}{2000}$, so $16 \times 2000 = 30x$ and $x = \frac{32000}{30}$ trout. Since $\frac{32000}{30} = 1066.7$, the ranger would estimate that roughly 1067 trout are in the lake.

29. $\frac{Mars}{Earth} = \frac{2}{5} = \frac{x}{120}$ so $240 = 5x$, and $x = 48$ pounds.

30. $\frac{1}{6} = \frac{4\frac{1}{2}}{x}$, so $x = 6 \times 4\frac{1}{2} = 27$ miles.

31. $\frac{1\frac{1}{2}}{700} = \frac{x}{3000}$, so $1\frac{1}{2} \times 3000 = 700x$ or $4500 = 700x$ and $x = \frac{45}{7} = 6\frac{3}{7}$ quarts.

32. $\frac{6}{4} = \frac{x}{25}$ and $6 \cdot 25 = 4x$. Therefore, $x = \frac{150}{4} = 37\frac{1}{2}$ feet

33. $\frac{2}{5} = \frac{36}{x}$, so $2x = 180$ and $x = 90$ females.

34. $\frac{12 \text{ feet}}{4 \text{ inches}} = \frac{x \text{ feet}}{6 \text{ inches}}$, so $12 \cdot 6 = 4x$, and $x = 18$ feet.

35. $\frac{20}{32} = \frac{6}{x}$, so $20x = 192$ and $x = \frac{192}{20} = 9.6$.

36. A. 5   D. 10.5   G. 86
    B. 0.5   E. 10   H. 75
    C. 10   F. 80

37. A. 13.6   C. 1.68
    B. 13.92   D. $1.17

38. A. Mental solution: 16 is 1/4 of what? Answer: 4 x 16 or 64 Algebraic solution: $\frac{16}{x} = \frac{25}{100}$; 1600 = 25x, therefore $x = \frac{1600}{25} = 64$

    B. $\frac{13}{x} = \frac{86}{100}$; 1300 = 86x, so $x = \frac{1300}{86}$ or approximately 15.1

    C. $\frac{10}{18} = \frac{x}{100}$, so $x = \frac{1000}{18} = 55.55...$ Thus, x is approximately 55.6%

    D. $\frac{17}{51} = \frac{x}{100}$, so $x = \frac{1700}{51}$ 33.33.... Thus, x is approximately 33.3% (or exactly 33 1/3%).

39. A. 16% of $32 = 0.16 x 32 = $5.12. The shirt now costs $32 + $5.12 or $37.12
    B. 15% of $6200 = 0.15 x 6200 = $930. The new price would be $6200 - $930 = $5270
    C. The mark-up is $1. The percent mark-up is $1 out of a price of $4 or 1/4 = 0.25 = 25%
    D. The discount is $4 out of a price of $60 or 4/60 = 0.0666... or approximately 6.7%

40. A. The total weight is 3 x 14 + 7 x 8 = 98 oz. Of the total, the grapefruits provide 42/98 = 0.4285...or approximately 43%
    B. If the grapefruits provide 43% of the total weight, then the oranges must provide the rest: 57% because 43% + 57% = 100%

41. C

42. D

43. We use the formula d = rt, except that we are interested in the rate of travel r. Thus, r = d/t. In terms of this problem, r is denoted by V and we have V = F-S/t

44. p + 0.2p or 1.2p

45. C

46. e. Let x be 1/2, 1, 2. The corresponding y values are -1 1/2, 0, 1 1/2. The expression x - 1/x is always increasing but it is negative when x is less than 1 and positive when x is larger than 1.

47. T/0.5 or 2T

48. If you let P = 1 and Q = 1, then R = 4 for equations a, c, d

49. b, d (Try substituting some positive, decreasing values for x; for example, x = 10, 2, 1. What happens to y?)

50. Total Cost

$$100 \times P + (T - 100) \cdot 8P$$

$p each for 100 books 80% of P (.8P) for each book over 100 (T-100)

$100P + (T - 100) \cdot 8P$

$100P + (T-100).8P = 100P + T \times .8P - 100 \times .8P$
$= 100P + .8TP - 80P$
$= 20P + .8TP$

Therefore, c is the correct response.

51. $.15 \times 20{,}000 + .28 \times (D-20{,}000)$
 $= 3000 + .28D - .28 \times 20{,}000$
 $= 3000 + .28D - 5600$
 $= .28D - 2600$

52. A. approximately 975 students
 B. 200 to 250 or 4:5
 C. 1 1/2

53. 23%

54. 35,000 gallons

55. A. 10 days
 B. Fran

56. Choice A is correct: If t doubles, d doubles, etc.

57. Choice D

58. A. City D
 B. 18 degrees/6 hours = 3 degrees per hour
 (The rate of decrease for city D was 4 degrees per hour.)

59. #1 gives 20/48 square feet per dollar (20/48 = 5/12)
 #2 gives 18/44 square feet per dollar (18/44 = 9/22)
 #3 gives 24/60 square feet per dollar (24/60 = 2/5)
 Comparing the order of these fractions, 2/5 is less than 9/22, which is less than 5/12.
 Thus, 5/12 square feet per dollar is the best Lee can do. Choice #1 is best.

60. A. 5
 B. The third quartile

61. A. Yes
 B. No. The correct figure will lie somewhere between 26% and 32%, depending on the ratio of men to women. Suppose, for example, that there are 200 males and 100 females in the $25,000 plus category. Of the males, 32% or 64 smoke. Of the females, 26% or 26 smoke. Altogether 90 out of 300 smoke, that is, 90/300 = 30/100 = 30%. Thus, 26% of the females are smokers, 32% of the males are smokers,

and 30% of the entire group smokes. (Note that 30% is closer to the male percentage of 32% than it is to the female percentage of 26%. This is because there are more males than females in the entire population.)
- C. You cannot tell. A higher percentage of males are smokers, but the absolute number of males who smoke could be smaller. Perhaps there are 300 people in this category; for example, 100 males and 200 females. 32% of 100 means 32 males smoke. 26% of 200 means 52 females smoke.
- D. You cannot tell. The correct figure will lie somewhere between 32% and 40%, but will not be 36% unless the number of males equals the number of females in the under $5,000 category. (See the answer to B above)
- E. Yes.

62.
- A. 2/6 or 1/3
- B. 2/6 or 1/3
- C. 4/6 or 2/3
- D. 0/6 or 0
- E. 4/6 or 2/3

63.
- A. On 7 of the 21 days, egg production was 5 or more dozen. Thus, the probability is 7/21 or 1/3.
- B. The probability of getting exactly 4 dozen eggs is 1/21. The probability of not getting 4 dozen is 20/21.

64.
- A. There are 600 students in all (246 + 54 + 280 + 20 = 600). Of these, 246 + 280 = 526 scored above the mean. The probability would be 526/600 (or 263/300).
- B. 20/300 or 1/15

65.
- A. 7
- B. 2/3
- C. The probability of either rain or sun is 1/3 + 1/6 = 1/2. The other half of the time you get neither rain nor sun. The probability of neither rain nor sun is 1/2.

66.
- A. 60 out of 73 students passed: 60/73
- B. 5/13

67.
- A. 0.16 × 5000 = 800
- B. 15/80 = .1875, which is larger than the statewide figure of .16. Since a score below 51 is presumably not good, your students did worse than the state as a whole.
- C. The probability of scoring in the 0-80 range is .16 + .24 + .30 + .20 = .90. The missing .10, therefore, must have scores above 80.

68. He needs to know the size of a tile so that he can decide how many tiles he needs.

69.
- A. $2474; 100 cameras
- B. $50.42; $2568
- C. $2568; 100 and $5042
- D. $24.74; no extraneous data

70. A. How many cubic yards of sand did the contractor use or how many cubic yards of both sand and gravel did the contractor use?
B. We need to know where Ampex and Cranmore are in relation to Bodwick. Do the three towns lie on a line with Bodwick in the middle (Figure 1) or with Cranmore in the middle (Figure 2)?

```
←·····38·····→←··20··→              ←·····38······→
●           ●         ●             ●         ●     ●
A           B         C             A         C←-20·→B
        Figure 1                           Figure 2
```

Do the three towns form the vertices of a right triangle, etc.?
C. What is the number of students in each class?
D. How many rooms are in that house?
E. No information is needed. 105 = .70x so 1050 = 7x and x = 150. The team played 150 games and won 105. They lost 45 games.

71. A. The information in the first sentence is extraneous. Alternately, if you use the information in the first sentence, then 1/20 is extraneous.
B. The 30 is not needed.
C. The first sentence is irrelevant.
D. We don't need to know that yesterday 30 students bought tickets; only the non-student data are relevant.

ESSAY WRITING

THE WRITING PROCESS

Under ideal conditions, writing involves a series of steps:

1. Pre-writing activities which facilitate understanding the purpose and the audience for a particular piece of writing and which might include generating ideas through brainstorming, notes, reflection, research, or discussion;

2. Focusing the material generated in step one by framing a thesis (controlling idea) and a direction (organization);

3. Getting the first draft on paper, using standard grammar, correct mechanics, and accurate spelling;

4. Assessing the success of the first draft by yourself or in consultation with a reliable reader;

5. Revising the draft by clarifying the thesis, topic sentences, supporting detail, and word choice; and

6. Proofreading for mistakes in grammar and spelling.

Ideal conditions do not always exist in the real world. Often you have to write under pressure and produce a clear statement. This is the case in a test situation. You must streamline the writing process to compose an acceptable essay in approximately one hour. This section will help you to practice necessary strategies by describing how you might do the following:

1. Turn the directions into a purpose statement.
2. Brainstorm for material to put in the essay.
3. Group and focus your ideas.
4. Compose your essay with clear signals for the reader.
5. Proofread for word choice, grammar, and mechanics.

TURN DIRECTIONS INTO PURPOSE STATEMENTS

For each of the following sets of essays, the directions specify a topic, an audience, and some possible ways to develop the essay. You have some choice about how to develop the essay, but you must stick to the topic given and a style appropriate to the audience. The directions consist of four sentences which give

1. an indication of audience,
2. a description of audience,
3. suggestions for development, and
4. a restatement of the topic.

You can distinguish the sentences that suggest development because they contain words which give options rather than commands; for example, the sentences that give you commands about the topic will look like this:

In writing, tell the panel why you are considering teaching as a career.

On the other hand, sentences that suggest development will look like this:
The reasons may include...
You might want to consider...
The experiences could be...

Your first step, then, is to sort out the essential commands in the directions and convert them into a clear purpose statement such as *I will explain my reasons for choosing teaching as a career.* The purpose statement must cover all the essential parts of the assignment.

EXERCISE B

For each of the following sets of directions, underline the sentences that give you commands about the topic and write a purpose statement, using your own words if possible.

Prompt 1
A committee of teachers and administrators is reviewing your qualifications for a scholarship. In writing, tell the committee about a special activity you engage in, either in school or outside of school. It could be a job, an organization you belong to, a hobby or sport you participate in, or something you do with your family. Tell the committee what your special activity is and explain why this activity is important to you.

Prompt 2
A superintendent of schools has reviewed your application for a teaching position. Before holding a formal interview with you, the superintendent wants you to provide a writing sample that tells what motivated you to choose teaching as a profession. You might want to discuss a special learning experience you had or your interest in a chosen field or subject. Tell the superintendent what your motivation is and explain why your learning experience or your interest in a special field or subject is important to you.

Prompt 3
Your college advisor has just notified you that the college has instituted an open curriculum. As a result, you may choose any three courses or activities you wish to take next semester. You will be given equal course credit for academic subjects and activities such as sports, cultural

activities (music, theater, art), school newspaper or literary magazine activities, fraternities, sororities, community projects, or any other activity whose importance you can justify. In writing, indicate what three courses you would select and how each one would make you a better person.

Prompt 4
You have just been given the opportunity to write a letter of application to the Director of Admissions at the college of your choice. Imagine that cost is not a concern to you; you may choose a college that offers a traditional liberal arts curriculum or one that allows you to study only those courses that relate to your field of interest. In your essay, tell the Director of Admissions the type of college you are choosing and identify the reasons for your choice.

Prompt 5
A committee of teachers is reviewing your application for admission into the teacher education program of your choice. The committee has asked you to write an essay that describes a book that made the most lasting impression on you or from which you believe you learned some valuable lesson. The book may be on any subject, fiction or nonfiction, that is meaningful to you. The book need not be something you read for a course. Explain to the committee what your impression or lesson is and why it is important to you.

BRAINSTORM FOR MATERIAL TO PUT IN THE ESSAY

The directions on the subtest often contains suggestions for areas to explore. The sample directions which ask for an essay on your reasons for choosing a teaching career suggest that you consider *examples set by other people, benefits you expect from a teaching career, or the challenges you think teaching offers.* Remember that these suggestions are only suggestions. Before you respond to them, you should think about how you would accomplish the writing task if the suggestions had not been made. To be convincing, the material in your essay must come from your own experiences and knowledge. Brainstorming can help you accomplish this.

There are different ways to brainstorm. Some people prefer to write freely for 5-10 minutes. Others like to make lists or sketches. Others mull over ideas and ask themselves questions before jotting down a few key words. If you have a method that works for you, stick with it. If you don't, try one of the three approaches just mentioned.

EXERCISE C

1. Think about your reasons for wanting to teach and jot down a list of those reasons.

2. Compare your list with the suggestions given for considering teaching as a career: (examples, benefits, and challenges).

3. Which reasons fit the category of the rewards of teaching?

4. Which reasons could be labeled challenges of teaching?

5. Which reasons are related to examples set by other people?

6. What labels or categories do your other reasons fall under?

7. Are some of your reasons related to experiences that you have had as a learner or teacher (e.g., sports, scouting, 4-H, religious classes)?

8. Are some of your reasons related to your interest in a particular subject such as mathematics or art?

9. Are some of your reasons related to particular qualities you possess such as patience, enthusiasm, or tolerance?

LISTEN TO YOUR INNER VOICE

The purpose of brainstorming is to come up with enough detail or elaboration to satisfy the evaluation requirements. You should aim to produce enough material for an introduction and at least three additional paragraphs. Once you list a few initial ideas, the best way to generate more detail is to imagine a voice saying, *Tell me more about that.* Let's suppose that your initial list of reasons for wanting to teach looked like this.

- I like kids.
- Summers off.
- Make a contribution to society.
- Encouragement from teachers.

Responding to that imaginary voice saying, *Tell me more*, might help you elaborate the first reason as follows:

I like kids...
because they all have some undeveloped potential.
because their responses aren't always predictable.
because they get so excited when they learn something new.

Another way to elaborate on the first reason is through examples:

- The two boys I used to babysit.
- The girl I helped to get over her fear of water.
- The special education student who was my *little brother*.

Imagine the voice asking for more information until you believe you have enough for a satisfactory essay. Not every statement will give you as much room for development as others, but you can expand upon all of the statements. Each time you elaborate, your writing becomes more specific. Including specific detail makes your ideas concrete and your writing more convincing. Specific detail is one of the criteria for evaluating your essay.

EXERCISE D

1. Go back to the list of purpose statements that you developed in Exercise C, and brainstorm for material you might include in an essay.

2. Go back to your list of reasons for wanting to teach and elaborate as much as you can on each one.

GROUP AND FOCUS YOUR IDEAS

A good essay is unified by a controlling idea or thesis which dictates a pattern of organization. The thesis should be stated in one or two sentences. The words you choose to write the thesis statement should repeat or echo the directions for the essay. This strategy will ensure that you state the topic clearly. One way to write a thesis is to do one of the following:

1. Look at your purpose statement.
   Example 1: I must explain my reasons for choosing teaching as a career.
   Example 2: I must explain how a learning experience motivated me to go into teaching.

2. Look at the list of ideas you generated by brainstorming and try to sum up the ideas in a sentence or two:
   Sample Thesis 1: I have chosen teaching as a career because I enjoy young children, particularly those who have a learning disability. Teaching is a career that will enable me to make a contribution to society.
   Sample Thesis 2: The experience that I had as a *big brother* to a special education student helped me to realize that everyone has the potential to learn. This experience strengthened my interest in teaching as a career.

The thesis prepares the reader for what is to follow. It is a promise that you will discuss certain ideas and not others.

You will not always use all the material you generated during the brainstorming step. In the sample that we have been discussing, you might have decided not to use material related to summers off or the encouragement of teachers. However, if you decide that there is some material you want to include in the body of your essay material which is not indicated by the thesis, you need to revise the thesis. Suppose you decide to include the information about summers off and the encouragement of teachers, how could you revise the thesis? Here is one possibility:

Revised Thesis: There are many reasons why I have chosen teaching as a career. The pleasure of working with children, the opportunity to make a contribution to society, the encouragement of teachers, and time during the summer to continue my own education and interests are a few of them.

You should understand that it is not necessary or advisable to give every reason why you would like to teach. Be selective. Choose reasons on which you can elaborate and ones you feel strongly about. This will make a more convincing essay.

OUTLINING

There are different ways of grouping brainstorming ideas. The traditional format is the outline. Here is one example, based on the thesis we have been discussing.

<u>Thesis:</u> There are many reasons why I have chosen teaching as a career; some of them are the pleasure of working with children, the opportunity to make a contribution to society, the encouragement of teachers, and time during the summer to continue my own education and interests.

I. I enjoy working with children.
   A. All children have potential.
   B. Their responses are unpredictable.
   C. They are excited when they learn something.

II. I will make a contribution to society.
   A. Many jobs have questionable social value even if they have high salaries.
   B. Teachers can help children develop a good self-image and give them necessary skills.

III. Teachers have encouraged me.
   A. They say I can express myself clearly.
   B. They see that I am enthusiastic about learning.

IV. Summers will be time to continue my education and interests.
   A. Teachers must be lifelong learners.
   B. Intensity of teaching requires time for pursuing other interests.

CLUSTERING

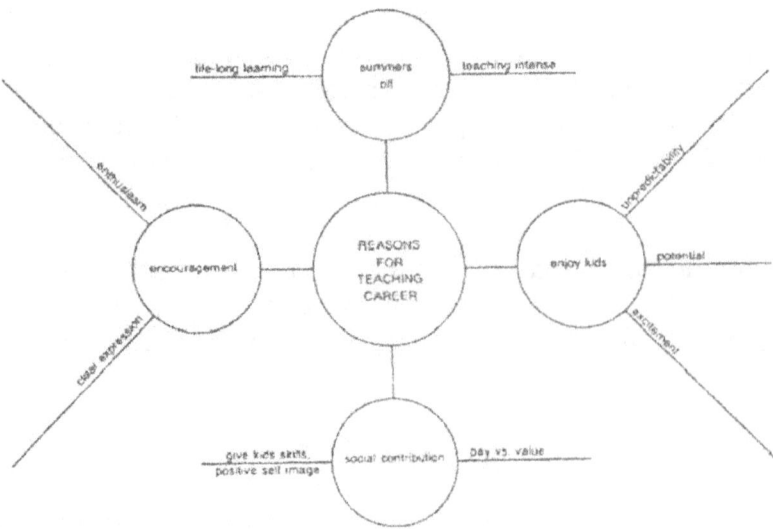

FLOW CHARTS

Still another way to map ideas is with the help of a flow chart. The main idea is placed in a box at the top, and other categories branch off below.

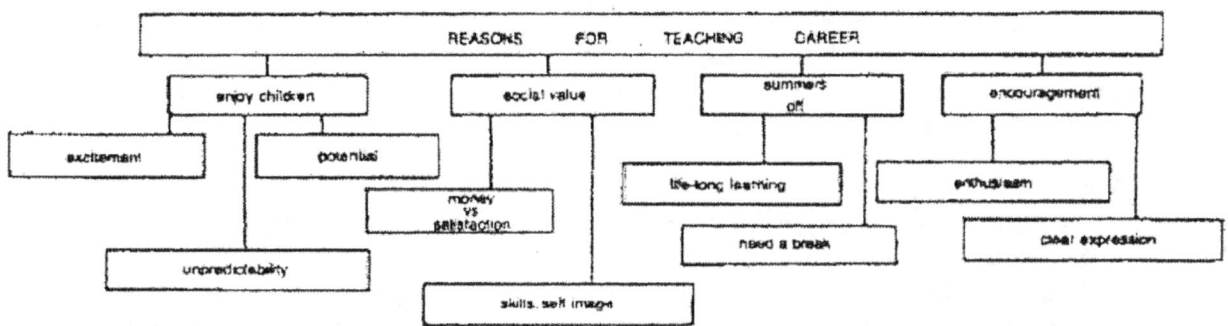

INFORMAL LISTS

An informal list is an easy way to group ideas.

My Reasons:

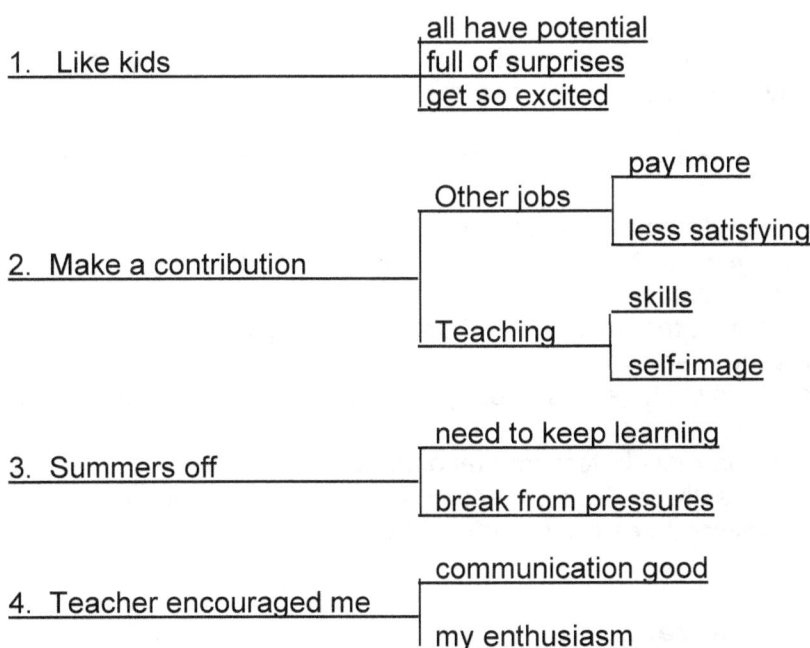

Regardless of which method you use to group your ideas, the goal is to pull together related bits of information and sketch the paragraph structure for your essay before you actually start writing your essay in the test booklet.

EXERCISE E

1. Go back to the material that you produced through brainstorming in Exercise D.2 and group the ideas by using one of the formulas illustrated.

2. Using one of the strategies mentioned previously, group the ideas given below in each set. For each set, read through the ideas in the set and identify or create a thesis statement; group related sentences; and find or create a sentence or phrase that will hold each group of sentences together.

   SET A.
   1. TV cartoons show characters recovering quickly from serious injury.
   2. Mr. Rogers never loses his temper.
   3. Ads associate happiness and good times with possession of a product.
   4. The ads show cereal boxes opening by themselves and dancing on the table.
   5. TV gives children a distorted sense of reality.
   6. Mr. Rogers always takes off his shoes when he comes inside.
   7. A character falls off a mountain top, shakes his head, and gets up.
   8. Positive role models, like Mr. Rogers, are unlike any real-life adult.
   9. Mr. Rogers never raises his voice.
   10. The ads are deceptive and manipulative.
   11. Characters who smash into walls are never badly hurt.

   SET B.
   1. I felt welcome when I went to see my math teacher during his office hours.
   2. The activity fair during orientation week had something to offer everyone.
   3. The counselors were helpful.
   4. Many teachers ask if students need help rather than wait for the students to get in trouble.
   5. The counselors helped with course selection.
   6. Resident advisors counsel students about adjustment problems.
   7. The counselors provided placement testing.
   8. Teachers talk to students after class rather than just rushing off.
   9. Students on campus are friendly.
   10. My experience at Winona College has been good, and I would recommend it to others.
   11. Teachers go over sample tests before you take the first test.
   12. The dorm council plans activities and projects to bring students together.
   13. The counselors offer minicourses on taking notes and tests.

   SET C.
   1. I don't belong to any organizations.
   2. I'm not involved in any special activities.
   3. I go to classes, work at the store, and see my friends on weekends.
   4. My job isn't special.
   5. I work at a supermarket.
   6. I need the job for spending money and college expenses.

7. I have learned some things from working.
8. It's not like school.
9. You have to be there to get paid.
10. The boss isn't always fair.
11. Sometimes she is impatient.
12. As a lowly clerk, you don't get any respect.
13. The boss seemed annoyed when I brought back the shopping carts.
14. There were long lines at the registers.
15. She told me to help bag groceries.
16. There's a pecking order in most companies.
17. My boss is under pressure from the manager.
18. I'm trying to stay on top of the situation rather than just reacting.
19. I ask the boss how things have been going.
20. I try to anticipate what she'll ask me to do and offer to do it first.
21. Sometimes I feel frustrated about being low on the totem pole.
22. The manager doesn't even know who I am.
23. There's not much incentive to do good work.
24. You can always be replaced by another minimum wage worker.

SET D.
1. DEATH OF A SALESMAN is a book that influenced me because of the connections between the play and my own life.
2. Each time I had a different reaction.
3. I read the play once in high school, again in college, and then saw it on TV.
4. In high school, Biff was a good-looking football hero.
5. The play is about a salesman named Willy, his wife, and two sons, Biff and Happy.
6. Happy was just an ordinary kid, living in his brother's shadow.
7. When Biff learned that his father was not perfect, he began to drift around.
8. I realized I was only hurting myself.
9. I had an older brother who was a star.
10. I was always trying to get my parents' attention.
11. I even tried to get their attention by doing poorly in school.
12. At first, I identified with Happy.
13. Biff had a big ego because of all the attention he received.
14. Biff became a bum because of all the attention he received as a teenager.
15. When I read the play in college, I sympathized with Willy.
16. He never received any respect from his boss.
17. I have been working at a supermarket.
18. Clerks are a dime a dozen, just like salespeople.
19. I want a career where a paycheck is not the only satisfaction you receive.
20. The TV version made me admire the mother.
21. She held the family together.
22. She was completely loyal to Willy.
23. We all want someone to stick by us like she did.

SET E.
1. Earning credit for my choice of courses and activities will give me a chance to integrate course work and real experience.
2. Reading Methods is a required course.
3. I'll learn how to assess a student's reading level.
4. I'll learn about various methods for teaching reading skills.
5. I plan to work as a literacy volunteer.
6. I want to know why people don't learn to read.
7. I'll learn about methods for teaching adults.
8. I'll learn how illiteracy affects a person's life.
9. I'll realize what's at stake if the education system fails.
10. I want to take either an advanced composition course or an independent study in composition.
11. I would like to keep a journal of my experience as a literacy volunteer.
12. I would like to write about the connections I see between the methods course and my tutoring experience.
13. I would like to write some feature stories about illiteracy for the college newspaper.

COMPOSE YOUR ESSAY WITH CLEAR SIGNALS FOR THE READER

Your essay is judged on how well the essay communicates a whole message. If you keep the reader in mind, your essay is likely to communicate more effectively. The most important signals to use are topic sentences to state the main idea of each paragraph and transitions to link sentences within the paragraphs. One basic pattern you might use in composing your paragraphs is the five paragraph essay. Here is one example of such an essay written in response to Prompt 1, Exercise B. Study the way in which the topic sentences give the reader a preview of what will be discussed.

<u>Paragraph I.</u>	Lead and thesis statement.
Lead	Some students may have time for sports, clubs, or volunteer organizations. Unfortunately, my schedule of classes and part-time work does not give me much time to devote to other activities. However, my job has been quite a learning experience.
Thesis	<u>Although I am just a supermarket clerk, I have gained insight into the demands of a job, the behavior of supervisors, and my ability to influence a situation,</u>
<u>Paragraph II</u>	Topic sentence developed with sufficient detail.
Topic Sentence	<u>I realized that the demands of a job re not always like the demands of school.</u> Maybe that is something that other people know from the start, but it did not work that way for me. In fact, I can remember how the equation between work and pay dawned on me; if I missed an afternoon of work, I missed an equivalent amount of money in my paycheck. The connection between work and rewards is not quite so clear in school. A student can study hard for a test and do poorly. On the other hand, a student can sometimes bluff through a test and get a good grade.

Paragraph III.	Another topic sentence with supporting detail.
Topic Sentence	<u>I did not work for very long before I also realized that bosses can be difficult.</u> At first, my supervisor seemed like a nice enough person. However, I had a look at her other side one day when I returned to the store, pushing a long line of shopping carts which she had told me to gather from the parking lot. Lines had formed at all the registers, and she snapped at me to bag for one of the cashiers. It was as if it my fault that she had sent two of the cashiers out for supper just as it was getting busy in the store.
Paragraph IV.	Another topic sentence followed by detail.
Topic sentence	<u>After my initial anger at the boss's behavior, I decided to try to influence the situation rather than just reacting to it.</u> I realized this approach might work as I was bagging groceries. I saw the store manager peering down at my box from her office window. My boss had a boss who had a boss who had a boss. She was part of the pecking order just like me. Now I try to make small talk with her, ask how things have been going, and so forth. Also, I try to anticipate what she might ask me to do and then offer to do it first. This gives me the feeling that I can be an actor rather than just a puppet.
Paragraph V.	Conclusion with restatement of thesis.
Thesis Restated	Sometimes I still get frustrated at work. As a lowly clerk, I do not get much respect in a large, impersonal company. <u>However, my job has shown me that even the most ordinary parts of my life can give me an opportunity to learn something about myself and other people.</u>

Topic sentences do not always occur at the beginning of paragraphs. In fact, at times it seems stilted to put the topic sentence at the start of a paragraph. You may need a sentence or two that makes a bridge with the preceding paragraph. For example, the fourth paragraph in the sample essay above might have been written more chronologically, following the sequence of events more closely.

Example:	After my initial anger, I noticed the store manager peering down at my boss from the upstairs office window. I realized that my boss had a boss who had a boss;
Thesis Statement	She was just a part of the pecking order like me. <u>I decided to try to influence the situation instead of just reacting to it.</u>

Placing the topic sentence at the start of a paragraph gives the clearest signal to a reader, but it is not always essential to place the topic sentence at the beginning. It is important, however, to have a sentence that holds the rest of the paragraph together. It can come at the beginning, the middle, or the end of the paragraph. Here is a paragraph without a topic sentence:

Ms. Rodriquez always had a word of encouragement on each test she handed back. Furthermore, she taught me the difference between an intelligent mistake and a dumb one. An intelligent mistake occurs when a learner applies a rule or procedure to a special situation where it does not apply. For example, if a young child says, "I taked the book," she is applying the rule to use a "d" sound for a past action. Ms. Rodriguez also had a way of making math problems exciting mysteries. We watched her solve equations on the board like Sherlock Holmes in pursuit of a suspect. The work was never easy, but she always made us feel that it was possible to succeed if we put in enough time.

One way to phrase a topic sentence for the paragraph above would be:
<u>Ms. Rodriguez was one of the best teachers I ever had.</u>

Even if you think that the point of the paragraph is perfectly clear without a topic sentence, put one in. You are now writing this essay for a sophisticated magazine; you are taking a test to show that you can get an idea across clearly to a reader.

EXERCISE F.

1. Each paragraph below lacks a topic sentence. Create a topic sentence for each paragraph and decide where best to place it.

   a. I would be happy if I could make some difference in the lives of the students I will teach. It might just mean making them more curious about the world or more accepting of themselves. I realize that it is difficult to reach each student, but that does not mean that I will not try.
   b. Mr. Wright began every class by putting the homework on the board. Then he would announce what we were going to do that day. Usually, we went over the homework problems first. Students were asked to put their solutions on the board. After discussing them and making necessary corrections, Mr. Wright would turn to the new material. Using three or four pieces of colored chalk, he illustrated and commented on the examples in the book. Finally, if we finished all of the scheduled lesson, there was time at the end of class to start on the homework.
   c. Every teacher spends a minimum of 35 hours in school. In addition, teachers must often supervise activities such as the drama club or school newspaper. Conferences with parents, staff meetings, and required professional development activities also add to the total hours required. A teacher usually has three different course-related preparations, each of which may take an hour or more, depending on the teacher's experience. English teachers who have 25 to 30 students per class may assign a short piece of writing each week, and may spend 4 to 5 minutes reading each paper. This may add 13 hours of additional work per week.

2. Go back to the material that you brainstormed and organized in Exercise D. Pick at least one batch of material and turn it into an essay following the pattern of the five-paragraph essay described previously.

TRANSITIONS

Transitions are signals to your reader about how your ideas are connected. Certain words and phrases prepare the reader for what is to follow. Examples of important transitions to use in your essay are:

1. Words that indicate sequence of events or ideas: first, second (etc.), finally, last, ultimately, eventually, later, meanwhile, afterwards;

2. Words that indicate examples: for instance, for example, specifically, in particular;

3. Words that indicate addition of similar ideas: and, also, furthermore, moreover, similarly, equally important, another;

4. Words that indicate addition of contrasting ideas: however, but, on the other hand, on the contrary, still, yet, in contrast, nevertheless.

Transitions between sentences can also be achieved by repeating key words, using synonyms, or using pronouns.

1. Example of a repeated key word: *Literacy* is not just a matter of learning the ABC's, *Literacy* means having sufficient control of the language to function in one's society.

2. Example of use of a synonym: *Literacy* is not just a matter of learning the ABC's. One's ability to read and write must be equal to the demands of one's society.

3. Example use of a pronoun: *Literacy* is not just a matter of learning the ABC's. It means having sufficient control of the language to function in your society.

EXERCISE G.

1. Look at the paragraphs you wrote in Exercise F and underline all the transitions.

2. Go back to the essay you wrote in Exercise F. Underline any transitions you used. Find places where you might insert additional transitions.

PROOFREAD FOR WORD CHOICE, GRAMMAR, AND MECHANICS

Under ideal conditions, you would complete a first draft and then evaluate it for content and structure. However, a subtest, lasting approximately one hour, does not allow time for true revision. You may want to think of your brainstorming as a type of first draft and your focusing as a type of revision. As you focus and compose your essay, you will do a certain amount of revision, deciding to change the order of paragraphs, inserting or deleting details, trying out sentences in your head before you put them down on paper. Once you have completed the essay, you need to proofread to make sure you have used words correctly and avoid errors that will detract from your essay and subsequently from the score you receive for your essay.

WORD CHOICE

In choosing words to express your ideas, keep in mind that the directions on the examination writing subtest are likely to specify an audience that requires you to use a professional tone. You should avoid slang and cliches. On the other hand, don't go overboard and complicate your essay with fancy terms and inflated language. Aim for a clear and direct expression of your ideas.

Here are a few examples of the kinds of words and expressions to avoid:

1. One activity that I've really *gotten into* lately is sailing. (Substitute *became involved in, become interested in, become enthusiastic about*).

2. The person sitting behind me talked *a lot* during the class. (Try to be as specific as possible about what *a lot* means in the sentence where you are tempted to use it. Here, you might use *continuously* or *incessantly*, but at other times, you might want to substitute *a great deal* or *often*.)

3. My first class was *awful*. (General words such as *awful, perfect, beautiful*, etc. are acceptable if you are going to follow up with more specific description. However, it is almost always better to use specific language. In what respect was the experience or the person awful, perfect, or beautiful? In the example above, was the class dull, disorganized, too demanding?)

4. I was faced with a *number of alternatives*. (Strictly defined, an alternative is a choice between two things. If you mean more than two, use *options* or choices.)

5. Computers are a *new innovation* in the classroom. (Innovation means *new*; therefore, the phrase is redundant. The same would be true of expressions such as *personal friend* and *advance planning*.)

Our language is constantly changing. At any period in history, some words and expressions are considered suitable for formal writing while others are considered colloquial and appropriate only for informal settings. As you prepare for the writing subtest, you might want to use a dictionary or a glossary of usage in a handbook. These references will provide guidance in currently acceptable choices. You might also want to keep in mind that no references will be available during the test. Therefore, if you have any doubt about the appropriateness of a word or phrase, you might want to avoid using it, and choose words about which you feel more confident.

Excess words are as much a problem as inexact words. When people don't know what to write, they often try to pad the paragraphs with sentences that say the same thing in slightly different words or fill up the sentences with empty phrases. Superfluous words and sentences may bore, frustrate, or even confuse your reader. You will be spared these problems if you practice brainstorming for relevant and interesting details before you compose your essay. Here are some examples of padded writing:

Wordy: Education faces a crisis today. At the present time, a number of problems are troubling concerned citizens. Not a day goes by that you do not hear about one problem or another.

To the Point: Many problems in education call for our attention.

Wordy: Due to the fact that a problem arose concerning the time our committee should meet, we decided in the final analysis that it would be best to postpone our decision until the new chairperson took over.

To the Point: Unable to agree on a meeting time, our committee postponed the decision until the new chairperson took over.

EXERCISE H

1. Find places in your own writing where you could eliminate words without losing meaning.

2. Trim unnecessary words from the following sentences and rewrite.

   a. The aspects of teaching that I imagine I will most enjoy are the diversity of students and the freedom to organize my own classes.

   b. The problem that I foresee causing the most difficulty in the future is that a few years from now we are going to have even more non-native English speaking students than we do now and people don't understand the need for bilingual education.

   c. In conclusion, the final point that I want to make is to say that the productivity of our economic system will decline unless we do something to tackle the problem of illiteracy among the many people who can't read at all or who can barely read.

EXERCISE I

There are a number of commonly confused words. Use a dictionary or handbook to check the correct choice for each of the sentences that follow.

1. I _____ your invitation to the party. (accept, except, expect)
2. I _____ to do well on my math exam. (accept, except, expect)
3. Everyone is going _____ Susan. (accept, except, expect)
4. I went to my guidance teacher for some good _____. (advise, advice)
5. I always _____ my students to take French literature. (advise, advice)
6. The _____ of the hurricane was horrendous. (affect, effect)
7. Does this test _____ my grade? (affect, effect)
8. _____ never too late to try. (Its, It's)
9. The committee reported _____ decision. (its, it's)
10. Please place the books over _____. (there, they're, their)
11. _____ my brother's friends. (There, They're, Their)
12. The boys have lost _____ shoes. (there, they're, their)

13. Most of the students could not choose _____ the four answers. (between, among)
14. Mary is trying to decide _____ two majors: History and French. (between, among)
15. John arrived at the game, _____. (to, too, two)
16. Please place _____ books on this corner. (to, two, too)
17. David gave the ball _____ Mark. (to, two, too)
18. Peter ran the mile _____. (bad, badly)
19. I feel _____ when it rains. (bad, badly)
20. Teachers often have to _____ packaged materials to the special needs of their students. (adopt, adapt)
21. Our school would like to _____ a dress code for all students. (adopt, adapt)
22. This corner will be the _____ for the reading materials. (site, cite)
23. Students must learn how to _____ source materials in a research paper. (site, cite)
24. Individualized activities are needed to _____ group activities. (compliment, complement)
25. Teachers should _____ children often on the work that they successfully complete. (compliment, complement)

GRAMMAR AND MECHANICS

An occasional error in grammar or mechanics in an essay written without access to a dictionary will not result in failing the writing portion of the exam. However, frequent errors will detract from the effectiveness of your message and can cause failure. There are so many possible errors, that they cannot be covered in this brief guide. A discussion of the most serious errors will be followed by a set of sentences you can use to test your proofreading skills.

1. <u>Sentence Boundaries</u>: Running two or more independent clauses together without linking words or proper punctuation violates basic rules. A grammatically incomplete sentence is equally distracting.

    a. Run-on, fused sentence, or comma splice: Teaching is not an easy field, the rewards aren't always there. (A comma is not sufficient to separate two independent clauses. Substitute a period, a semi-colon, or a linking word, such as *because* for the comma.)

    b. Fragment: The best example being the difference between the way we see a character on TV and the way we visualize a character in a story. (The *ing* form of the verb creates a fragment. Substitute *is* for *being* to correct the sentence.)

2. <u>Agreement of Sentence Elements</u>: Verbs must agree with their subjects; pronouns with the nouns to which they refer. Similar elements must have parallel structure. Parts of the sentence must fit together grammatically.

    a. Lack of subject-verb agreement: The problems that young readers have seems to come partly from the environment. (*problems* calls for the verb form *seem* not *seems*. In sentences where several words come between subject and verb, it is easy to lose track of the elements.)

b. Lack of pronoun agreement: Everyone wants to achieve their potential. (*Everyone* is singular and calls for *his/her*, not *their*.)

c. Lack of parallel structure: I learned to operate the computer, write some simple programs, and the fundamentals of word processing. (*Operate* and *write* set up a pattern which calls for a similar word. Therefore, the last part of the sentence should be rephrased to include a verb; for example, *...and use the fundamentals of word processing*.)

d. Lack of grammatical fit: While taking an elective course in design my freshman year sparked my interest in art. (The introductory phrase, *While taking an elective course*, calls for a subject to come before the verb. This sentence could be revised in at least two ways:
While taking an elective course in design my freshman year, I became interested in art.
Taking an elective course in design my freshman year sparked my interest in art.

SELECTED CAPITALIZATION RULES

A few of the rules governing capitalization are reviewed below. Consult a dictionary or handbook for more complete coverage of this topic.

1. Capitalize proper nouns and adjectives.
   Example: Capitalize: *Judy Blume* and *Southington High School*.
   Do not capitalize *the author* or *my high school*.

2. Capitalize titles when they precede proper names, but not when they follow proper names or are used alone.
   Example: Professor Kent Curtis
   Kent Curtis, professor of history
   the history professor

3. Do not capitalize the names of academic years or terms.
   Example: spring semester
   my sophomore year

4. Capitalize the names of specific courses, but not fields of study unless they are languages.
   Example: Capitalize *English, Spanish,* and *Math 101*
   Do not capitalize *math, physics,* or *education*.

5. Capitalize the important words in titles of books and underline the titles.
   Example: <u>Catcher in the Rye</u>
   <u>Grapes of Wrath</u>

PUNCTUATION

Punctuation is another area that you should review with the help of a good handbook or dictionary. One simple rule to remember is: Do not use the dash as a substitute for the proper punctuation. Example of a punctuation error: Although I took up swimming—the doctors said it would be good exercise—but I found that I did not have the ability to make the team

(The problem with relying on dashes is that, as in the example, dependence can lead to sloppy sentence construction. The sentence above should be revised: I took up swimming because the doctors said it would be good exercise, but I found that I did not have the ability to make the team.)

EXERCISE J

1. Proofread the following essay to identify errors in grammar, mechanics, and word use. Underline or cross out all errors.

2. Rewrite the essay, using correct grammar, mechanics, and wording.

The extent of illiteracy in the Country is documented in Illiterate America—a book by Jonathan Kozol. When I read this book and realized the extent of illiteracy gave me a shock. Kozol claims that 25 million people can not red warning labels or a simple news story, another 35 million do not read well enough to survive in the Modern Age—Like being able to follow printed instructions. For someone who can't read and has to support himself or a family could be a real disadvantage.

The problem of illiteracy will be difficult to solve. There being many causes that go deep into our society. Schools have failed to halt the problem and may be contributing to it. My parents say that the problem with schools today are a lack of respect for authority. Years ago, everyone know what would happen if they disobeyed a teacher. Today, teachers must contend with students who are often bored, rarely prepared and frequently they defy the teacher. Some respect and discipline is needed to create a learning environment.

Another problem with the schools is poorly prepare teachers. Students graduating from college without being able to read or write well. During the 1960s was the decline of strict academic standards. Students failed to learn what they should of learned. The decline may be ending, new tests and requirements are in place. For example, the college of arts and sciences at Northeastern State University changed their requirements because entering students were so poorly prepared. Some of them unable to identify Sophocles or locate spain on a map.

Kozol's book interested me in the larger issues of literacy—it is more than learning the ABCs. Literacy is when you can read and write well enough to survive in a complex technology and making informed opinions about government policies. Teachers can help to create a literate America. After reading about the problems of illiteracy facing this country, I want to become one,

19

PUTTING IT ALL TOGETHER

PRACTICE TOPICS

You will not know in advance the topic on which you will be asked to write an essay for the examination. However, the topic is likely to involve your education, education in general, or your choice of a career.

The best way to prepare for the writing subtest is to practice the skills presented in this book and to write whole essays under conditions similar to those found in examinations. Below are several topics you may use for practice.

Practice Prompt 1

The Academic Standards Committee of your college is considering changes in the current grading system and they have asked you to write a statement about the impact of the letter grade system (ABCDF) on learning. You may want to consider how the letter grade system affects certain types of students, how it is viewed by students, teachers, or prospective employers, whether there is a practical alternative, or whether modifications should be made. Write a statement of your opinion of the letter grade system and the reasons for your opinion.

Practice Prompt 2

A screening committee is reviewing your application for a teaching position and has asked you to submit a statement of your strengths and weaknesses for the position. Imagine a specific teaching position for which you might apply and write a statement about how well you qualify for that particular job. You might want to consider how your educational background, work experiences, internships, or special interests make you a suitable candidate. You might also want to consider whether there is anything about the position, the type of students you might face, the location, or the responsibilities that might be a challenge to you. Describe the teaching position for which you are applying and explain why you would be a good candidate for the position.

Practice Prompt 3

The committee considering your application to enter a teacher training program wants to learn about your awareness of students' non-academic needs. They have pointed out that a teacher must often do more than teach subject matter. Consider the psychological, physical, social, and economic problems that affect a student's ability to learn. Describe your understanding of the ways in which the role of a teacher goes beyond teaching academic subjects.

Practice Prompt 4

Your college is hosting a conference for state high school teachers to address the problem of the inadequate preparation of the average student for college work. The conference is focusing on the average student because college teachers are concerned about the many students entering freshman courses who are unable to meet the demands of college. You might want to describe how serious the problem is, whose problem it is, and to what extent high schools should consider changing what they are doing. Use your experience, observations, and knowledge to write a statement which gives your perspective on the gap between the academic requirements in high school and those in college.

POST-TEST

Writing Subtest Directions

This part of the examination consists of one writing exercise. You should allow approximately 60 minutes to complete this assignment. You may NOT use a dictionary during the subtest. Make sure you have time to plan, write, review, and revise what you have written.

Before you begin to write, read the topic carefully and take some time to think about how you will organize what you plan to say. Your writing exercise will be evaluated on the basis of how effectively it communicates a whole message to the intended audience for the stated purpose. Your writing exercise will be judged on the success of its total impression by a panel of language arts experts. When evaluating your ability to communicate a whole message effectively, the scorers will also consider your ability to:

1. state and stay on the topic;
2. address all specified parts of the writing assignment;
3. present your ideas in an organized fashion;
4. include sufficient detail and elaboration to statements;
5. choose effective words;
6. employ correct grammar and usage; and
7. use correct mechanics (spelling, capitalization, paragraph form).

PROMPT

The screening committee considering your application for a teaching position is concerned about teacher stress and burn-out. They would like to learn about your awareness of this problem and your susceptibility to it. You might want to discuss how you have handled stressful situations in the past and any techniques that you use to cope with stress. Describe in writing how you would confront the problem of stress and burn-out in the teaching profession.

NOTES/OUTLINE

KEY (CORRECT ANSWERS)

In some cases where there is no one right answer, possible answers are given. If your answer is significantly different, discuss it with a teacher or tutor.

EXERCISE B

1. I must describe an activity and tell the committee why it is important to me.

2. I must explain to the superintendent why I want to teach and how an experience or subject helped me make this decision.

3. I have to select three courses or activities and justify why they would be worthwhile.

4. I have to write a letter to the director of admissions at the college of my choice and explain why I want to go there.

5. I have to describe to the committee a significant book and concentrate on what I got out of it.

EXERCISE C

Answers will vary.

EXERCISE D

Answers will vary.

EXERCISE E

1. Answers will vary.

2. A. An ideal wheel:

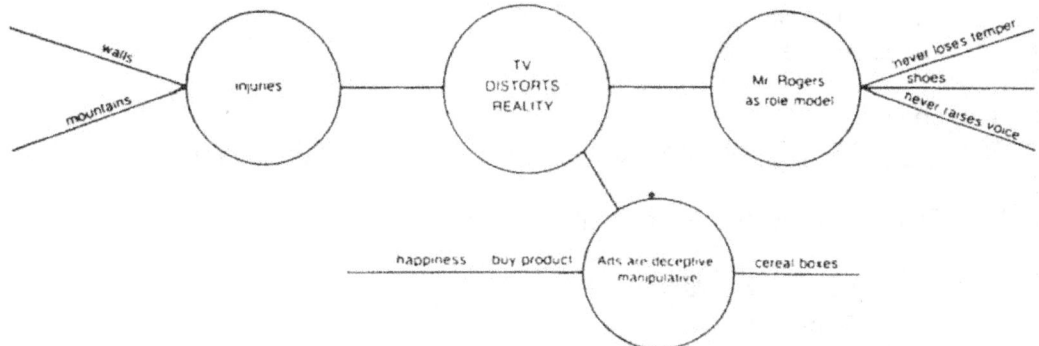

B. A flow chart:

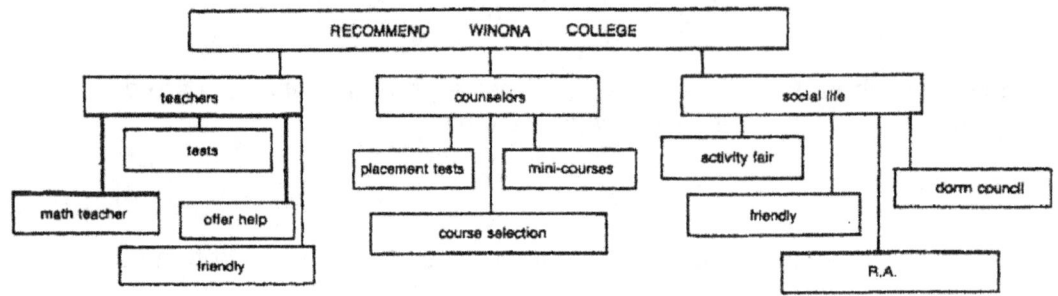

C. Using an outline:

Thesis: My job as a clerk has taught me about the reality of work and how to get along with supervisors.

I. I don't have time for special activities.
   A. School
   B. Need job
   C. Friends

II. Work is not like school because if you don't work, you don't get paid.

III. Boss is not always fair.
   A. No respect for clerks
   B. Gets impatient
   C. Got annoyed about lines

IV. I'm trying to get on top of the situation rather than just reacting.
   A. Boss is part of pecking order
   B. Make small talk
   C. Anticipate orders

V. I am still frustrated.
   A. No recognition
   B. No incentive
   C. Easily replaced

D. Using a list:
Death of a Salesman – connections between the play and my life

1. Different readings – different reactions

2. Describe characters
   Willy: salesman
   Linda: wife
   Biff: good looking, football hero breaks with Willy, drifts around
   Happy: ordinary, shadowed by Biff

3. Identified with Happy
   My older brother
   Wanted parents' attention
   School troubles
   Realized I was hurting myself
   Attention hurt Biff

4. Sympathy for Willy
   No respect from boss
   My job as a clerk, dime a dozen
   Want more than a paycheck

5. TV version – admiration for Linda
   Held family together
   Loyal to Willy
   Want someone like her

E. Another list:
Choices: integrate courses and experiences

1. Reading Methods Required – would choose it
   What I'll learn; assessment, skills

2. Activity – literacy volunteer
   Why don't people learn
   How to teach skills
   Effect on a person's life
   Failure of system

3. Course or individual study in writing
   Keep journal
   Make connections
   Write feature stories for newspaper

EXERCISE F

1. Answers will vary.

2. A. One benefit of teaching is personal satisfaction.
   B. Mr. McGrath ran a tightly structured class.
   C. Many teachers work harder than people realize.

EXERCISE G

1. Example: furthermore, for example, also, like, but
   A. but
   B. then, after, finally
   C. in addition, also, another

2. Answers will vary.

EXERCISE H

1. Answers will vary.

2. A. I will enjoy the diversity of students and the freedom to organize my own classes.

   B. The failure of people to understand the need to provide bilingual education to the increasing numbers of non-native English speaking students will be our biggest problem.

   C. Finally, failure to tackle the various forms of illiteracy will cause a decline in our economic productivity.

EXERCISE I

1. accept
2. expect
3. except
4. advice
5. advise
6. effect
7. affect
8. It's
9. its
10. there
11. they're
12. their
13. among
14. between
15. too
16. two
17. to
18. badly
19. bad
20. adapt
21. adopt
22. site
23. cite
24. complement
225. compliment

25

EXERCISE J

The extent of illiteracy in this ~~C~~country is documented in <u>Illiterate America</u> ~~,~~ a book by Jonathan Kozol. When I read this book and realized the extent of illiteracy ~~gave me a~~ shock, I was ^ed. Kozol claims that 25 million people can⌒not read warning labels or a simple news story; because they are un another 35 million do not read well enough to survive in the Modern Age, ~~Like being~~ able to follow printed instructions. ~~For~~ Someone who can't read and has to support himself or her or a family is at ~~could be~~ a real disadvantage.

The problem of illiteracy will be difficult to solve. ~~There being many~~ Its causes ~~that~~ go deep into our society. Schools have failed to halt the problem and may be contributing to it. My parents say that the problem with schools today ~~are~~ is a lack of respect for authority. Years students ago, ~~everyone~~ knew what would happen if they disobeyed a teacher. Today, teachers must contend with students who are often bored, rarely prepared, and frequently defiant of ~~they defy~~ the teacher. ~~Some~~ Respect and discipline ~~is~~ are needed to create a learning environment.

Another problem with the schools is poorly prepared teachers. Students graduating, from college without being able to read or write well. During the 1960s ~~was the decline of~~ strict academic standards declined. Students failed to learn what they should ~~of~~ have learned. The decline may be ending because new tests and requirements are in place. For example, the College of Arts and Sciences at Northeastern State University changed its ~~their~~ requirements because entering students were so poorly prepared. Some of them were unable to identify Sophocles or locate Spain on a map.

26

Kozol's book interested me in the larger issues of literacy. Literacy means more than learning the ABCs. It means reading and writing well enough to survive in a complex society and making informed opinions about government policies. Teachers can help to create a literate America. After reading about the problems of illiteracy facing this country, I want to become a teacher.

---

www.ingramcontent.com/pod-product-compliance
Lightning Source LLC
Chambersburg PA
CBHW082026300426
44117CB00015B/2368